Riding the Century

A Memoir

As revealed to

Olgard Dabbert and Ray Hutchinson

with Margaret Lang

San Diego, California

Riding the Century: A Memoir

For information, contact Silver Threads, 3830 Valley Center Drive, #705, pmb 102, San Diego, California 92130 (858-794-1597)

Silver Threads is an imprint of Silvercat™

ISBN -13 978-1-893067-07-3
ISBN-10   1-893067-07-6

All artwork, including the icons at the head of each chapter, are from the works of Alexandra Dabbert

Library of Congress Control Number: 2006921900

printed in the United States of America

Riding the Century

A Memoir

Contents

To Mother

Боже,
помоги мне пробиться,
отбиться и не разбиться

God, let me break
through, fend myself off
without crashing

Disclaimer

During a century of wars and revolutions, many interpretations are offered. Alexandra's interpretations were, at times, at variance with current historical notions and political correctness, yet her opinions were never malicious. She expressed what she thought was the truth. As with all memoirs, her stories are as she remembered them.

Ray Hutchinson and I tried to preserve Alexandra's tale as she told it. Many events described are part of my own memories and thoughts related to particular events. Some hearsay stories could not be confirmed. Some of the dialog isn't verbatim, but as closely remembered as possible, and true to the personalities portrayed.

Olgard Dabbert, M.D.

Preface

My mother was born to a Czarist officer in the Russian Army into a world on the edge of the cataclysmic changes of the twentieth century. After minimal training at age sixteen, she found herself on the Russian Front during World War I, nursing wounded soldiers, revolution moving ever closer, and ultimately chasing her out of her homeland. Her life would take her through the political and economic chaos of post-war Germany to Ethiopia, where, she managed to support her family as a dentist. Whether her patients were ex-patriates in exotic Djibouti, natives on remote plantations, or members of the royal family of Haile Selassie, Mother treated them all and created a paradise for her family, only to have it all wiped out by World War II. Rebuilding her life and that of her family in Italy, and then again in Peru, and yet again in California, Mother's story is one of dazzling resilience.

Her most treasured image of herself was on horseback, the horse an allegorical instrument of her will, overcoming obstacles, jumping every hurdle, and escaping in the nick of time. Where others panicked or gave up, Mother worked hard, and through daring, resolve, self-promotion, and faith in God, she succeeded beyond reasonable expectations, refusing to submit to events. She had the audacity to make her word better for herself, her family, her patients, and those who had the opportunity to meet her.

After Mother's death, I felt compelled to write of her story, to provide a lasting memory of truly remarkable human being.

Foreword

Refugees flood the world in such numbers that we become ambivalent about them. In America they live among us in the millions, legal and illegal. We recognize the suffering that drove them here and try to sympathize with it, but sometimes we resent them for being foreign, despite their sorrows.

During World War II, a new coinage for the dispossessed appeared: "Displaced Persons." This comfortable abstraction and its bureaucratic blandness nicely softened the reality it defined. Abbreviated to "DP," it served as a handy pejorative to conjure away the distrust and distaste many people felt toward this exotic detritus of the war: the exile.

Some exiles never get over their loss of country and property—never come to terms with their new condition—and so manage to stretch the attenuated sympathies of their hosts almost to the breaking point. But for the most part, they cope and make valuable—even distinguished—contributions to their new lands. Now and again we encounter among these exiles some who, by their remarkable qualities of character and an extraordinary ability to overcome all handicaps, fall into a special category.

One such rare and inspiring individual is Doctor Alexandra Drosdovsky Dabbert, whose "memories" appear in these pages. Uprooted not once, but many times, each occasion spiritedly began again somewhere else and involved learning a new language, moving among "strange" peoples, and making new friends. She enriched the lives of those around her with her courage, her enormous practicality, and her keen sense of humor and honor.

Alexandra responded to the challenges that life presented to her and became a nurse on troop trains and battlefields, a successful dentist in four countries on three continents, a companion to—and finally guardian of—her aging parents, a wife and mother, the discoverer of archeological finds now in museums in California, and all the while an accomplished artist whose watercolors, oils, and icons are cherished by art collectors in many lands. Gifted in several languages, in addition to her native Russian, she spoke French, German, Amharic (Ethiopian), Italian, and Spanish. As for English, she admitted she came too late for mastery. In her ninetieth decade, she remained acutely aware of political events around the world. She was an avid reader of books and periodicals in several languages and corresponded with friends all around the globe—from Canada to Swaziland.

Her strength was combined with a finely honed, life-saving pragmatism—the legacy in great part of her father's military lineage, no doubt, as well as of her maternal grandfather's medical and scientific interests.

Alexandra had a realist's understanding of man as "paragon of animals" with a trace of romantic sentimentality. She kept and rode horses and mules, admiring them for their beauty, yet loving them for their utility. She always had dogs and carefully preserved their memories in albums. Her love for nature is reflected in dozens of delicate watercolors of flowers and landscapes. But people were her real passion.

She collected friends the way others collect stamps, and she kept them for life. The "memories" (the word was her own choice) in these pages clearly illuminate this passion for friendship, focused on players both great and small in some of the epic events of our century—from the Bolshevik Revolution through World Wars I and II, to the rise and fall of Haile Selassie in Ethiopia, and the rise of Marxism and the "Shining Path" in Peru. Among the murdered; among the prisoners in gulags throughout Europe, Asia and Africa; and among the exiles scattered about the world were most of her family and many of her friends. They look out now from the pages of her twenty-three photo albums, some smuggled out of a British prison camp. She would show visitors her photographs and remark, "Almost all are dead now, except for me." But all of them lived on in her daily reflections.

Doctor Dabbert's reading of the history of our times is, therefore, full of personal associations. She cannot view Russia, Ethiopia, Germany, Italy, or Peru with detachment. History for her is the story of the life she lived, though it takes a special gift to look at that history, find it tenanted with one's family and friends—many cruelly put to death, jailed, or sent into penniless exile—and yet keep one's outlook unsullied by rancor and partiality. This is the achievement of Doctor Alexandra Dabbert.

What it means for our future generations is this: An endowment of virtue and strength is being handed on to us, an inheritance from all those Displaced Persons that we have been blessed with in America, a legacy that has come to us from all the ruined cities and obliterated societies of the world.

Alexandra's memories can show only a millionth part of that legacy, but it is my hope that reading them will make us grateful that those who have persevered have come to us to share their pilgrimage of exile and rebuilding.

Raymond Hutchinson

One

A White Lie

*O*n Saturday evening, January 10, 1919, a colonel in the German army occupying the Ukraine, von Makovsky by name, rang through the Kiev telephone exchange to a twenty-year-old second-year dental student, Alexandra Drosdovsky.

"You must be at the railway station on Tuesday morning, the thirteenth," he told her bluntly. "There will be a ticket at the ticket booth in your name. Be on the train leaving for Berlin at eleven o'clock."

Her father had asked Colonel von Makovsky to "look after my daughter; warn her when the danger in Kiev is such that she should leave." Alexandra would have to abandon her familiar world—her hopes and plans, a missing fiancé, friends and relatives, her few possessions—and head for Germany, another war-torn country completely unfamiliar to her.

Between the upheaval of war and revolution, the Ukraine had made a valiant effort to become an independent country, despite power grabs all around it. Under the Treaty of Brest-Litovsk, which ended the war between Germany and Lenin's Russia, Germany kept the Ukraine safe from the Red Army in exchange for "foodstuffs." But the former "breadbasket of Europe" was in shambles, and Germany had occupied the Ukrainian lands delineated by the treaty. The White Russian Army aimed to reestablish the old order and defeat the Bolsheviks

Alexandra said of her passport photo, "I looked like one terrorist."

(communists). The League of Nations had given Poland the Ukrainian lands of the area called "Galicia," and Poland began the equivalent of an ethnic cleansing of Ukrainians from their own homelands. And from the east had come the dreaded Bolsheviks, ready to occupy Kiev.

Alexandra had only two days to prepare. Her father had also left instructions for retrieving his back pay before she left Kiev.

Her father, General Lev Drosdovsky—with this wife Katerina Liatoshinsky Drosdovsky and nine-year-old son Roman, Alexandra's younger brother—had gone to Switzerland a few months earlier as military attaché for the Ukraine. His mission was to study the organization of the Swiss army to try and build an army capable of resisting the Bolsheviks and other aggressors. Unfortunately, his position was soon cancelled by the fall of the Ukraine to the advancing Red Army.

Alexandra got busy. She was wearing a navy-blue skirt and a new dark-blue jacket. It was the jacket of a Russian military aviator that she had seen on a manikin in a fashionable Kiev shop. "It was reasonably priced, so I bought it. I sold the trousers to an officer friend, Captain Boris Chigewich. I was quite smart-looking.[1]"

Alexandra was still able to obtain a Ukrainian passport, and the photo—issued in Kiev at this chaotic time—shows her in the aviator's jacket with a man's shirt and tie, her dark hair tousled, and her eyes large and determined. As she says, "I looked like one terrorist." Thus

[1] Captain Chigewich and his wife lived out their years of exile in a housing project on Broadway in New York City. When he was in his 70's, Chigewich was attacked by youths in the elevator of his apartment as he was returning from cashing his Social Security check. In spite of his years, he successfully fought them off. He died in 1975.

decked out, she presented herself at the office of the Finance Minister of the Ukraine, a man her father had known before he rose to this position of eminence in Kerensky's short-lived government in Russia.

"I wish to speak to Herman Hermanovich," she said to the minister's secretary with the insouciant tone of a young woman who has known the minister all her life.

Impressed perhaps by her use of the familiar form of address, the secretary welcomed her, offered her a chair, and assured her that the minister would receive her as soon as he was free. She did not have long to wait.

"I am the daughter of General Lev Drosdovsky," she told the minister when she was ushered into his office.

He may have noted her penetrating eyes and pretty face. Not the prettiness of a fashionable debutante, though she possessed a strength, a purposefulness in her glance that endowed her with an air of authority beyond her years: a kind of dominating quality that would serve her well.

"Ah," he said warmly, "And how can I help the general's attractive daughter?"

"I have to get my father's backpay and have it changed into German marks. It is impossible at this time to depend on the mail in the Ukraine and Germany. My father has asked me to carry out the money myself."

Cities and towns fell with the advance of the Red Army, and bureaucracies were in chaos. Still he replied, "That is no problem for us. We have a record of the amount owed to the general. I can get the money for you, of course, and write a note to the director of the State Bank. He will see that you get the sum changed into German marks. But as for your carrying that much money—" He shrugged and gazed at her, sizing her up.

"Thank you, Herman Hermanovich, but there is no need to be worried. It will not occur to anyone that I have that sum of money with me." She spoke with such confidence that he smiled again, perhaps wondering if such pluck would indeed be enough to protect her from the desperation of the times.

"All right," he said after a pause. He scribbled a note with the amount owed, stamped it, and gave it to her.

"Here is your father's money. You may count it if you wish."

"There is no need. I will go now to the bank and have it changed into German marks."

The State Bank building stood nearby. The office of the bank director was on the second floor, up a massive marble staircase. Alexandra's note from the Finance Minister earned her swift entree into his office.

"I come from Herman Hermanovich," she said, once more using the familiar term of address. "I need to have this money changed into German marks. I have a note from the Finance Minister."

To her surprise, the director frowned nervously. "Yes, I received a phone call from him only a short time ago. It is a very big sum you want changed," he said at once. "Five million is a lot. I am not sure we can handle such a sum."

Five million! He had confused her with someone. Who it was did not matter. There was no need to call his attention to this case of mistaken identity.

"Yes," she said calmly, "you're right. Five million is a lot. Perhaps then you could change just a small part of it?'

"How much?"

"Perhaps thirty thousand marks? If you write me a check for thirty thousand marks, that will be sufficient." *If he thinks I am a millionaire,* she reflected, *that is a misunderstanding that I have done nothing to foster. Surely it will grease the wheels of this entire money-changing process.*

"Ah, yes." His nervousness disappeared. "Thirty thousand marks is nothing." Relieved, he went through the business of writing a note. "Take this to the cashier downstairs. He'll change your money for you without question and write you a check on the Bank of Berlin. And how is the General, your father?"

Her pleasant reply belied the anxiety of the moment. In the main lobby, her heels echoed on the marble floor. How permanent the bank seemed! How enduring! Perhaps as solid as the German mark itself, she speculated. The Ukrainian government offices were also about to evacuate Kiev.

At the proper window, a cashier wrote out a check for thirty thousand German marks. Alexandra smiled her thanks and stuffed the check inside her blouse. It was time to return to her apartment for she had much to prepare.

Her mother had written recently about the shortage and extremely high cost of food in Switzerland. "We get only one egg per person each week," she had complained. So Alexandra purchased enough eggs to fill her hatbox and added a large piece of ham fat, much prized in the Ukraine. She then put in flour for making vareniki, a pastry like dumplings or piroshki, except that they are boiled in salt water instead of being baked. Then she packed her things into a second suitcase.

She protected her Ukrainian passport, ornamented with the impressive double eagles of a Russia that no longer existed, and stamped with the democratic Ukrainian Peoples Republic emblem that featured the trident of Neptune[2]. A young woman alone, traveling among increasingly desperate people, loaded down with the thirty thousand mark check—a piece of paper on which her family's survival depended—a suitcase with the last of her worldly goods, and a hatbox full of eggs and ham fat and other groceries, Alexandra boarded the eleven o'clock train from Kiev bound for Berlin the morning of January 13, 1919.

She held a precious possession in her hands as she contemplated her destination in Germany where firearms were outlawed, especially to aliens and refugees.

When I was nine years old, papa took me to fire range and taught me to shoot. When I went to the Front, I had my Browning—for protection. I always had pistol.

---

[2]   See photo, page 16.

Standing between two train cars, knowing that I could not keep my faithful handgun that had been so close to me—it seemed for years—I started disassembling it and throwing its parts along the railway.

A Jewish man saw me and kept imploring me to sell it to him, but I could not and would not let anybody have it; it had meant too much to me!

Alexandra cried silently, saying goodbye to a way of life she would never see again. She straddled the rail cars, just as she straddled borders, a victim of opposing social forces that swept her toward life in exile—if all went well. She wondered whether it would be forever, or if her nightmare would end with the defeat of the Bolsheviks.

Two

A Peripatetic Life

*A*lexandra was about to lose her homeland, her extended family, roots, stories, traditions—the only world she had ever known. Looking back, her Russian childhood may have prepared her for the turmoil that lay ahead of her.

Alexandra was what Americans call an "army brat," born on November 14th, 1898 in a part of Russia called Rovno, a town located about two hundred miles west of Kiev in the Ukraine. Russia's territory extended three thousand miles north to south and seven thousand miles west to east. Rovno was near a military post that was closer to the border with Poland where her father Lev served as an artillery officer. She would begin life in a country changing so drastically that it would become the most powerful catalyst of global change in the twentieth century. And she would enter it as the daughter of one who had fought for Czarist Russia, which intended to change through an evolution that did not destroy tradition, pitted against those who insisted on erasing the old ways through revolution.

Son of a Prussian

To be in the Russian army in 1898 was to defend the tsar's policies in the time of a rising clash of intense political extremes. Just four years earlier, Nicholas had become tsar, succeeding his father, Alexander the III, who died after a short reign of six years.

The policies of Alexander III had turned repressive after the assassination of his father. Bombs thrown at the carriage killed the more liberal Tsar Alexander the II on the eve of granting the first Russian constitution. His father's brutal death so angered the son, Alexander III, that he quashed the constitution and sent thousands of dissidents to Siberia. Ruling as an absolute autocrat, he stabilized Russia, allowing modernization and capitalism to take hold. Industrial output would quadruple from 1895 to 1914. Cotton and grain harvests would increase drastically. Yet despite the tsar's quashing of democracy, workers unions were recognized, including the right to strike. U.S. President Taft said, "Your emperor's worker's legislation stands higher than any available among the democratic states." Public elementary schools would be free and obligatory by 1908.

Alexander III hadn't prepared his son Nicholas to lead a drastically changing nation in a changing world, yet Alexandra's parents could not have imagined the total collapse ahead of them, and Lev was eager to serve his country in the army of the tsar. Lev's future in the Russian army was limited, unless he could win admission to the General Staff Academy at St. Petersburg. He had passed the examinations with twenty or thirty other officers in the early 1890's under the tighter reign of Alexander III, but was refused admittance because his father had not been a Russian citizen.

"But he served in the armies of the tsar," Lev protested.

"Yes, but he was a citizen of Prussia." A typical bureaucratic contretemps as found everywhere in every age.

Lev's father, though an officer in the Russian army, had died owing large debts. As a result, Lev lived a somewhat spartan life in the early years of his service and needed to supplement his income. Since he had completed a classical education, which included Latin and Greek, he decided to teach language classes.

Katerina Liatoshinsky and two of her sisters went to Warsaw to improve on their foreign languages and general education during their high school years. Of ten siblings, Katerina was the only one still single. She wanted to study Medicine in Moscow, which was taught in Latin.

To pass the entrance examinations, she needed to learn Latin. Lev began giving Katerina private classes. Soon they fell in love and married on June 30, 1896.

Two years later Alexandra entered their military world, and then in 1900 when Alexandra was two, Lev was posted to St. Petersburg, the capital, for four years. Alexandra remembered her first trip with her father to the stables

Lev and Katrina recently married

when she was five. She became a passionate equestrian.

After years without rising through the ranks, Lev received good news. A reprieve came in an unlooked-for manner, a hope that had almost been forgotten.

Help from a Princess

Back in 1894 when Tsar Alexander III had died in the Crimea, his body was shipped by boat to the railhead at Odessa. Among the notables aboard the ship carrying the tsar's body was Princess Olga, daughter of the late tsar, and also Nicholas's sister, later to become the queen of Greece. Also aboard was a Russian navy captain of the second class in the Black Sea Fleet. His name was Alexander Liatoshinsky, Katerina's brother, and soon to become Lev's brother-in-law[3]. During the voyage to Odessa, Captain Liatoshinsky told Princess Olga the story of Lev Drosdovsky, who was refused admittance to the General Staff because his father was not a Russian citizen but who had

---

[3] Alexandra's uncle, Alexander Liatoshinsky, would attain the rank of admiral of the Black Sea fleet by the time of World War I.

served honorably. Olga took an interest in the matter, and sometime after her return to the capital, she set in motion the ponderous and creaking machinery of the Russian bureaucracy.

Finally in 1904, ten years after Princess Olga's intercession on his behalf, Lev was admitted to the general staff. A photograph taken in Dvinsk—near Riga in Latvia at the summer home of Colonel Alexander Kedrov and his wife Anna, one of Katerina's sisters—fixed his appearance in that year. Lev is typical of army officers of the period: short, cropped hair; a steady gaze from under dark brows; a cool, confident look; and the inevitable mustache, this one twisted at the ends into sharp points. Lev wore clips on the ends of his mustache after waxing it in the mornings to hold it until it set. Alexandra remembered a morning in St. Petersburg when her father abstractedly left their apartment for the electric tram that would take him to work and forgot to remove the mustache clips.

Separation

In 1904, when Lev finished the General Staff academy course, he was sent to the Siberian Far East. During that time, Alexandra and her mother lived briefly with Katerina's relatives near her birthplace of Zhitomir[4] about a hundred miles west of Kiev in the Ukraine and then with Katerina's brother, Alexandra's Uncle Nicholas Liatoshinsky, his wife Olga, and their two children Boris and Zina, Alexandra's cousins, in Kiev.

Aunt Olga, who taught Alexandra to "read" tarot cards, was very attractive with black hair, smilingly called a gypsy. Aunt Olga was gifted at "opening the cards," as Alexandra phrased it. "I believe in it so much," she added, "and became so good at it."

During her year with Uncle Nicholas, Alexandra's regular evening playmates were her cousins Zina and Boris. Boris, perhaps influenced

---

[4]   Also spelled Dzhitomir and Gitomir.

by the proximity of the Kiev Opera House two doors away, took a deep interest in music.[5]

Pogroms

A Jewish family lived on the lower floor below Alexandra's aunt and uncle. The lower the floor, the higher the rents, so this family could obviously afford more. Jews usually lived better than the average Russian because, according to Alexandra, "They were smarter, worked harder, and had more money."

Alexandra, age 4 (1904)

One day, the Jewish family's cook, a Christian Ukrainian woman, came running to the door. She asked if she could borrow one of Uncle's icons because word was out that a pogrom would be made soon.

Six-year-old Alexandra didn't know what that meant. She knew that icons were treasured religious paintings, plaques, and carvings of images sacred to Russian Orthodox Christianity, but did not understand how they would help. Alexandra's family loaned the cook two icons for the Jewish family to display as a protection against the pogrom looters of Jewish properties who bypassed houses with icons.

As for this pogrom, some Jews lived in restricted areas called ghettos, but her Uncle's apartment building was not in a ghetto. Walking a Kiev street with her mother one morning, Alexandra saw sheets and blankets flapping from the balcony of a nearby apartment.

"Look," her mother said, "there was a pogrom there."

---

[5] Subsequently he made a great reputation as a composer in post-Revolutionary Russia. He received an award from Joseph Stalin for an opera he composed (with three ballets) for the Kiev opera house. Tourists to Kiev who have visited No. 5 on Theater Street have seen a plaque placed by the Soviet government on the front of the apartment, memorializing it as sometime home for the famous composer Boris Liatoshinsky. He died in the 1950's.

Envious workers or peasants who made the pogroms stole the possessions of the Jews, broke in, destroyed things, and then hung the bedclothes on the balcony as a sign that they had already been there. There were no statistics, but Alexandra didn't believe that thousands had been killed. "I was small and don't know if there were killings, but I know the police always come too late."[6]

Tsar Alexander III and Nicholas II had both turned a blind eye toward the revival of the repression of Jews. "There were very few Jews in the army—they detested being soldiers and were not admitted in the officer corps except as medical doctors," Alexandra recalled, "but none on the general staff."

Papa Goes to War

Leaders of the impending revolution, intellectuals—many of whom were Jewish dissidents opposed to tsarist rule—and students agitated workers and peasants, yet the government still continued its expansionist policies in the east, which were similar to America's vision of a "manifest destiny." In 1550 A.D. during the reign of Ivan IV, "The Terrible," Russia had first started expanding to the East, eventually acquiring Siberia and Alaska, advancing as far down to the northern shores of California.

The Russian expansion into Manchuria in 1904 and eventual takeover of the Korean Peninsula triggered the Russo-Japanese War of 1904–1905. Lev was ordered to join the Siberian Campaign.

Now as Captain Drosdovsky, he would serve one year as secretary to General Alexeev, first commandant of the army in Siberia to be replaced by General Kuropatkin. From St. Petersburg, it took Lev twenty-eight days to reach his destination in Manchuria.

One can only imagine the difficult logistics of transporting troops and supplies across Siberia. The Trans-Siberian railway had recently

---

[6] According to Alexander Solzhenitsyn in his book, *Two Hundred Years Together,* thousands of Jews were killed, but not millions.

been completed, and having only one railroad track was quite inadequate. Yet before the railroad, it took six months to reach the Far East from European Russia. It was faster to reach Moscow from the Russian Pacific harbor Vladivostok going by ship to San Francisco, taking the American trans-continental train and crossing the Atlantic Ocean.

The Japanese, inspired by the lessons learned from Admiral Perry, had decided to modernize their military and naval forces and did not tolerate this Russian advance. They made a surprise attack on Port Arthur—occupied at the time by the Russians. Possessing the first Asian army to defeat a European army, Japan may have been inspired to use the same technique in their 1942 raid on Pearl Harbor.

Although outnumbered perhaps ten to one by the Russians, the Japanese inflicted such heavy casualties that Russia was defeated. Weakened, the tsarist government faced the first serious challenge at home by the liberal and leftist insurgents. The infamous "Bloody Sunday" occurred in January of 1905 after this defeat. Strikers protested outside the imperial palace in St. Petersburg, and Nicholas sent Cossacks in to mow them down.

Japan pursued its imperialistic aims in Korea, Manchuria, and China to the relief of the Western Powers (England, Germany, France, and Italy) who thus manipulated the containment of the expansionist drive of Russia for the next decade.

Civilized

When Captain Lev Drosdovsky returned from duty in Siberia, the family went to Moscow to meet him, and there is a photo in the album commemorating his return, dated 1905. In it he is wearing a papakha, the round fur hat favored by the Cossacks, and a goatskin burka or cape. The photo is adjacent to one taken just before he left for Siberia[7].

"Look," Alexandra said with a chuckle, comparing the two photos, "Papa looks much more civilized before he went to Siberia."

[7] See photo, page 28.

Lev's homecoming in Kiev from the Russian-Japanese war

In Siberia, Lev acquired a preference that he adopted permanently. "Papa discovered Chinese silk shirts." One of the chief benefits of these shirts was that they seemed to repel lice. From then on, he wore only Chinese silk shirts.[8]

In Russia, before the Revolution, Chinese men came through the larger cities, selling their goods (which they carried on their backs) from door to door. The silk, called chesucha, came in many thicknesses. Mama made from this silk jackets and coats as well as Papa's shirts. It was very washable, this silk.

"Civilization" had reached Russia in stages. What finally linked Russia to the West was Peter the First, "the Great," the reformer (1696–1725) who was the architect of Russia's adoption of Western ideas and practices. "Enlightenment" never permeated through the "Russian Soul" unconditionally. The French expression "Scratch the Russian and you will find the Tartar," and Kipling's statement "Russia is not the most Eastern of the Western countries, but the most Western of the Eastern countries" makes the point.

In the nineteenth century, Russia was among the European great powers that included Great Britain, France, Austria, and Germany. Following the French Revolution and the Napoleonic epoch, Russia—after defeating Napoleon in 1814[9]—rapidly achieved new heights in industry, agriculture, education, science, economy, and finances. It

---

[8] Michael Ignatieff in *The Russian Album* (Viking Press, New York, First American edition 1987.) mentions that his grandfather has a similar preference for silk and for the same reason, as a protection from lice.

[9] This victory was immortalized by Tchaikovsky's symphony which includes the famous "1812 Overture."

was exporting oil, gold, and agricultural products. There was an extraordinary output of literature, music, and painting. Serfdom (slavery) had ended in 1861. The Trans-Siberian railway that had enabled the Russo-Japanese War was completed in 1903. "Civilization" was penetrating ever more deeply.

On the other hand, one of the effects of European "Enlightenment" was the progressive philosophical, social, and political unrest that peaked with the American and French Revolutions followed by widespread strife in the rest of the World, and nowhere was the unrest more pronounced than in Russia.

Three

1905–1910
Scorpions and Other Tales in the Caucasus

In 1905, Lev headed a company of his Bendersky Regiment, which took its name from the city of Bender, then a part of the Ukraine.[12] The company was sent to the Caucasus, a region of Southern Russia limited by the Black Sea, Caspian Sea, Turkey, and Iran. Since the Russian conquest in 1827, the Caucasus had always been in turmoil, not unlike today. It needed pacification, so many military families lived there while the men were stationed in this volatile area. Alexandra would see the ashes of a general's house that had been burned in an uprising. Lev's first assignment was in the booming town of Baku[13] on the Caspian coast near the border of present day Iran.

To be with her papa, Alexandra and her mother made a journey that would have been close to two thousand miles from St. Petersburg. They traveled by railroad to Kiev and then to Odessa, riding on the tracks Lev's own father worked on in the 1850s and 60s. From there they would skirt the Black Sea and then have to cross the mighty Caucasian mountains, which boasts the highest peak in Europe.

---

[12] It is now in Moldava between the Ukraine and Romania.
[13] Baku is in the region now recognized as Azerbaijan.

With its rapid industrialization around rich oil deposits, the city of Baku had attracted a swarm of conflicting interests, both within Russia and internationally, including the Nobel brothers from Sweden of future Nobel Prize fame and other entrepreneurs. Such sudden modernization in an area of ancient traditions along with exploitation and political agitation was a breeding ground for trouble. Lev's assignment was to keep law and order, especially in the nearby town of Saliani[14] at the mouth of the River Cura[15] that emptied into the Caspian. A factory there processed the finest Russian black caviar, but the workers were out on strike. Soldiers kept matters under control in this important factory. Lev and many of the troops came down with severe tropical malaria from mosquitoes in outlying swamps.

While the family lived in Baku, Lev bought beautiful Persian rugs in January of 1906, which the family cherished for their added warmth. Alexandra learned to love them for the rest of her life. Also that month, they crossed the southern region of the Caucasus traveling west into what is now recognized as Georgia to within fifty miles of the Black Sea, staying for four months in the town of Kutais[16]. In May they stayed for a month in the town of Borjom[17] about thirty miles to the southeast, and then to Batum[18] on the Black Sea just a few miles away from the border with Turkey.

Scorpions

Lev was sent to nearby Turkey to see "what the Germans were up to." They were building a railroad from Constantinople, currently called Istanbul, to Baghdad in Iraq, but the Russian General Staff wanted Lev

---

[14] Also called Salyan.

[15] Also called Kur.

[16] Also called K'ut'aisi.

[17] Also called Borjomi.

[18] Also called Bat'umi.

to find out if that was all they were doing. He was sent to a town in Turkey called Erzerum[19] with a guide, probably a Russian-speaking Armenian. Lev came back with a story about his unusual sleeping arrangement because of enemies who were not human.

One evening just as they were about to camp for the night, they reached the railroad line. Since it was not yet completed, there were no trains running yet.[20]

"You must sleep between the rails," the guide told Captain Drosdovsky.

"Why?" The rough ties and rock ballast did not look to Lev like a particularly comfortable bed.

"It is because of the scorpions. There are many of them. But they don't climb the rails, so we'll be safe between the tracks."

Schooling and Playmates

Until 1906, Alexandra went to school at home, taught by her mother Katerina, a skilled tutor. Alexandra spoke excellent French and German, and at age seven in 1906-07 passed the entrance exams for public school. Alexandra at eight years of age was a tomboy, and large for her years, so most of her playmates were boys. One of these playmates was Mstyslav Vesalovsky, son of Colonel Vesalovsky in charge of logistics (obvos) in Batum, a position that was considered rather dull and less prestigious in the military world. Mystslaw, was small for his age at twelve. His companions called him Lialia, and they used to play war games.

"One time," Alexandra recalled, "Lialia had me by the hair with a very firm grip, but he did not hurt me. It was strange to have had a childhood friend who later would become a man of brutal violence."[21]

---

[19] Also called Erzurum.

[20] During the First World War, those railroads were repeatedly attacked by Lawrence of Arabia and his Arab insurgents.

[21] Fifteen years later Lialia became an aide to General Baron Ungern-Sternberg, who was from the Baltic and who commanded a White Russian army in

In 1907, Lev and his family went back to Kutais for one year. The city with its many trees and gardens was built on both sides of the Rion[22] River. One of the oldest cities in the Caucasus, this ancient capital of Colchis was famed as the home of the Golden Fleece stolen by Jason and his Argonauts. Kutais had been attacked throughout history by Persians, Mongols, Turks, Russians, and others, leaving a highly mixed ethnicity. Alexandra, then age nine, often went with her father to a firing range where he taught her to shoot using handguns.

Tiflis

Lev, Katrina, Alexandra, and Roman on vacation

Finally, after three years with no time off, Lev was given a vacation and took the family on a brief trip to Kiev in the summer of 1908. When they returned to Georgia in the Caucasus, the destination would be Tiflis. The final segment of their journey brought them to Wladicavcas[23] where they had to resort to an older form of transportation. They boarded a horse-drawn carriage and traveled on the Georgian Military Road (Voyenno-Grusinskaia doroga) through

---

Siberia on the Mongolian border. During the Civil War between the "Whites and the "Reds," Lialia's duties had changed from the years in Batum. The General had other things in mind for him. When Red Army prisoners were captured, the general interrogated them at length to discover if they were just simple peasants dragooned into the army by the Reds or if they were instead deeply committed to the Red cause. When he was convinced by the answers to his questions that a particular prisoner was a fully dedicated Communist, he would signal Lialia by a movement of his eye or nod of his head, and Lialia, standing behind and to the side of the prisoner, a revolver already in his hand, would raise the weapon and fire a shot into the prisoner's head at short range. Both Lialia and General Ungern-Sternberg were later killed by the "Reds."

[22] Also called Rioni.

[23] Also spelled Vladikavkas.

the famous Darial Pass, a narrow defile with vertical crags of rock rising on either side. Every fifteen or twenty miles the coach stopped for a fresh span of horses. After a day in the pass they made about sixty of the two-hundred mile journey and stopped for the night in Kashek, a way station at the top of the pass. Though it was July, snow covered the ground. From Kashek they went down the mountains to Tiflis, the Russian name for Tbilisi, meaning warm springs in the Georgian language. Part of this capital city looked ancient and Oriental, and part of it bustled with modernization.

A House of Mirrors

In 1909, Alexandra was eleven years old with a new baby brother, Roman. Another new addition, almost a part of the family, was the new horse Lev acquired: the noble Barinia. Lev often took Alexandra horseback riding. Part of military courtesy for officers was to pay respect to other officers by making a visit at certain times. "Mama did not like such calls," Alexandra recalled, "so Papa and I rode our horses to make social calls."

Lev and Alexandra rode out to visit Colonel Przewalsky and his wife. The colonel was the son of the famous General Przewalsky[24] and was, like Lev, a General Staff officer and about his same age. Przewalsky had been military attaché in Belgium. He was small with dark hair,

---

[24] The Russian General Przewalsky had spent years exploring Siberia and Mongolia in the 19th Century. One of his contributions was the naming of a horse species that he discovered and has since been known by his name. General Przewalsky was one of the Russian protagonists in the "Great Game" scheme that pitted British political interests in defending India and the "Northern Frontier" from Russian aspirations to conquer Afghanistan and reach an outlet to the Persian Gulf (immortalized by R. Kipling's Kim and the fascinating books on the struggle for Central Asia by Peter Hopkirk.) "I knew General Przewalsky's son." Alexandra said one day as she was reading "Zoo News," a magazine put out by the San Diego Zoo which had an article about their Przewalsky's horse. "He was, like my papa, a General Staff officer, about the same age as papa. It was in 1910 in Tiflis, capital of Georgia in the Caucasus.

shaved, and fine-featured. Alexandra recalled that their house was full of mirrors brought all the way from Belgium.[25]

An Operation

While in Tiflis in 1910, twelve-year-old Alexandra developed pain in her left ear that became worse. She began having chills, fever, tenderness, and an ominous swelling. Doctors diagnosed that she had an abscess of the mastoid that needed to be incised, drained, and curetted. Though a daring enterprise before the age of antibiotics, they knew that she would be safer if the operation took place at home away from the less hygienic conditions of a military hospital.

> I had my head shaved for mastoid surgery. Three doctors performed the operation on a special table, made just for the occasion, in the kitchen in our house. Doctors say no need for hospital if we clean the kitchen properly. They instructed us to scrub the walls and ceiling with white bread.
>
> One day a carpenter came to the house and said he wished to measure me. He took my width and height, and I was very scared. I thought he was measuring me for casket, but I find out he is measuring me for the table to be used for surgery.

The operation was successful, although it slightly impaired her hearing for life.

When Lev completed his military duty in the Caucasus, he was given a small gold and silver medallion, like a tiny book with several pages on which are inscribed the date, 1910; place, Tiflis; his name; and

---

[25] Later, during the First World War, General Przewalsky distinguished himself by breaking through the Turkish lines in the Caucasus and occupying Erzerum in Turkey, threatening Constantinople (at the time, that was the only good news for the Allies who had evacuated Gallipoli with great losses and were bogged down in the trenches of the Western France). He was killed later, during the Russian Civil War between the Reds and the Whites.

the names of all the generals, Yudenich's included, who served there with him[26]. He wore the medallion on his watch chain until he died.[27]

---

[26] The Germans were very active in Turkey and had long-range plans of conquest at the expense of British and Russian interests. (Read Peter Hopkirk's *Like Hidden Fire*. During World War I, the Germans sent their own version of Lawrence of Arabia to Persia and Afghanistan to promote a major uprising of Muslims in India, the Crown Jewel of the British Empire.)

[27] Alexandra preserved it along with other military mementos of Lev's life.

Four

The Goat in the Blue Dress

St. Petersburg

After the Caucasian stint, Major Lev Drosdovsky was transferred to St. Petersburg to join the Imperial Russian General Staff. He was promoted Colonel and his office was opposite the Winter Palace of Tsar Nicholas who had inherited the most extensive and valuable collection of art in all of Europe and which was housed in the palace.[28]

As the Capital, St. Petersburg was the most desirable place in Russia to be assigned to. In 1910 the Drosdovskys moved to Smolni Prospekt 6, Apartment 63. The house belonged to the Empress Mary, the mother of Nicholas, and the apartments in it were rented only to army officers and government employees. The apartment offered a marvelous view across the Neva River.[29]

To the right of the apartment rose the beautiful Peter the Great Bridge, *Most Petra Velikovo*, which led to the Ochta district. It had two long spans with arching trusses, and in the center, between tall towers, a lift section accommodated river traffic. To the left was the Smolni

---

[28] It would later become the famous Hermitage Museum.

[29] Alexandra's nephew Bogdan visited the city a few years ago and reported that the building and the apartment were still there.

View of the Neva from the St. Petersburg residence, ca. 1915

Institute—a long multistoried stone structure with an ell at its far end. Next to that stood the domed Smolni Cathedral.

> We did not know how poor we were. Papa's salary as a colonel was three thousand rubles a year. That came to three hundred English pounds— twenty-five pounds a month. A governess who taught English could earn twenty pounds a month. A French governess got less, perhaps half. Teachers from Switzerland were more appreciated because they could teach both French and German.

Lev had earned extra money for combat pay in the Caucasus. In St. Petersburg, he also gave lectures in three different officers' schools, including teaching artillery in the Military Academy to earn extra income.

If the apartment on Smolni Prospekt was situated in a prestigious location with the cachet of being part of a building owned by the Empress, it was nonetheless quite humble by current standards. The bathroom contained a toilet and nothing else, not even a window—just a small vent near the ceiling, which "gave off" to the kitchen.

We had water in a small tank mounted on the bedroom wall with a spigot for daily wash-ups. We also had a big copper tub, which we kept in the attic. Each apartment had a nice attic. Every Saturday out comes this tub and water was heated on our wood stove for our baths.

Before I would use this restroom, I banged the door back and forth very hard to scare the cucarachas. Whenever I do that, they fall from the ceiling like rain. I think they make a busy traffic back and forth from the kitchen.

The family always had help, including a nanny for Roman and often a maid. In St. Petersburg and other big cities, Alexandra says, "We had a horse as well as an official car and driver. Our driver was Ali, a Muslim Tartar from Crimea."[30] And Barinia was still with them.

Barinia in Russian means Madame or Señora. When a Russian entered a home, he would say, "Barinia doma?" Is the lady of the house at home?

Mama did not like this name for Papa's horse. One day before the war, a servant entered our dining room while we were eating and said to Papa, "Barinia is limping this morning." Mama was angry. "Couldn't you change the name of that horse?" she scolded him. "People will think I'm ill."

A custom in the Russian army (as in the British) was for each officer to have a personal orderly, what the English call a "batman." This aide served the officer and his family as servant, valet, cook, and jack-of-all-services. Orderly Gvosdenko had served Lev since 1905. He

[30] Tartars were the descendents of the Mongolian hordes that had come from Mongolia with Genghis Khan and occupied large portions of Russia, but had later shrunk to the southern part of the Volga region and Crimea. They were all Muslims. They suffered much, and were exiled to Siberia by Stalin for having cooperated with the Germans during World War II.

was considered part of the family. He had been mustered out of the army after the first four or five years and went back to the country to live with his parents, but only for a short time. He found that he preferred the Drosdovskys and was soon back in their service.

As one of the entitlements to officers of the general staff, twelve-year-old Alexandra was able to enter a seven-year high school program at the Smolni Institute, THE prestigious school for the daughters of the aristocracy and military officers.[31] One of her favorite subjects was art, and Smolni Institute had good art teachers.

Zhitomir

Lev's position and modest income provided occasional time and leisure in those last few years before the world changed so irreversibly, to travel to the homeland of Alexandra's mother, Katerina. The summer of 1910, the family took a vacation to Zhitomir, seventy kilometers west of Kiev.

Grandfather Leonty Liatoshinsky was a doctor there—a man of medical and scientific interests. He was for many years chief physician of Zhitomir, capital of Volinya in the Western Ukraine. Before Katrina married Lev, she'd wanted to be a doctor like her father. As other doctors did, Dr. Liatoshinsky had to go to small towns to examine newly recruited soldiers. His travels also included an annual trip to Carlsbad (now called Carlovi Vari in the Czech Republic) to undergo the "treatment of waters" for "weak stomach," a condition that would worsen into a perforated ulcer. Because of all this traveling, he possessed an English suitcase that Alexandra would later use in her journey—an enduring link to the past.[32]

---

[31] It was in this Institute that Lenin, two years later in 1917, made his first headquarters and masterminded the October Revolution and the birth of the Soviet Union.

[32] Alexandra kept this suitcase during her odyssey. Eventually Oksana, Alexandra's cousin who lived in New York, inherited it.

Alexandra's grandfather also worked in the city prison. It was in an old castle, built when Zhitomir was Polish. The church in the prison was very poor, so the doctor decided to have all his children baptized in the prison church. It became a populist fashion to have baptisms and weddings there by the well-to-do, and the church prospered. The country's religion was an important part of peoples' lives.

The Russian State originated in the ninth century A.D. as a principality attached to the Ukraine, and its link to the West was determined by the adoption of Christianity as its official faith. The Russian Orthodox religion (987 A.D.) became a major building block of national cohesion that stood fast during the Mongol (Tartar) invasion (1236 to 1480), which effectively retarded the progress of the Russian civilization for two centuries.

Alexandra's grandmother's sister had become a nun when her fiancée went to Crimea to fight the British in a battle Tennyson immortalized in "The Charge of the Light Brigade" and never returned. She made several pilgrimages to Jerusalem and brought back many things from the Holy Land, including a cross made of olivewood—yet another family treasure, and this one would become especially important to Lev.

Interestingly, in Dr. Liatoshinsky's own family, his wife—Alexandra's grandmother—prescribed more down-to-earth remedies for common ailments. When their children had whooping cough, for instance, she went to the nearby Orthodox seminary and gave the guardian five kopeks in return for which he gave her a dozen or so lice that had been combed from the seminarians' long hair. She wrapped each louse in a tiny pellet of bread and gave it to the sick child. The prescription called for five lice per day for five days. The children suffered no ill effects. Other superstitions held sway as well.

Of course, if you see a cat cross the street, you must turn your head to the left and spit three times, or misfortune will happen. If I lose or can not find something, one must 'bind the old man's beard down' by taking a white handkerchief and tie it to one of four legs of a piece of furniture with three knots.[33] Within twenty-four hours you will find the lost object. And before a journey, all must sit down in the room, in a loose circle for a minute of silence to be safe. It works.

The Goat in the Blue Dress

In those less complicated times, perhaps they simply made do with what they had. The same principle applied to entertainment. Goats were very common in the Russian rural areas, and Alexandra remembered the family trip of 1910, featuring a friend and a goat.

> I played with Kolia [Nicholas] Strashkevich.[34] He was a little older than I. He took one of my blue dresses—which I did not like—and put it on a milk goat that belonged to Aunt Olga, the one who taught me to divine the future with cards. The goat in the blue costume escaped, jumped over a fence. I ran after the goat and caught her in our neighbor's stable. Mama was not angry over the damage to the dress, but Aunt Olga was very upset: the goat might stop producing milk from stress.

Family Events

Sadly, Alexandra's grandfather died from the complications of his perforated ulcer and was buried in the family mausoleum in Zhitomir. Grandmother Liatoshinsky moved back to the town of her birth, of her daughter Katrina's birth, and of Alexandra's birth—Rovno—some two hundred kilometers west of Zhitomir where she later died.

Her body was to be buried in the same family mausoleum in Zhitomir alongside her husband, but transportation over the two

---

[33] Even after eighty years of Communism, many Russians still swear by this method.

[34] During the Revolution, Kolia and his wife were able to flee to Poland. He became a banker.

hundred miles between the two towns was a problem. A Jewish butcher with a horse and wagon was found and hired to transport the body without attracting attention. "He was smart," Alexandra said. "He covered the casket with bricks. The summer was a hot one. Anyone that passed him would only see bricks. The journey would take a week."

The faithful family orderly Gvosdenko accompanied the butcher. He reported that after two days, he noticed flies following the wagon. Every day more and more. Finally, "There were troops of flies," he said. "They knew what was under the bricks." By the time they reached Zhitomir, the wagon was black with flies. Burial was not delayed.

On another vacation, the family gathered in 1913 for a photograph. Both Uncle Alexander and Aunt Olga appear in the photo on the occasion of the birthday of Ludmila Kedrov, daughter of Katerina's sister Anna, who was married to Alexander Kedrov. Nicholas was darkly handsome, according to Alexandra, and entirely bald with a luxuriant drooping black mustache. Anne, in white, looks solemnly at the camera from a broad, sweet face. Fifteen-year-old Alexandra is in the photo

Family gathering, Zhitomir, 1913; Alexandra standing on the right

at the right, also in white, with dark braids reaching almost to her waist. She said her hair would have been longer still if it hadn't been for the operation in Tiflis where they'd shaved her head.

Family Ghosts?

The family spent summers and holidays, when time allowed, at a property in the Ukraine belonging to Katerina's relatives. In 1914, these relatives wished to sell half of the property to Alexandra's parents.

> When we make our trip to the property, we always go by train. And we take along with us always our bathtub wrapped up and put in the baggage car of the train. The trip from Petersburg takes part of one day and all of one night, going west on the Riga-Orlovsky line.
>
> We arrive in evening at Pochinok, a village about fifteen *versts* [ten miles] from the property. There was waiting a driver with two-horse team and carriage for us, and also farmer with a cart for our baggage. It was dark, perhaps 9 P.M. There were my parents, my brother Roman, then about five, and his *niania* [nursemaid].
>
> When we arrive at the house, half of it is empty. It is in anticipation of the coming sale. The other half is furnished. We are to sleep in this main house. We go to eat with the family.
>
> The niania goes to eat with the employees of the house. When she returns she says to us, "The servants told me that in the room where we are to sleep there are bad spirits."
>
> When Mama hears that, she says, "I won't sleep in a room with bad spirits. And I won't live in a house with bad spirits." So the sale is off. More than that, Mama insists we move out of the main house and into a small guesthouse nearby where there were no bad spirits. The guesthouse, it turns out, is new and better than the main house. It has bathroom, complete with toilet, bath, tub, and wood-burning heater that takes about one hour to heat enough water for three baths. So

because of the bad spirits, we did not need to carry our bathtub all the way from Petersburg.

St. Petersburg had been a hotbed of political agitation, yet it seems not to have touched the daily lives of Alexandra and her family. In late June of that same summer of 1914, perhaps even as they packed their bathtub on the train, Archduke Ferdinand was assassinated. The July that followed was a month of international ultimatums and alliances honoring commitments. On the first of August, Germany declared war on Russia because of Russia's pledge to help defend Serbia. Austria-Hungary followed suit on the fifth.

In an atmosphere of progressive worry and unrest, buying a property in the country could have meant keeping a semblance of tranquility away from the turmoil in the cities.

Lev, Alexandra, Roman, and Katerina, 1914

Five

1915
Little Sister

In the Spring of 1915, Alexandra would soon finish her studies at the Smolni Institute. Her father was concerned about the outbreak of war, but they discussed what course of studies she would follow after the Institute. She told her parents that she preferred art. "I like to paint. I think I shall take up painting. Perhaps I shall paint on porcelain like Kira." Kira was the daughter of a Russian general.

Colonel Drosdovsky objected. "No," he said, "Painting is very well as a hobby. There are many practicing this hobby, but very few are stars. My military pension is small. You should take up a more remunerative profession." Lev wished for his daughter to be independent and practical about the future.

Swayed by her father's words and an interest in medicine that ran in the family, Alexandra decided she would choose dentistry. When she told her fellow students of her choice, they were surprised.

"You will be taking bread[36] from Jewish women," they cried.

Dentistry, like medicine in general, was much favored by women in Russia at this time—a practice that continues to this day.

---

[36] "Bread" means livelihood here.

To that Alexandra replied, "If they study it, it must be good profession, for they are very smart."

Roaches

For Alexandra, her mother, and her little brother, life on Smolni Prospekt was not without its humorous side, in spite of the war. Alexandra was still studying in school, and the lesson one day was about electricity. She decided she could repair the bell that rang in the kitchen when a button was pushed at the front entrance or in the dining room. The button there hung from a cord over the dining table.

> I get ladder and climb up to investigate and I find out why the bell doesn't work. It is full of cucarachas, small brown ones, not the big black ones. No, I did not get rid of them. I am doctor. I only make diagnosis. The maid get rid of them.
>
> One day, around 11 A.M., General Yudenich (while in the capital) came to tea at our apartment.[37] But at this time, around 1915, he was commandant of troops on the Turkish Front and a good friend of my parents.
>
> Mama put out the best silver service. She sit on the general's left and I sit on his right. While she is pouring coffee from the silver coffee pot into his cup, I notice a cucaracha is swimming in his coffee. Happily he does not notice for he is busy talking with Mama. So I quickly take away his cup. Mama asks me what I am doing and I make some excuse, I don't remember what, so he will not see the cucaracha.

Later Alexandra described a fascinating book by a man named Levenson, all about how wonderful life was in St. Petersburg before the Revolution. "But Levenson did not mention cucarachas," she said laughing.

---

[37] He would die in the 1930's in the south of France, and Alexandra's parents would correspond with him to the end.

While finishing high school, Alexandra began attending night classes for wartime nursing. She was still able to complete her education at the Smolni Institute with honors and won the coveted gold medal, received from the hands of the mother of Tsar Nicholas—the Empress Maria herself—who still owned the roach-infested building in which Alexandra lived. Alexandra would never forget the invitation by Her Imperial highness to hot chocolate and cookies and to receive a scholarship. The award entitled her to take any course of studies she chose without taking an entrance examination. But since she lived at home with her family, she renounced the scholarship in favor of another student who did not live at home.

Siestriza

Suddenly there was a great need for nurses. Before the Revolution, nurses were called *siestra miloserdia*—sister of compassion, or simply, *siestritza*—little sister.[38]

In late May of 1915, Alexandra and her friend Lena finished their crash course in nursing. The diploma that Alexandra and her friends received at the end of their accelerated six-week night school course in nursing qualified them as wartime nurses, but not as peacetime nurses and not as R.N.s.

In early photos, Alexandra had no red cross on her nurse's uniform. When she completed her six weeks of training, the red cross was added. It belonged to

Alexandra in nurse's uniform

---

[38] After the Revolution, the Communists abolished the word compassion from their dictionary, and nurses became *med siestra.*

the order of Saint George. "There were different orders, like nuns." Every big city had its own order of nurses.

They finished the course on a Saturday and on the following Monday were at work in the Warsaw station in Petersburg meeting sanitary (hospital[39]) trains as they steamed in from the front lines with their loads of wounded men. At that time the Polish city of Warsaw was being evacuated, the Russian army was in retreat, and trainloads of wounded men were rolling into the station day and night.

She received a telephone call at home whenever a train rolled into the station. Sometimes the calls would come in the early morning, but usually in the daytime. These trains might once have served in elegant express passenger trains, or they might be sway-backed freight cars with dirty straw on the floor. Whatever was handy and serviceable was pressed into this important duty.

And so, in a frenzy, Alexandra's nursing career in World War I began—a few months of night classes, then the trips to Petersburg's Warsaw depot to assist with the wounded being carried from the front lines by the thousands. Another chapter in her life had started. It would help add more steel to her character—steel sorely needed so much in the years to come.

Sixteenth Summer

Not long after Alexandra began her nursing duties, a doctor from one of the hospital trains came into the barracks where she was working and told the chief surgeon that he needed two sisters to go to Warsaw that very evening on the hospital train.

"Can you give me two sisters?"

Alexandra interposed quickly, "My friend Lena and I can go."

The chief surgeon Frau Doctor Tenner, a German from the Baltic region, knew that Alexandra was only seventeen. "You can go," she told the girl, "but only if you get permission from your parents."

[39] "Sanitary" didn't necessarily mean immaculate.

Alexandra hurried to a telephone. Her father at that time was still earning extra money as a professor in a military academy outside Petersburg. By the time she was connected with his office it was 9 P.M. and he was unavailable. She told the person on the line to tell Colonel Drosdovsky "first thing in the morning" that she had left the night before on the hospital train to Warsaw. That was how she got "permission" to work on the hospital trains.

She stayed in Warsaw, then a part of Russia, until September of 1915, and then accompanied a trainload of wounded on the six-day trip to Moscow. When the train's twenty-two cars were cleaned and disinfected, she returned with it to Warsaw.

She was given the last two cars in the train to work in, and Lena was put in the operating room. The sleeping and dining cars were in the middle of the train, which entailed a trip "through" the officers' car from the tail-end cars. Since entry to that car was strictly forbidden, she had to detour around the car by walking outside of it on a small running board and holding on to the handrails. Every trip back and forth necessitated this arduous detour. Sometimes, as she inched along the outside of the officers' car, another train steamed by on the adjacent track in a thunder of smoke and steam, and she clung tightly to the car side to keep from being swept off.

When the train went empty from Moscow to Warsaw, Alexandra was assigned to the kitchen car. Her charge was to select the menu for the two cooks on duty there. Since it was very hot summer weather, she chose yogurt soup for the first meal. That was what her own family often had in the hot days of July and August.

> I tell the cooks to take large basin of yogurt and put in diced red beets, which turn the whole mixture bright pink, potatoes, fresh cucumbers, cold boiled beef, and lots of dill. There were twenty persons on the train—half Russian, the others German and Jewish physicians. All twenty ate heartily of my yogurt soup. All of the non-Russians came down with diarrhea.

Alexandra was promptly relieved of her duty in the kitchen and asked if she could do anything else.

"I can paint." She was thinking of her art lessons.

"Good. We need someone to repaint the plaques on the cars. They're all weather-beaten. You can repaint them for us."

Each car had two plaques on the sides. Alex first had a soldier paint each plaque with white enamel. On that background she painted a large red cross and the car's identification number with the words, "Of the Russian Red Cross."

After finishing one such plaque, she absent-mindedly sat down on it before it had dried. Nothing would remove the red paint, even washing in gasoline. She had only two nurses' uniforms in her suitcase, gray dresses that reached to her ankles. An older nurse cut off the stained section from the back of the skirt, cut a section the same size from the Front, and exchanged the two. The stained piece was then nicely concealed by the white apron, which was a standard part of her uniform.

A German aerostat [small balloon] flew over our train but did not put bombs on us, because we had red crosses painted on the roofs of all our wagons. The roofs were white. In those days every army respected the Red Cross. It was not like today.

Because of the retreat of the Russians before the German advance, the train was unable to go into Warsaw proper, but was stopped and turned at a town called Chervony Bor, which means Red Forest. From her car at the rear of the train, now headed back toward Moscow, she could see the Russian sappers already at work removing the rails behind the train so as to delay the advance of the German army.

While the train was being loaded in the very hot sun, she noted one young officer in particular lying on a stretcher.

He was very handsome. His stretcher was full of blood, dark red blood. And I remember thinking at the time that he is swimming in his own blood. I said to the soldiers carrying his stretcher to hurry at once to the operating room of the train. But then I see it is too late, he is already dying.

I had a patient who was an older German soldier, a prisoner of war. I spoke fluent German and was able to talk easily with him. Later he gave me his helmet and the bayonet from his rifle as relics of the war. I was very proud of them. The bayonet, I remember, was not smooth like the edges of the Russian bayonets, but very rough like a machete.

Here for the first time, on the side track at Chervony Bor, I saw a man die. I remember it so well because the man looked much like my father. It happened inside my car. There were two tiers of stretchers along the sides of the cars. The upper tier was for less important soldiers. Officers were on the bottom tier.

"This man is dying," someone said to me, nodding toward the man who looked like my father. I told them to give him some water, but he could not drink. And quietly, almost casually, he died.

From Chervony Bor the fully loaded train returned to Moscow. For the entire six days the operating room was kept busy—while in the cars, food and medication were given out by the nurses with the assistance of one or two soldiers in each car. During the two-day layover in Moscow, the wounded were transferred to hospitals, and the train cleaned up for its return trip to wherever the front line might be. On its return the train stopped short of Chervony Bor because the Germans had taken the town during the trip to Moscow.

I don't know just where the train stop on second trip to pick up wounded. But I notice when we are returning to Moscow with a full load of wounded men, it is our second day, and I had hole in the sole of my shoe. All the nurses had them. It was not from wear but from the constant motion of the floorboards of the wagon against our feet as we worked. I put some pieces of carton in my shoes.

On her last day, she received some money from Frau Doctor Tenner for her service. It was the first payment she had received. The chief nurse was the sister-in-law of Doctor Tenner. That was how she spent her sixteenth summer.

Six

1916

$\mathcal{I}$n the fall of 1915, Alexandra turned seventeen and had returned to start her university courses full time. Lev was off to the Front on the Austrian border to his artillery unit.

The Grand Duchess

The following spring, 1916, Alexandra decided that if she were going into war zones as a nurse, she would want to go to the Austrian Front where her father was serving with the 137th Infantry Regiment, the special regiment of the Grand Duchess Maria Pavlovna. Lev wrote in answer to her letter that she must first get permission from the Grand Duchess before she could serve with the 137th.

Grand Duchess Maria Pavlovna was the widow of a son of Tsar Alexander II, the great uncle of the then reigning Tsar Nicholas. She lived in a palais on *Millionair Uliza* (Millionaire Street) in Petersburg. But a visit with this celebrity required that an appointment be made through the duchess's secretary, Colonel Serebriakov, who lived in a villa by the River Neva in St. Petersburg.

She went at once to the villa and was admitted inside by a Negro servant, the first black person she had ever seen. She knew upon seeing this servant that Colonel Serebriakov was from old aristocratic family, going back perhaps to Peter the Great when blacks were imported from Constantinople via the Turks, or from Ethiopia. The famous Pushkin's father was a Negro.

> I already know about Serebriakov from my childhood time in Batum on the Black Sea. In 1904 there was a rebellion by revolutionary workers in Batum. One of their deeds was to burn down the house of Serebriakov. I remember seeing its ashes, but I never thought I would get to meet the famous owner of such ashes.

Serebriakov made an appointment for her the following day at the duchess's palais. For her meeting with this grand personage, Alexandra wore her best nurse's uniform under a leather overcoat. The servant who admitted her took her overcoat and ushered her into the receiving hall.

The meeting was brief. Alexandra explained her wish to be a nurse in the 137th regiment. The old woman, speaking in Russian—Aristocrats usually spoke in French, especially among themselves—gave permission, congratulated her, and wished her a safe return.

At the door, as the duchess' servant was putting Alexandra's leather coat around her shoulders, he said in a quiet voice, "My son is a lieutenant with the 137th regiment. Would you give him a greeting from me?"

Alexandra noticed that the servant knew all about the reasons for her visit with the duchess. "What is your name?" she asked the servant.

"Trubezkoy," he replied.

Trubezkoy was a very aristocratic name, she knew. But she wondered how this mere servant came to have it. When the slaves were freed in Russia in 1861, many of them took the names of the families who had been their owners. [40]

---

[40] This was the case in the United States after the Civil War. "In Peru also," she recalls, "there were many blacks I met named Prado, the name of the former president of Peru."

The Austrian Front

In May she left by train for the Austrian Front, changing trains at Kiev for Kremnitz, about sixty miles southeast of Olmutz.[41] Her father's

longtime orderly Gvosdenko met her there and took her by car the half-hour ride to the front-line camp.

A photograph shows her in this camp with Doctor Dupertuis, a volunteer from Switzerland, two Red Cross inspectors in the front row. Two Jewish medical students stood on the left, and on the

Alexandra with medical officers, Austrian front

right, a Russian in charge of supplies. One of the tent-residences is partially visible in the right background.

"At Front I meet and give greeting to Lieutenant Trubezkoy, as his father (the duchess's servant) ask me to do," she said.

The Godfather and Other Unseen Help

Despite her youth, Alexandra knew many people and made friends and connections easily. She also was able to see her father on occasion.

She told a story about her father that perhaps revealed a certain sense of divine protection, which may have, in turn, contributed to her own courage. Twice, bullets had avoided Lev rather spectacularly. Deeply religious, Alexandra knew God's role in her father's luck.

---

[41] This is inside modern-day Czechoslovakia, but about a hundred miles north of Budapest in Hungary, which was then Austria-Hungary, and a hundred fifty miles south of Krakow, Poland.

Papa's mother had six children, but all died as babies. That was in Southern Russia, in the Province of Podolsk where my grandfather Drosdovsky was building the railway from Kiev to Odessa.

When papa was born in 1869, there was a superstition to pick as his godfather the first person you see on the street, going to the church. Grandmother (Drosdovsky) thought, "It can not hurt," and so the first person they saw was a man sweeping the street. He became godfather of Papa.

In 1916, one time I stood by Papa. He was looking through his binocular, on the Austrian Front. Suddenly a bullet came from the air and struck the binocular and lodged there. Papa was not injured, and for long time he kept the binocular as souvenir. His regiment gave him as a present a new one, shaped like letter Z, the kind used in trenches.

Another time a bullet went through the front of his shirt, but did not touch him. The shirt was repaired. So, the street sweeper was good godfather to papa.

Still in her teens and in a war zone, she needed peace and quiet, even if it meant slipping away to a graveyard.

Hospitals were always near cemeteries. On Sundays, I went to the cemetery and put my mirror against a stone cross, and I combed my long hair. When I got one hundred lice, I said, "Enough for Sunday." I was by papa's regiment—the only woman. I helped the doctors.

Near Kremnitz, on the Austrian Front in the western Russian province of Volinia, there was an old and once-revered Russian Orthodox shrine, much of it then in ruins. Alexandra took time away to visit this shrine called Pochayevskaya Lavra. It had been desecrated by the presence of the Russian and Austrian armies using it for military purposes and had been abandoned, save for an octogenarian monk who preferred to die rather than leave. In a grotto on its grounds, Alexandra saw impressed in a rock the marks of two footprints believed by devout Orthodox Christians to have been made by the feet of the Madonna.[42]

According to a legend, Russian believers in 1240 were escaping from the invading Tartars (Mongols), and found refuge by a forested, rocky mountain dotted with caves. One of the devotees saw the Mother of God standing on a fiery stone. Under her right foot, the rock melted like wax, leaving her footprint copied in the rock from which flowed clear water with miraculous curative powers. Over its history, it has attracted hundreds of thousands of Christian Orthodox and Catholic pilgrims from Eastern Europe.

First Battle

Alexandra had only been at this camp on the Austrian Front for a little over two weeks when the war started for her with a big bang.

> Around May 20 order come for big offensive, and the regiment moved off to engage the Austrians. It was my first battle. It was called Sopanov after little town near Kremnitz. The Austrians were driven back that day a few miles.

During an artillery barrage, Alexandra was in the stable by the local school building. She watched half a dozen rabbits calmly nibbling in the hay while shrapnel rattled on the stable roof, and the air was filled with the roar of high explosives. "If the rabbits are not troubled by the noise," she told herself, "then perhaps it is not so dangerous."

She was put to work assisting the surgeon in the operating room, which had been set up in the school building. "For two nights and one day I work without stopping," she said. "At the end of that time I was so

---

[42] "I saw similar sets of footprints [in photographs]," Alexandra said, "also made in the rock, one in the stone lintel of a Greek monastery on the Via Dolorosa in Jerusalem, and the other in a stone on the beach in Portugal, covered whenever there was high tide. They too were believed to have been made by the feet of the Madonna."

tired that I sleep through artillery barrage, much to amusement of Doctor Dupertuis."

Prisoners

Most of the patients were ambulatory, and there were thirty or thirty-five Austrian prisoners among the wounded. One young officer was too tall to fit on the stretcher. Another officer prisoner told Doctor Dupertuis that the money he had been given to pay his troops with had been stolen from him in the time when he was moved from the front lines to the school. The corpsmen who transported the wounded from the front lines in this area were mostly musicians, many of them Jewish. Doctor Dupertuis called them together and told them that money had been taken from this prisoner.

He said sternly, "Whoever took it will return it by tomorrow morning. Leave it in the bathroom. No questions will be asked. If it is not returned by morning, I will have every other corpsman flogged."

By morning, the money was returned mysteriously.

Shots of Another Kind

During the moments of less intense fighting, inoculations were given. Many of the soldiers were shy and fearful about getting their cholera shots.

"It is nothing," Alexandra scolded them. "Here. I will show you." She offered her own arm to the needle.

Apparently the shot was too strong, for she quickly fell sick and got diarrhea. An older married soldier tended her in the tarp-covered wagon where she slept and kept her belongings. Tenderly he nursed her, did her laundry, emptied her waste, and brought her food and medicine until she recovered.

While recuperating in this wagon, she overheard the soldiers complaining one night about the next day's offensive. They had just been given their allotment of cartridges.

"Only ten bullets," one of them complained. "Give me more."

"We have no more."

The artillery was equally short of shells.

Grown to the Ground

The Russian soldiers were holding their lines, but at increasingly high costs. After she returned to duty, a weeping soldier came to Alexandra and told her that his lieutenant had been killed in the night. He asked her to help him put a clean shirt on the officer for his burial. Together they went to the officer's quarters and found a clean shirt. But when they went with it to the body lying in a nearby house, they found that rigor mortis had set. It was impossible to change shirts because of the stiff limbs.

"He was already hard," Alexandra remembered. "All we can do is wash his face and arrange his hair."

The corpsmen had laid out the bodies of a dozen young dead officers on the grass behind the stables. Papa was there and went to see them, and he did not know that one of these officers was not yet dead but still dying. Just after Papa walked up, the dying man groan and move suddenly. Papa fainted.

But it no impressioned me. I remember once after big battle in the hot summer on Austrian Front, bodies of dead soldiers lie on battle-field for two or three days. When sanitary corpsmen go to pick up these dead for burial, the bodies are stuck to the ground and only with much difficulty can they pick them up. They tell me that the dead bodies have "grown to the ground."[43]

---

[43] In Spanish they say *crecido*, grown together with the ground.

The Return to St. Petersburg

Going through Poland on one of her return trips, Alexandra was nearly eighteen, but she'd seen much violence, even though it didn't "impression" her in the intensity of the moment when she had to keep her wits in order to survive.

She detoured about forty miles northwest of Krakow to stop and visit the serene and famous Sanctuary at Yasna Gora.[44] For centuries Christian pilgrims have venerated its main icon, Our Lady of Czestochova. She was very impressed with the old painting of the famous Black Madonna that had endured fire, invasions, and vandalism—and around which many legends and miracles were attributed.[45] The image was so lovely and powerful that it inspired her artistically for the rest of her life. The icon of the Virgin of Czestochova has been—and still is—venerated for centuries by Christian pilgrims.

Ironically, a short distance from Krakow in the opposite direction of the shrine lay what would become one of the most infamous manifestations of human inhumanity: the German extermination camp of Auschwitz.

In the first week of September of 1916, Alexandra returned to St. Petersburg to begin dentistry studies at the Dental Institute of Doctors Pashutin and Efremov. "Very good school."

During the day Alexandra attended classes at the dental school on Nevsky Prospekt (the institute is still there), and from 8 P.M. until

---

[44] A short distance from Krakow, rests one of the most infamous manifestations of humanity: the German extermination camp of Auschwitz. In the opposite direction from the city one can visit the serene and famous Sanctuary at Yasna Gora.

[45] Alexandra said, "I painted her four times. One is in Mama's casket; she wanted to be buried with that icon. One is in the library of Duke University in Durham, North Carolina, donated by Olik where he was in training in orthopedic surgery. One is with my friend Elizabeth Meier in Germany, who bought her for $400, and one was bought by Mr. Panek of San Diego. It was the best—like a miracle. He made all my tablets and frames for icons. When he saw Her, he said, "How beautiful," and paid immediately.

Alexandra and cousins Kolia (left) and Gleb, who was executed in Poland by the communists in 1947 for having been a Guard officer 30 years earlier

midnight she helped tend the wounded. They were laid out in barracks containing forty stretchers each, with two nurses per barracks. Part of her work involved cleaning and dressing the wounded—and feeding the men in the short time they were in the barracks and prior to being sent on to the hospital or returning from operating rooms. Nursing and dietetics in such conditions did not constitute exact sciences.

One night Alexandra gave some especially appetizing food—red beans with chunks of pork in it—to a wounded soldier. He took it with pleasure and proceeded to gobble it down. When he was done, he called out to her, "That was very good. But now please give me my milk diet. I have been wounded in the stomach and can eat only a milk diet."

Such docility before authority has been a mark of the Russian peasant for centuries.[46] Docility was on the wane as more and more daring revolutionary activists managed to rouse the docile masses to action so powerfully that the social structure teetered on collapse at that point. Many in the aristocracy no longer accepted the will of the tsar without question, and Prince Yousupov and other nobles murdered the notorious monk, Rasputin, thereby ending his influence over the Romanovs

[46] And it has continued into modern times.

in December of 1916. Alexandra remembered it, however, mainly as a time of a pleasurable evening with a friend.

When Rasputin was killed, I had a Jewish friend, also a dental student. We had the same name, Alexandra Lvovna. Her brother was a journalist for "Retch" or "Speech"—a very liberal paper in Saint Petersburg. I remember invitation at her uncle's home: big table, nice china, crystal, wonderful food like we never had at home. Chicken, better than in restaurant, and on a weekday. We have chicken at home, maybe four times a year, on special occasions.

Life carried on even though much of the country was exhausted by the prolonged war, and the country's markets offered little. Friends still gathered though the Russian winter worsened the shortages. Young people still met and dared to dream of a future.

That winter Alexandra was the object of attentions from someone other than wounded and ailing soldiers, although the young man had already been wounded twice. A captain in the Russian army of Polish origin, Anatole (Tolia) Yaroshewsky,

Tolia Yaroshewsky, sitting between friends

came to Petersburg at the Christmas season, fell in love with the eighteen-year-old dental student, and proposed marriage. Anatole's father had been a kapellmeister (band director) in the Russian army and had spent twenty years in Siberian exile, accused of political agitation against the tsarist government.

Alexandra's father, however, said while on leave that a marriage was impossible until the war had ended.

Well, they had to wait.

Anatole had a severe cold and Alexandra's mother gave him for a handkerchief an enormous piece of white brocaded material, two by four feet in size. Captain Yaroshewsky tucked it into a coat pocket from which it cascaded with a flourish as they visited the Petersburg museums. The young girl laughed every time he pulled this enormous piece of cloth from his pocket and applied it to his reddened nose. Young and optimistic despite everything, they were just three months away from the abdication of Nicholas Romanov, the last tsar.

Seven

1917

The Russian Army suffered terrible losses, inadequacies, and demoralization within the ranks. This together with the general economic hardships, the longing for peace, and socialist activism brought about the disintegration of law and order. Tsar Nicholas gave commands, but those in charge of enforcing them refused in increasing numbers or even joined the ranks of the protesters. That March, The February Revolution took place, so-called because of the differences in the old Russian calendar. Nicholas II abdicated on March 15, 1917, the ides of March. A provisional democratic government was handed to Alexander Kerensky. The Russian provisional government headed by Kerensky was committed to keep fighting the Germans and Austrians on the side of England and France, however, so Lev was still at the Front, now promoted to General.

Katrina prepared to leave St. Petersburg, never to return. She sent two big steamer trunks to her niece Zina, then living in Moscow, for safekeeping. The trunks contained the Drosdovsky's family heirlooms: silver, Lev's dress uniforms, fur coats, and all the Persian carpets Lev had purchased in 1906 at Baku on the border of "Persia." Then she and eight-year-old Roman left for Zhitomir, traveling over a thousand miles with Gvosdenko and the first load of the Drosdowsky family's possessions.

Six times Gvosdenko made the trip from Zhitomir to St. Petersburg and back, bringing Mama's things. It was the time of the revolutions and the trains were so crowded that he had to ride on the roofs of the railroad wagons. And there was much danger. Still Gvosdenko went six times to Petersburg.

Alexandra's Dental Institute was still operating, despite the riots and lack of stability. In the spring, it was the inevitable time for exams, so she stayed behind.

One professor told us that in preparing for our exams, we should hold a skull in our hands so that we can understand better the construction of the mouth and jaw. But the problem is to find a skull. That is not so easy. It was Easter time, and I went to Church to make my Easter Communion. In the church I saw a large crucifix and under it, a skull. It was a symbol to the faithful of impermanence and of the blood of Christ running down the cross to the head of Adam, redeeming him and all of us for our sins.

With good inspiration, I borrowed that skull when no one is looking. Later my professor asked me, "Drosdovsky, how did you prepare for your exams? Did you study with a skull, as I suggested?"

"Yes," I told him. Now every one of the students wanted to know where I got a skull. I told them, "I used the skull of Adam." They were mystified.[47]

I passed my exams with good high marks.

That spring, Alexandra was alone for two months in the St. Petersburg apartment on the fifth floor—no elevators—at 6 Smolni Prospekt, #63. As revolutionary activity mounted, she "buried" two pistols and some ammunition in the attic of the apartment. The builders

[47] Perhaps 60% of the students were Jewish. They could not get permission to live in Petersburg unless they were engaged in higher studies such as medicine, dentistry, and pharmaceutics.

put soil between the heavy joists above the ceiling. In this soil, she made a hollow and put in it the Austrian bayonet, jewelry, and cartridges.[48]

The Front 1917

A letter reached her from Tolia, her sweetheart, telling her he'd been wounded again, but that he was still alive and would heal. In the first week of May, 1917, Alexandra went to visit her mother and brother for a few weeks in Zhitomir, and at the end of that month, her father—now a General under the provisional government—sent Gvosdenko to bring her to the Front, this time as a dental nurse.

The Front in the summer of 1917 was in much the same place it had been the year before. Papa was living in the Castle of Vischnewez,[49] a place of great historic interest in Polish history. Papa took me to the dental station in his auto.

The chief dentist was very nice to me. Her name was Olga Sergeevena Geist, a Jewish lady from Moscow. I slept in a tent with another nurse. There were four or five nurses like me. They fix up barber chair for me to put my patients in and I begin work. But dentists are so scarce that they put me to work as dentist, an eighteen-year-old girl, with one year of dental school. I know only theory. I have no practice.

The Dancing Tent

I remember well my first extraction. The patient was not ordinary soldier, but is elegant officer of the Life Guard Semenovsky Regiment.

---

[48] "Perhaps," she says with a smile, "it's still there. My nephew Wolfgang Zeidler visited the building in 1986. At every one of its six entries was posted Soviet flag. So the entire building is used for government offices."

[49] Russian spellings often differ from local spellings. It refers to the castle of Wisnicz about fifty miles east of Krakow. Alexandra had pointed out that the borders of Russia extended further into what is now Poland. The Front may have been a hundred miles further north than the previous summer, but when traveling a thousand miles between St. Petersburg and Kiev, a hundred miles probably seemed like the same neighborhood.

His name is Baron Engelgardt. He had a German name. He is perhaps third or fourth generation of his family in Russian service.

A soldier brought him to see me, and he said, "Little sister, please take out my tooth." I see that his jaw is swollen.

"We have here corpsman," I told him. A *felcher* is soldier who is something like male nurse, but higher. He can do vaccinations.

The officer said to me, "I don't want one of those damned soldiers to touch me. You can take out the tooth."

I put him in my barber chair and looked at his tooth. It is molar in his lower left jaw and it is moving. With my forceps I pulled it out without difficulty. I did not use cotton, then or later in my practice. I tell my patient to suck and spit, suck and spit. That way they get up all blood and pus. I never use cotton. Captain Engelgardt went away happy.

Alexandra's quarters, Austrain front

Two soldiers always assist us in our work, keeping order and seeing that no more than a hundred patients were in our tent at one time. Sometimes the tent dance over our heads as the soldiers waiting were too many and were sent away, but tried to stay and clung to the tent ropes. We worked from morning till evening.

Hunting

One afternoon of that summer, Alexandra went with the cook when he went out to hunt for game for the mess. He carried a rifle; she, her sturdy Browning pistol. The cook was after wild boar. His plan was for them to climb a tree near a waterhole where boars came to drink. They climbed some nine meters up the tree and waited. The tree, like all the rest of the forest, was the private hunting preserve of the Emperor of Austria.

After half an hour or so, they heard a group of boars in the underbrush all around him. But the boar, perhaps smelling the hunters, would not come out into the open to drink. The hunters had no choice but to wait in the trees. Sounds of movement in the undergrowth continued until dark and then it was too dangerous for the two of them to walk back to the camp. The two of them sat all night, uncomfortably, in the tree.[50]

A Last Summer with Barinia

General Drosdovsky was living about ten kilometers from Alexandra's medical station. As worried as he was about his daughter's proximity to the Front, he may have wanted very much to give her something a normal teen would look forward to. Every Sunday morning when the fighting wasn't too intense, he sent his horse Barinia to Alexandra so that she could enjoy an afternoon ride. She never rode alone, but was always accompanied by someone, usually one of the doctors.

On one such Sunday in August, they rode through fields crimson with poppies to the house used as quarters by General (then Colonel) Kutiepov, commandant of the Preobragensky Regiment, the first regiment established by Peter the Great. As Alexandra and her escort cantered up to General Kutiepov's house, they saw a crowd of some two hundred soldiers standing out front, listening to someone giving an address.

It proved to be a propaganda harangue by a Bolshevik. "The officers could do nothing to prevent these harangues," Alexandra said. As soon as the soldiers—most of them peasants and perhaps a few workmen—saw Alexandra, they began to whistle.

---

[50] How dangerous is the wild boar? A Bulgarian hunter friend of Alexandra's in Ethiopia would later describe how he came across the body of an Abyssinian native in the forest. He had been gored in the belly by a boar and bled to death before he could get help.

Instinctively she kicked Barinia's flanks and galloped up to them, reining in her horse just short of their ranks in a shower of dust. They must have been a bit taken aback at her daring as well as her horsemanship.

"Bratzi!" the eighteen-year-old shouted. "Brothers! Have you never seen the girls in your villages ride horseback?"

They did not reply.

"Which one of you has toothache," she screamed, "and did not come to me at the dental station and I take care of it? There I work from dawn to dark as voluntary nurse, without pay. Have we turned any of you away? No. Every day we treat a thousand patients. And when you have toothache again, you may come to us once more."

The soldiers began to mutter among themselves.

"Goodbye then," she responded.

"Goodbye!" the astonished peasants cried. Then, "Goodbye, little sister. Goodbye."

Again she wheeled the noble Barinia about and galloped back to where the doctor sat his mount quietly smiling in amusement.

The memory of that moment must have been satisfying, and also sad because that summer was the last she would see Barinia. Eventually things would go badly for General Kutiepov as well. The General, in front of whose house the soldiers were protesting, would live briefly in exile in Paris. After the war, he would be kidnapped by the Soviets, together with General Muller, and returned to Russia and shot.

Bolsheviks Reveal Themselves

In that summer of 1917 there occurred an event that changed Alexandra's whole outlook. The Bolshevik leaders were attempting to take power by establishing local soviets. They had ruled that the soldiers should hold elections for revolutionary committees. The soldiers elected Alexandra as a medical representative on their committee.

"One of the soldiers who is on the committee is going to Kiev and I give him a note to Mama so she will give him suitcase full of my warm clothes for fall."

She thought she was still needed on the Front, but her compassion stopped at betrayal.

When the soldier return, he say my suitcase of clothes is stolen on the train. I think to myself, "It is God's will; nothing can be done about theft." But a little later some other soldiers tell me he sell my clothing for two rubles.

This incident, in Alexandra's words, "kill my sympathies with the Russian soldiers." She decided to get on with her own life.

In September of 1917, I could not return alone to Petersburg because of the revolution, and so I go to Kiev for my second year of dental school. There I attend Dental Institute of Doctor Projeico on Bessarabca Square. He is Ukrainian, but very old man. There were two or three French dentists on the faculty, one is named Martin. Another one is Lebedinsky, a Russian Jew.[51]

While studying dentistry that Fall of 1917, Alexandra went to live again with Uncle Nicholas and Aunt Olga in Kiev at Number 5, Theater Street. She hadn't lived with them since the Siberian Campaign. Cousin Lina had moved to Moscow, but Boris the musician was still there.

And Where Was Lev?

Sometime in October, the proud old Russian Army fell apart and stopped fighting Austria. General Lev Drosdovsky was made a Ukrainian prisoner of war.

---

[51] "Lebedinsky became a Frenchman. Many years later I met his son in Paris."

Papa was sleeping in the local school of a small town when the Austrians occupied it. The Austrian commander came to him at the school and together they arranged the surrender.

The former enemies discovered a basis for mutual respect and became friends. Lev clipped a lock of Barinia's mane and put it in his pocket. He'd owned and loved the horse for eight years.

"Papa said to the commander, 'Take my horse. I don't think I have any more need of it.'" His face probably showed only professional dignity, and in the Russian way betrayed nothing of the sorrow he was inevitably feeling.

The Austrian was delighted to get such a fine animal. Shortly thereafter, Lev was released and assumed a new position as the Austrians and Germans recognized the Ukraine as an independent country apart from Russia.

Eight

The Last Year in Russia

*L*enin's promise to end the war won him many supporters. His Marxist ideology stressed the dissolution of borders. There would be an international proletariat of workers in a "New Order of Nations." Borders were "old order" concepts. World War I had been a typically misdirected waste, benefiting only the exploiters of the masses. Class struggle was the only valid aggression. And so, with this paradigm, it was easy for Lenin to accept the harsh territorial demands made by the Germans at the Brest-Litovsk Conference. "Give them what they want," was his policy. "Just get an armistice signed and hand them [as buffer States] Finland, the Baltic States, the Ukraine [which had been the breadbasket of Europe]. At the end, it will not matter. Just stop the war." Exhausted Russians wanted the horrible war over with. Lenin fulfilled his promise.

The Ukrainian nationalists didn't like the notion of being merely a buffer state, however. It had suffered a turbulent history and saw the opportunity to secede from Russia and become independent. The rich soil, abundant minerals, and a crossroad between East and West made the area a target to numerous invaders that ranged from the Khazars, the Huns, Tartars from the east, the Turks from the south, Austria/Hungary the German Teutonic Order, Poland and Lithuania, and the Swedes from the west and north.

While the October Revolution was taking place in Russia—actually in November because of the calendar difference—the Ukraine optimistically longed for freedom, especially from a Russia run by Bolsheviks. The Ukrainian Peoples Republic formed its own provisional government, which was recognized immediately by the Central Powers (Germany and Austro-Hungary) who hoped that besides being able to move their troops to the Western Front to win the war against France, England, and Italy, to also overcome hunger at home through the anticipated availability of Ukrainian harvests. This gave a breathing spell to the new Ukrainian republic, and incidentally made the Germans—the former foes—allies of the independent Ukraine.

The new republic printed stamps, ran a postal service, and established its own army, turning to former officers in the Russian Army for direction. General Lev Drosdovsky—freed from his oath to a deposed tsar and from loyalty to the failed provisional Russian government—joined the army of the new nation.

> Papa became the third highest official of Ukrainian army. First is Minister of War whose name I do not remember. Then is General Slivinsky, chief of General Staff, and then was Papa, First General Quartermaster. He has in his hands organization of entire Ukrainian army.

Collaterally, Lev found friends among the former German enemies, such as General Von Makovsky who would eventually alert Alexandra if Kiev should prove too dangerous in the seesaw of events. The Red Army was advancing, the counter-revolutionary anti-communist White Army battled in a desperate Civil War, the Polish Army was attacking from the west, and the Germans themselves were near collapse on the Western Front.

During a school recess in December, Alexandra accompanied her father from Kiev to St. Petersburg to retrieve his life savings, but St. Petersburg and much of Russia was under Bolshevik control. If they had discovered Lev's rank, they probably would have shot him.

"Papa removed all his military insignia. He was in half uniform. I was dressed like nurse," Alexandra said.

Their train came to the border of Bolshevik Russia at Mogilev, a little more than third of the way to St. Petersburg. They got off the train there to visit a relative who was chief of artillery there. His name was General Barsukov and he was married to Alexandra's cousin Mary, the daughter of her mother's sister Anna and her husband Colonel Alexander Kedrov.

Papa phoned General Barsukov from the railway station. He invited us to lunch with him and sent a two-horse sleigh to bring us to his office. It is the last time I was in such a sleigh. Everything was snow. All the buildings were small and all of wood. I saw no stone or brick, and few buildings of more than one story. General Barsukov's office was in just such little wooden building as the rest.

While we were talking with him, his door suddenly burst open and a sea soldier—how do you call him, a sailor?—walked in with two pistols strapped to his waist. He stared at us without smile.

"Who are these people?" he demanded to know.

The General said, "They are relatives of mine. They are Ukrainians." Ukrainians then were foreigners to Russia and protected by Germany. The sailor looked at Papa and me some more and then left. We asked General Barsukov who he was. "He is my commissar," the general replied with a smile, but only little smile. "He is charged with seeing that I am true to the doctrine of the Bolsheviks."

Before getting back on the train, General Barsukov tell Papa to give his *shashka* [saber] to the commandant of the depot. "You will not need to be armed," he told Papa. So Papa give up his saber that he has had since he was first an officer.

Two days later, December 17, 1917, father and daughter arrived in St. Petersburg at about ten at night in bitter cold and took the electric tram to their apartment at 6 Smolni Prospekt, fifth floor, #63. The building was built of gray stone around a central courtyard. Their own apartment, unheated for a year, was intensely cold in the subzero weather.

I wrap myself that night in all warm clothes and several coats, but I cannot sleep much because of the cold.

General Drosdovsky went at once the next morning to the bank to take out his deposit. It amounted to sixty thousand rubles and represented his life savings. The ratio then was ten rubles to one English pound.

"It was considerable sum," Alexandra said, "and would buy nice property."

"We are sorry," the bank official told the general, "but all the money is gone."

"Gone!" he exclaimed. "Gone where?"

"It has been confiscated by the government."

"And what of the jewelry in my safe deposit box?"

They shrugged. "It has been confiscated too. All is gone."[52]

That night, while trying to sleep in the cold, she became aware of a sound in the opposite corner where her father was sleeping. At first she did not recognize it. She lay still, trying to make out this strange sound. And then it dawned on her.

It is sound of Papa's weeping that I hear. At this moment I realize I must become good dentist. At this moment I realize I must take all responsibility. Papa is then fifty years old, an old man for those times. He lost all. He has no pension, no insurance, no life savings. All gone. I realize then I must take responsibility for family.

---

[52] Alexandra revealed that much of this property confiscated by Lenin's government was later sold to Armand Hammer, the United States businessman long friendly with Soviet regime. "For this reason," she said, "I do not like Armand Hammer. He is like jackal."

In the apartment on Smolni Prospekt, a dozen icons still remained, some worked with silver and gold. Every room had its icon, and there were five in the bedroom. Nothing could be taken.

We left everything, even our icons, in apartment. We gave apartment to a widow, Mrs. Kholodnaya, who had two sons, officers in Russian army. She had lost everything in Finland sometime before.[53]

Train Wreck

A week after their arrival in St. Petersburg, they took the train back to Kiev. On the first night out, under Bolshevik-managed railroads, it collided with another train. One of the steam lines was broken in the accident, and escaping steam scalded scores of passengers. A call went up and down the train for medical personnel to assist the injured. Alexandra in her nurse's uniform went off at once to help. Her father came slowly behind.

Despite the fact that he'd seen horrible injuries in battle, this high-ranking general never seemed to get used to the sight of suffering.

Papa was sensitive. When the train accident happen, some of the passengers are horribly disfigured by the steam. I do what I can to help. But when Papa come and saw the injured, he becomes faint and they had to put him in one bed until he recovered.

Cards

Lev may have been demoralized, but he didn't give up. He returned to his duties in the Ukrainian army, and Alexandra returned to her classes. Four and a half months later after her school examinations in

---

[53] "Mrs. Kholodnaya lived in our apartment on Smolny Prospekt at least until 1928. We have letters from her to this time. And then all letters stopped. I do not know what happen," Alexandra said.

May of 1918, Alexandra went to Zhitomir to spend a few weeks with her mother. "That summer I spend one month working as dental assistant at a German dental section. All of Ukraine was occupied now by the Germans."

Still, the Ukrainian Peoples' Republic remained hopeful that Germany would at least halt the advance of the Red Army until the Ukrainians would be fit to keep their freedom. Lev would travel as Ukrainian military attaché to observe the organization of the Swiss army.

Alexandra read her cards, which indicated a sudden visit.

Papa was trying civilian clothes for his trip to Switzerland. I opened the cards[54] for myself and see my fiancée. I was by the window and see a man in civilian clothes coming up the alley: It was Tolia! I did not recognize him out of uniform. Is it not a wonder? Papa gave Tolia his uniforms because he was joining the White Army and they were the same size. He was three days with us.

Former Tsar Nicholas and his family had been executed in July, the White Armies unable to reach them to save them. Like so many officers after the Bolshevik revolution, Tolia wanted to fight the Reds.

"I saw him leaving with numb thoughts." From then on, she learned not to "open the cards" for herself. Sometimes it was best not to know what they foretold.

Broken Dresses and a Mother-in-Law's Lost Head

In September of 1918 when Alexandra returned to dental school, her father left for Switzerland. Katerina and little son Roman accompanied him. Alexandra stayed with Uncle Nicholas Liatoshinsky and Aunt Olga, and cousins Boris and Zina. Not long after, the Bolsheviks had reached Kiev. The conflict between the Reds and Whites had escalated into a Civil War that would last two years. The war-weary Allies tried to

---

[54] As she had learned from Aunt Olga.

help the Whites, but may have done more harm than good since the Reds told the people that foreigners were still attacking them, and that the Reds were keeping them safe.

> I was in Kiev during bombing. By artillery, not airplane. The Germans came to the aid and the Reds retreated. We were having dinner with the mother-in-law of a colleague of the owner of the house when an artillery shell went through the house and cut off her head! It exploded in the closet full of dresses. They were all ruined. The colleague talked more about the ruined dresses than of the mother-in-law.
>
> People were told that when the Reds will come, all young men will go to Siberia or Red Army. My cousin Nina had poison tablets against conceiving of child. Her husband decided to kill himself and took those tablets. Then, he changed his mind and was taken to hospital. They washed his stomach and he lived many more years.

Word came that Tolia was wounded again, though still alive. Her parents and Roman had spent a week in Berlin before going to Berne, Switzerland. In Berlin, they stayed at the hotel on Friederichstrasse. A revolution was also going on in the streets there outside the hotel.

Lev did not wear his military uniform, but his bearing gave him away. When he entered the dining room with his wife and son in civilian clothes, all the young German officers in the room stood up at attention. Lev snapped his heels and bowed.

"They could see that he was officer," Alexandra reported proudly.

In December of 1918 Alexandra took her last examinations in Russia. She took one of the exams in the chemistry professor's kitchen and the next in the dining room of another of the professors. She went to the office of the University of Kiev to obtain copies of her high school and dental school diplomas. They told her to come back in March. She knew that was going to be too late.

In that December, the Revolution and the Civil War were in full swing and many started leaving the country. "How do you know when to leave?" was a question many asked.

A friend of the family, General Voronetz, told Alexandra, "You can swim with one arm holding a boat—you are not ready. When you

think you can swim with both arms, without holding to boat, then you are ready to emigrate."

The Bolsheviks had overrun and occupied most of Kiev. Tolia had been wounded yet again. They killed many

The CHEKA Building, later the KGB building

people, including General K who was a good friend of the family. He was taken out of his house and killed in front of the CHEKA building.[55]

"I came to his wife and she said, 'Do not go to main door, but use side door.'" Another general had lived there and was also taken out and shot. Their bodies were still lying in the gardens. Madame K wanted to bury the body of her husband, and also she knew that he had his last payment of three hundred rubles in his sock.

When she went to the gardens, the guard had said, "No, you can not bury your husband. He will have a common grave. A dog's grave is enough for a dog."

Alexandra went to Commissar Churnovsky to see if she could get permission for Madame K to bury her husband. He had been her patient. She went dressed in her nurse's uniform because she could better pass through the guards dressed so. When she asked if she could see Commissar Churnovsky, they let her in. She would always remember the long corridors to his office.

"I recognize you, of course," he said. "Do you wish to work with us?"

---

[55] This would become the KGB building. (The Cheka were the original Bolshevik enforcers.)

"No, thank you," she told him. "I am studying in dental school."

"Oh, good."

Alexandra found him tall, good-looking, and well shaven.

"I wish to get permission to bury the body of my friend's husband, still lying in the city gardens."

"Ah, good" he said, and without questions drew up a paper and gave it to Alexandra.

The general was buried and the three hundred rubles retrieved. Madame K's husband had been shot in the back of the head.

"It is Bolshevik manner. It is good—instant death," Alexandra later said.

The same "good" fate lay ahead for Commissar Churnovsky. The Whites later captured him and shot him.

It was at the apartment of Uncle Nicholas and Aunt Olga Liatoshinsky that she received the phone call from Colonel von Makovsky telling her to get out of Russia immediately. When the colonel called Alexandra on January 19, 1919 and told her to leave the country, Alexandra abandoned her plan to get her diploma from dental school.

Tolia was still alive and fighting the Reds, but he wouldn't stop until he had given his all. If he somehow survived, Alexandra knew that finding each other would be virtually impossible. She also knew that those three days together at the end of the summer would probably be the last time she would ever see Tolia.

"Our love was doomed by the breakdown of Russia," Alexandra said.

There was no time for sorrow, however. Her family needed her. And so Alexandra had collected the check for her father's backpay and headed for Berlin, which was also in a state of chaos.

Standing between the railroad cars and throwing away the treasured Browning pistol that she had dismantled piece by piece, Alexandra—with tears in her eyes—understood there was no point to looking backward. Looking ahead was more her style.

Nine

Back to Russia

*T*hrough obvious tenacity and determination on the part of the disintegrating Ukrainian government, the Ukrainian embassy continued to operate in Berlin to help the flood of Ukrainian refugees escaping into the country that had attacked them, occupied them, and was now experiencing the chaos of its own revolution. Nineteen-year-old Alexandra, carrying the important check and her hatbox full of eggs and ham, learned there that her parents were not in Berne as originally planned, but were staying at Lindau, a small town in Bavaria on the edge of Lake Constance, also called Lindau-am-Bodensee. They had fled Switzerland's high prices, which were roughly five times higher than those in Germany.

They were together in Lindau only two months when her father received a letter from the Ukrainian government telling him that he had money coming, a kind of "liquidation payment" to be made before the Ukrainian government fell completely to the Reds. Since the money couldn't be delivered, someone had to go to the Ukraine in person to collect the sum, another thirty thousand marks. It was imperative that someone go for the money since they could not foresee when the general would have employment again. But that someone could not be the general himself. Katerina and Alexandra both insisted that he not return.

"You will not be allowed to leave," Katerina cried.

Alexandra knew he would be shot like General K. "I can do it," Alexandra said. "I know all those people in the government, and I can stay with Aunt Vera in Rovno."

On March 14 she took the train for Rovno. The Red Army had overrun Kiev, and the Ukrainian government had moved its seat to this town on the Austrian border. Alexandra knew the town of her birth well.

Her first layover was in Vienna. "I visited a museum," she recalled. "There was not much to eat there unless you had food stamps. I had none. All I could get without them was herring and sweet wine. I could not even get bread."

All of Eastern Europe was in disarray after the war. She arrived in Budapest during a day of demonstrations by Hungarian army officers who were angry at having been denied a pension. Hundreds of them were out in the streets, in full and magnificent military regalia, shining the shoes of passersby in an attempt to shame the government into yielding to their demands. Next morning she took a train through the Carpathian Mountains where she caught the local to Rovno.

I stayed with Mama's sister in Rovno. The Ukrainian government offices were in a little . . . bungalow. After I showed them my passport and the letter Papa had received telling of the money, they paid me thirty thousand German marks Papa was owed—only they didn't have marks and paid it in Austrian krone. They completely filled one of my suitcases. And the grip did not have a lock, only two leather straps that buckled around it. Next day I said adieu to Aunt Vera. It was the last time I ever saw her.[56]

[56] Vera escaped to Poland with her son Nicholas and his wife, and lived in Warsaw until her death. I wrote to them over the years and sent them clothing and money. Vera died in the kitchen of that tiny apartment, of stomach cancer which she had suffered for three years, with vomiting and everything. . . .They had only one room plus kitchen. Now her son is also dead of cancer of the shoulder. He had a large swelling there. It proved to be cancer.

When the train from Rovno reached the Austrian border, Alexandra—burdened with her two suitcases, one full of clothes and the other of money—was told she must have her passport stamped in the station. She did not have the time or strength to carry her suitcases with her and she was afraid to leave them even for a short time.

Looking about the railway car, she noticed a Polish army officer and his wife. She decided to ask him to watch over her bags while she was gone. Standing in line, she heard the train already starting to steam down the tracks. Alexandra ran back from the station office, praying she'd make it. She had to leap aboard the moving car. It was the Polish officer who caught her and pulled her back aboard.

Somewhere she changed trains and was consigned to a boxcar. The few existing passenger cars were mostly restricted for special use. Every available car carried people, in between and on top, masses of humanity trying to escape. "A Russian helped me board the boxcar and he protected me. I am sure he was a Cossack officer who had escaped the Reds."

At Stanislau, where the West Ukrainian government had an embassy, she was forced to lay over once more. It was Easter week, 1919. She had to go again to the station to get her passport stamped. Many Russian soldiers were lounging about the station. She walked boldly up to one of them.

"*Bratzi* [brothers]," she said, "can I leave my luggage with you for a few minutes? I must go to the commandant and get my passport stamped."

"Of course," one of them replied with a laugh. "We are in no hurry here. Our train will not be in till midnight."

In the railroad station office, she discovered that there was no train going in her direction until the next day at the earliest. She would have to stay at least overnight, but the hotels were full of refugees. She wondered where she could go.

Aunt Vera's daughter-in-law still lives in the little one-room apartment in Warsaw. Conditions are terrible there, still. We do not realize here," Alexandra said in her later years.

"I had found," she remarked, "that when you need to know something, ask a Jew." They depended on networking and were very connected. So that was what she did in this instance. She walked with her luggage into the town and accosted the first Jewish man she met.

"I know of a woman who rents rooms," he told her. "She can put you up for the night. I will tell you how to get to her house."

She found the house and took the room. It was satisfactory, though the decorations hung about the bed—some sort of black hangings—were somewhat unusual. When the laundry woman came to the room in answer to her request to the landlady, she made the sign of the cross as she crossed the threshold.

"Why did you do that?" Alexandra asked.

"A lady died yesterday in this room—a Jewish lady. In that very bed, in fact."

"What was wrong with her?"

"She had typhus."

Alexandra crossed herself. Hygiene did not exist in such social upheaval. After settling in, Alexandra walked to the West Ukrainian ministry, which was in an unpretentious little house. The chief of the ministry, Doctor Gregorovich, knew her and her family. She explained what she was doing there.

"Well, we will have to arrange something," he replied.

"We have a mission that is leaving in a few days for Italy. It is headed by Major Ivan Kossak. I will make you his secretary. You can travel with him; it will be safer." Embassy envoys could count on diplomatic immunity.

Gregorovich had a new passport made for her that she would keep all her life. In the photograph she is wearing her aviator's jacket, but the "terrorist" look has been softened. On her head she wears an attractive felt hat and she has flung a gauzy white scarf casually around her neck. "In this photo I look more like Mata Hari than like terrorist."

After ten days waiting in her rented room, now officially a secretary of the Ukrainian foreign mission to Italy, she received word that their train was about to leave and did not have time even to allow her washing to dry. She had to pack it damp and rush to the station. With Major Kossak and two officer-aides, Alexandra left Stanislau in late April of 1919.

After one day on the train, they commandeered a military truck and drove the rest of the way, buying eggs and other food from farmhouses as they went. Going through Hungary, they drove north of Budapest and avoided other population centers because the Hungarian Communist Bela Kuhn was running the government and Ukraine was, of course, anti-Communist.

On May 1, they arrived in Prague and the situation improved. They were promptly invited to the opera as members of an official diplomatic mission. Jan Masaryk, ill-fated president of Czechoslovakia, sat in a nearby box. Major Kossak, who knew Prague well, gave her a tour of the city and also of Vienna later. He dropped her off in Lindau with her two suitcases and drove away into the darkening night. She lugged her two suitcases to her parent's little rented house and rapped wearily on the door.

"I have come with your money, Papa," she said to the general when he opened to her knock.

Ten

Exile

Between the enormous fluted Ionic columns
There seeps from heavily jowled or hawk-like foreign faces
The guttural sorrow of the refugees.

    —Louis MacNeice,
    inspired by a visit to the Reading Room of the British Museum[57]

By 1918, the Russian body count was placed at just below two million, ranging from as high as nearly three million, and they would experience another three years of Civil War and subsequent brutal famine. Alexandra and her family had left it in favor of Germany where Emperor Wilhelm the II had abdicated and fled to Holland. President Woodrow Wilson's "Fourteen Points" appeared acceptable at first, and the Weimar German Democratic Republic was proclaimed on November 18, 1918. The "Fourteen Points" were soon forgotten, however, in favor of the harsh Armistice terms and the Versailles treaty that followed. Germany lost fourteen percent of its territory, half of its iron ore, twenty-five percent of its coal deposits, and ninety percent of its merchant navy. Its colonial empire dissolved, foreign investments

---

[57] *The New Oxford Book of English Verse*, edited by Helen Gardner (New York and Oxford, 1972), p. 927.

and patents (like Aspirin) were lost, and astronomical reparations imposed. Germany had lost close to two million people, roughly ten percent of its population.

The number of people exiled by modern states, like the number of the dead, is so huge as to defy comprehension. Millions endured the stripping away of all they knew and loved—home, friends, work, culture, even language. Unlike death, however, exile is a repeatable experience and can be prolonged over many years, as it would be for Alexandra and her family. Yet Alexandra would become another kind of refugee. When her original world was destroyed, she would keep it alive, carry it off into exile with her. She gave it shape through her creative, practical, and artistic talents, and through her memories—all the while adjusting to new circumstances.

The German Revolution started one year after the Russian Revolution, almost as a mirror image, but with a difference: There was enough discipline left in the military ranks to bring back a semblance of law and order to the Weimar Republic's democratic experiment. The money Alexandra retrieved for the Drosdovskys was helpful, but inflation was already beginning and the general was out of work. No salary, no income. The former third highest-ranking officer in the Ukrainian army became a shoemaker. The Germans, quite aware of their own post World War I miseries, were sympathetic and helpful to the former enemy general who made many friends for life.

While living with her parents in Lindau on Lake Constance in 1919, Alexandra went to the movies one evening with a friend. Quite by accident, they met the friend's nephew there, a German dentist. When he learned of Alexandra's dental training and experience, he encouraged her to seek a job in Germany.

"I will be happy," he told her, "to place an ad at my expense in one of the German dental magazines. I assure you, you will receive a job."

To her astonishment, the advertisement produced eight job offers within a few days of the appearance of the magazine. Such a response was not at all surprising. Because many had died during the war, few young men had gone into the dental schools in Germany between 1914 and 1919. Dentists were in great demand.

A Woman on Her Own

Alexandra accepted a position with Orts Krankenkasse Zahnklinik, a dental insurance clinic near Hamburg.

> My parents and brother accompanied me as far as Meersburg. From there I took the train alone. I cried and cried leaving my family. I felt that I was so desperately alone—just four months short of being twenty-one years old, and I was on my own. I was assured that I could study and complete my additional two years required to receive my German Dental Diploma while working with them. That is why I chose the Hamburg position, because it gave me time to study.
>
> First of July 1919 I started working at Dr. Ritter's dental clinic as his assistant. I soon earned his confidence and had a separate office and nurse, with my own patients under his friendly supervision. I received three hundred fifty marks a month of which two hundred marks were spent for room and board at my employer's house—I had a hundred fifty marks left for small expenses, but I lived with a pleasant, supportive, and cultured family.

It was in Hamburg that she learned "there was escape from Europe," as she puts it. She met a German colonial family that had lived in several German colonies. Their son was working in South America.

> In Russia, I met no colonial families like this since Russia had no colonies. It was first time in my life that I meet colonial people. So I learn in Hamburg that I can escape too from Europe.

The Civilizing Effect

In December, six months later, she left Hamburg to work in Dresden for a similar position for Dr. Herman Petry's dental clinic at Lindenauer Strasse #5, on the corner by the *Technische Hochshule* (Technical High School). Her salary was five hundred marks per month, to which was added ten percent of all the work she performed. Since this ten percent averaged two hundred to two hundred fifty marks per month, she made twice her Hamburg salary. Both Dr. Petry and Alexandra had an office and an assistant. Hers was ten years older than she. She lived for a time with an elderly Catholic lady with whom she went to Sunday Mass.

> I much prefer Dresden. It had good museums and theater. In the summer Rachmaninoff used to visit his wife's parents, the Satins, in Dresden. He stayed in the Hotel Weisser Hirsch and almost every day he practiced piano in the lobby of the hotel from eight in the morning till noon. I used to go with friends to the garden of the hotel to listen to such concert.
>
> Also, in Dresden I know that there are three things that characterize the young woman who has finally come into her own. She must read French romances, she must eat chocolates, and she must smoke cigarettes. I started to do all three. I read many French romances, ate many chocolates, but I did not like cigarettes and soon stopped smoking.
>
> In Dresden I learned to paint in the modern style. There were many distractions in Dresden, wonderful art in the museums, and one of finest opera houses in the world. Many opera singers were our patients, and I often received complimentary tickets to opera. I remember especially *Eugene Onegin*. I cried when I heard it. I think that I heard all of Wagner, but I did not like him. But I did paint Wagner's music in my modern style. I discharged my impression of *Lohengrin* and *Die Meistersinger* by painting. Dresden had a very civilizing effect on a Russian immigrant girl.

Back in Lindau

Alexandra's parents had a welcome rendezvous with someone from Russia. By a strange irony, Queen Olga of Greece—aunt of the late Nicholas II—met Lev and his wife. All three were exiles at Lindau-am-Bodensee in Bavaria. That same year, 1920, sad news came out of Russia concerning the family. Uncle Nicholas, whose family had so generously shared their apartment in Kiev with Alexandra while she went to dental school and at other times in the past, should have lef when Alexandra did—along with his brother-in-law, Uncle Bogdan Sinegub.

> Uncle Nicholas Liatoshinsky was a school director in Zhitomir for many years. He was imprisoned by the Communists. He suffered from lice and died of typhus.
>
> Uncle Bogdan Sinegub had married my Aunt Larissa [Katerina's sister]. He was an employee of the port of Sebastopol and was liked by his workers. They begged him to stay, so he did not escape. "You have been good to us. We will tell the Bolsheviks [the communists] that you always helped us." He remained, and in 1920 they arrested him with all other supervisors in the administration of the port district. They were put on a train. At the second station they were taken out of the train, lined up along the tracks, and shot. There were hundreds of them.

Uncle Alexander Liatoshinsky, an admiral of the Black Sea fleet who was married to a much younger German teacher, had better luck and managed to escape with his wife to East Prussia.

Passport

Alexandra had to work hard to get by in 1920. She had heard about a job in Switzerland that paid four times what she was earning in Dresden. She applied immediately, but was turned down because of her Ukrainian passport. Had she a German passport, she would have gotten the job in Switzerland. She remembered that experience and learned from it.

Love

As part of her preparation for the examination in dentistry, Alexandra took a course in chemistry at the Technical University.

It was there that I met Herman Dabbert, an engineering student who had two more years to go before he received his degree. He became my patient. We found that we both liked to draw and paint. We loved animals, especially horses. We were both poor. He had lost his brother Heinrich on the French Front in World War I in the Battle of Langemark in 1914. We started exploring together the theaters, gardens, and museums of Dresden.

During the First World War, Herman had been assigned to the Eastern Front as a Rittmeister, or squadron leader. He told the story of being severely reprimanded for disobeying orders when ordered to attack the Russians over an icy field and had his men wrap the horses' hoofs with straw, thereby successfully guiding the attack over enemy positions. The general felt he should have obeyed orders immediately. "The German Cavalry is not an arm of the Humane Society."

Reminiscing World War I, we realized that while we were in the same area, we were on opposites sides of the Frontline.

I soon married Herman because he was good looking, and a name that sounded distinguished. Dabbert, of Huguenot origin, meant that his family had also once had to run for their lives from persecution by the Catholics in Southern France in the sixteenth century and had moved to Germany. We wanted to escape reality and create a dream.

And he was German—and I would get a German passport and forget being a destitute Russian that was refused access to most countries because of the Revolution.

I also loved him.

Newlyweds

Not long after their marriage in 1921 they attended a costume ball given by the students of the university. Alexandra, in elaborate white wig, went as Marie Antoinette. On the tram en route to the ball, they saw a gentleman in his fifties sitting alone with whom they struck up a conversation. Since he had no plans for the evening, Alexandra invited him to go to the ball with them.

> He enjoyed himself very much, dancing with many of the ladies in our party, and in the end he insisted on paying for our table. His name was Droste, he said, and he was in the candy business. A week after the dance I receive an enormous box of chocolates. The box has his name on it, Droste. He was owner of Droste chocolate factory. He died not long afterward.

In April of 1923, she passed her examinations and was ready to open her own dental practice, but she had no idea where she would get the money to buy one. Oddly, a man came to her office one day to tell her of a dental practice for sale.

"I think you should come to look at it," he said.

"How can I? I have no money."

"Well, come and see anyway."

They took the train for three or four stations from downtown Dresden to where the practice was located in a "nice villa." The dentist was selling out in order to get enough money for his marriage to the daughter of a butcher. All his tools and furniture were for sale: dental chair, electric drill, cabinets, a couple of tables, everything she needed.

> I saw the equipment was good and asked how much they wanted for the practice. They said one million marks. I had only ten thousand marks, but I said I would see about it. I wrote my parents at once in Lindau. Two or three days later I got a reply with a check for one million marks. Mama had

put up her diamond broach as guaranty with a friend in return for the million. The broach was worth three times that amount. That is how I opened my practice. In three months I had made enough to repay the million marks. I cannot remember [how much one million marks were worth in the spring of 1923], but I know that six months later in November one English pound was worth two billion (with a B) marks.

In these days of Germany's astronomic inflation, workers insisted on being paid at the end of each day so that they could spend their money on the way home, since its purchasing power would be halved, or worse, next morning.

Of the furnishings that came with the practice was a column with a vase on top into which the patient spat during treatment. An elegant affair, like a silver urn atop a square column, it would later be taken to Ethiopia. But when Alexandra looked into it in the office in Germany, it was full of bloody sputum. The dentists had never bothered to empty it.

Alexandra and Herman rented an apartment with a living room and bedroom. They turned the living room into the practice room, and the bedroom became the sitting room. For themselves, they rented a little apartment in the same building where they slept and cooked.

Most of her patients were from well-to-do families—many of them foreign, some from Sweden and Bulgaria—and they included Rachmaninoff's father-in-law, Herr Satin.

But the rich did not come to me themselves at first. First they send their servants and cooks. If it is all right, then they bring their children. Then they come themselves if I do painless work.

The cleaning lady in the building told Alexandra about a German general living in a nearby villa for whom she also worked. His mother lived in a nearby apartment in Dresden, but was unable to visit a dentist because of arteriosclerosis, which had literally cost her an arm and a leg. Alexandra went to see the old woman and soon made her a patient. "They were good people," she said. "They did not put the mother in a nursing home."

> The cleaning lady also told me of another rich family with twenty-six-year-old daughter who is mentally retarded and they wished for a dentist to come to their home to do work on their daughter. I went to their home and this young woman was sitting on the floor playing with her toys. I had the nurse hold her while I made fillings for her.

Still, both her income and Herman's salary as a member of the faculty of the Technical University did not amount to much. "We had enough only to eat," she says.

She first thought of Ethiopia in the spring of 1923 when one of her patients left for that country to be married.

> There were only two countries I knew of at the time that would take immigrants without requiring someone to be their financial sponsor. They were Ethiopia and Brazil. Brazil seemed more attractive to me. I went to the annual fair held in Leipzig where there were products displayed from all over the world. At the Brazil booth I got information and pamphlets. I thought that the Portuguese language might be a problem.
>
> Back in Dresden a few days later I met Rachmaninoff's mother-in-law, Madame Satin, in the Russian church. Her husband is my patient, and I tell her of my trip to Leipzig.
>
> "But why would you think of going to Brazil?" she asked. "Why don't you consider Ethiopia? Graf Rehbinder, who is Countess Keller's brother, is even now in Abyssinia. And already in one year he has forty-five porks [pigs]."

In Germany at that time, to have one pig was to be rich. Madame Satin was "in society." Graf Rehbinder was married to the granddaughter of the famous statesman Bismark.

"I will write to Graf Rehbinder for you," Madame Satin told Alexandra.

"At the mention of forty-five porks in one year," Alexandra said, "all thoughts of Brazil vanished."

In a few weeks Graf Rehbinder wrote Madame Satin saying that Ethiopia was ideal for a young dentist because dentists were in short supply. Moreover, it did not have the terrible inflation that crippled Germany.

Alexandra and Herman wrote for an appointment with Count Keller and his wife at their farm, about an hour outside Dresden by train. She learned there that the Count had been a good friend of her Uncle Alexander Liatoshinsky, formerly an admiral of the Russian Black Sea fleet.[58]

Countess Keller read aloud letters they had received from her husband's brother in Ethiopia, including the part about the forty-five pigs. With the help of the Kellers, Alexandra and Herman arranged for their emigration to Ethiopia. The fact that French was spoken there was important, since both of them were fluent in that language.

Once more they faced the hurdle of obtaining cash for the trip. Alexandra went to the Swiss friend of her parents, the same man who had already loaned her one million marks against her mother's broach. This gentleman, a resident in Lindau, owned a soap factory in Dresden.

Since I repay the first loan so quickly, he is prepared to make me this second loan. He loaned me one hundred English pounds. My husband Herman got additional loan of fifty English pounds from his cousin, Molly Dabbert, whose father was a retired English sea captain. His brother, Herman's father, was for long time officer in the Prussian army.

With one hundred fifty English pounds, we were millionaires.

---

[58] Uncle Alexander may be seen in one of Alexandra's albums in his dark-blue naval uniform. On the right breast is an insignia with a torpedo, his specialty. He died during a World War II bombing on the German-Poland border.

She made twenty-six visits to various offices of the French consulate on her bicycle in order to arrange the various permits and transit visas, which would allow her to reach Ethiopia via Djibouti (French Somaliland.)

"I feel at home in French consulate offices," she said. "They were very kind to me, perhaps because I speak such good French."

After tearful goodbyes and mixed emotions, the day had arrived for the great new adventure: Africa-Ethiopia.

Eleven

Africa

*A*lexandra and Herman took the train for Trieste, Italy on the first day of December, 1923, where they were to catch the steam passenger liner to Aden. A local passenger ship would carry them from Aden to Djibouti. The passage for two from Trieste to Aden—third class, with no cabin—cost them twenty pounds each.

One of her memories of this boat trip is a sign in the port city of Port Said, Egypt:

> *No Landing Permitted*
> *To Chinese, Russians,*
> *Dogs or Cats*

Djibouti was at the time a French colony also known as French Somaliland. With its hot, dry climate, the tiny colony's main wealth grew out of the trade through its harbor on the Red Sea and its railroad hub at the beginning of the line that connected the coast with Addis Ababa, the capital of Ethiopia.

In Djibouti they caught the train to Dire Daua, their destination in Ethiopia.

Ethiopia

Twice the size of Texas, and on the northeast corner of Africa, Ethiopia was the only kingdom in that continent, except for Liberia, that had the distinction of having survived an uninterrupted period of independence—at least since being described by the Greek historian Herodotus who lived in 450 B.C. The challenging rough geography of deserts and mountains had deterred many foreign attempts to subdue this kingdom, which was predominantly Christian at the time of Alexandra's and Herman's arrival. This feudal society was recovering from the passing of Menelik II—the emperor that had defeated the Italians in the famous battle of Adowa in 1896, enlarged his possessions, and started the modernization of his country, which included the first railway—a five-hundred-mile-long French enterprise that joined Addis Ababa to Djibouti.

Halfway between Addis Ababa and Djibouti lay Dire Daua, a town in an arid, hot, volcanic valley, similar to Calexico, California. It served as a crossroad for the voyagers taking the railway from or to ships heading to Europe or India and beyond. It also served as a gateway for an exotic passage to the wilderness of the interior. At the colorful local market, agile women of the fierce Danakil tribes—bare-breasted and wearing dyed long skirts—knelt at their stands, selling or exchanging the meager products of their farms.

Savage-looking men with their inseparable curved daggers and spears would attend to flocks of sheep, goats, lean long-horned cattle, camels, horses, and mules. Hungry dogs and flies circled stands where food was being prepared—injera, pita-like pies, fierce red-hot sauces, and charring meats—while vultures spiraled in the sky.

In its desire to modernize and improve health, the government was grateful to have dentists, especially those with Alexandra's education and skills. No examination was required for her to practice in Ethiopia. She rented a small office and put up her German dentist's sign. It was December 17, 1923—sixteen days since the journey to Africa had begun.

The only major disappointment was that her valuable dentist chair—which would be nearly impossible to replace and which she couldn't have afforded even if a replacement were available—had broken. The chair had been insured "CIF," but neither she nor Herman knew what "CIF" meant. The crate had been off-loaded at Djibouti for Dire Daua, and they had sent it on to the railway without inspecting it. When Alexandra and Herman opened the crate in Dire Daua, they found the chair broken in pieces.

"I cried and felt so powerless and exhausted!" Alexandra said.

Additionally, the insurance company was unwilling to pay compensation because "CIF" meant it was insured to the point of disembarkation. Had they opened the crate on the wharf at Djibouti, the insurance would have paid for the damage to be repaired. Alexandra would have to make do with a rattan chair. In fact, there were many items and procedures with which European immigrants, used to a certain way of living, had to make do.

There were many fleas in Ethiopia. The accepted method to get relief was to sprinkle horse's urine in the house—just like using eucalyptus tree branches and leaves to dissuade ants to invade the house. There was some difficulty to collect horse's urine, as they would get anxious of the noise and stop if a tin pot was used to get the urine.

We also put the metal legs of our beds in cups of water to keep crawling bugs away. In the low lands like Dire Daua everybody used mosquito nets, but eventually almost everybody would get malaria.

Wildlife often fascinated and surprised Europeans. In Dire Daua, Pan Vazek, who worked in a bank and also provided German zoos with wildlife, saw on opening the gate to his garden a telephone pole across his path. He pushed it with his foot, and it moved. It was a boa constrictor. These snakes lived in the cactus groves in the outskirts of town.

After a month, Herman left Dire Daua at the suggestion of new friends to look for an engineering job in the capital Addis Ababa. There he rented a small house and bought two horses, one named Ajax for Alexandra, hoping she would join him before long.

For two months she took lessons in Amharic, the native language, from Yohannes Asbe, a young Ethiopian who taught the children at Mere St. Melard's mission in Dire Daua. He was a Catholic "with excellent manners."[59]

> At night, before sleep I run through the more than three hundred fifty letters of Amharic, memorizing them and writing them in my mind. It was excellent preparation for sleep.

The nuns, always eager to be helpful, had introduced Alexandra to the instructor. This wasn't the first time she had been alone in a totally new and challenging situation.

Two of her first patients in 1923 in Dire Daua were nuns: Sister St. Melard and Sister Anne Marie Chantal. The order wore big white caps that the natives called airplane hats. "Never came out one sister alone. Always accompanied by another sister or a Catholic native." A priest in Harar had previously found Sister St. Melard in a far away mission unconscious from malaria in her tent with a snake, "but the good snake went away."

Sister Anne Marie Chantal was a university-trained mathematician. Her fiancée died in the First World War, and she became a nun.[60]

Alexandra saw them both frequently, but on this memorable visit, they came with a black maid and a baby. It had been found beside the dry riverbed where women abandoned unwanted children to be washed away by sudden floods when it rained in the mountains. A

---

[59] He was later killed in a brawl in a local nightclub, most of his face cut away by the blow of a saber, or so his friends told Alexandra.

[60] Several years later, she would be decorated by the French Government with a war medal because during the Italian invasion, she stayed behind in the mission to protect the children.

Franciscan friar who regularly checked the river after the rains in the highlands had found it and brought it to the mission.

The little patient had unaccountably grown a big canine tooth, and Sister St. Melard asked if Alexandra could remove it because the baby could not keep from hurting the wet nurse. She extracted the tooth, and the procedure brought her French patients because the nuns had praised her work. New patients came from all parts, including the priest from Harar who rode sixty kilometers on his motorcycle. "Priests and nuns were good and interesting people," Alexandra said.

Money Matters

Because of her growing reputation and many patients, Alexandra began earning a respectable income and was able to send money back to her lender, the owner of the Dresden soap factory. "I pay off this loan very quickly, sixty percent of it within two months of my arrival in Dire Daua," she said.

The silver thaler used in Ethiopia was also used in commerce all over Africa at the time. The thalers were minted by Austria of pure silver with an embossed figure of Empress Maria Theresa on one side. and on the other the double-headed eagle with single crown—the emblem of the Austro-Hungarian Empire. Alexandra has such a coin with the date 1780 on it, the year in which the die was made. Currency exchange at the time: two thalers for one American dollar.

There were other smaller coins for making change. These included the alat, one-half a thaler; the rup, one-fourth a thaler; the tamun, one-tenth a thaler; and the bessa, one-sixteen a thaler. The Ethiopian women carried many such coins with them when they went to the marketplace to shop. But because they had no pockets in their dresses and did not carry purses, they carried all their coins in their cheeks. When they were told how much they owed the shopkeeper, say eight bessa, they would expertly juggle their cheeks and spit out into their hands the correct number of the proper coin. They had pretty hands with delicate fingers.

Among her patients was Madame Hetz from Strasbourg, wife of the director of the Franco-Ethiopian Railway, whose home was in Djibouti. The ladies always came to her in twos. Alexandra told them that she had been in Djibouti en route to Dire Daua.

"But why did you not stay?" asked Madame Hetz. "There are five hundred whites in Djibouti, and we have had not a single dentist for the past six months."

"But I cannot stay in Djibouti as I have only transit visa."

"I'll speak to my husband about that," said Madame Hetz.

And that was how Alexandra got permission from the French government in Djibouti to stay in the French colony.

Within three months of her arrival in Africa she returned to Djibouti where she set up private practice again.

Peripatetic Dentist

Herr Hetz, the railway director, was one of Alexandra's first patients in Djibouti. He sat in the rattan chair while she worked on his teeth. In a corner of the room sat her original dentist's chair in five pieces. He asked about the chair, and she explained the situation.

"Do not worry," said Herr Hetz. "I will have my railway mechanics pick it up and fix it for you."

In two or three weeks it was back in her office fully restored. Moreover, when Hetz's dental work was done, he approved of her work to the point of offering her a position as dentist to the railway. It required a month's work each year in Dire Daua and a month's work in Djibouti. She could practice privately in between. She quickly accepted.

The railway would transport her, her family, and a servant back and forth first class at no expense, and supply her with an apartment or—as in Dire Daua—a house of a vacationing railway employee at the railway's expense.

The railway did not pay me for this work. It supplied me transport and a furnished house or apartment, and I would be given a free ticket to Europe every five years.

It was the railway employees who paid me receiving twenty-five percent reduction off my regular charges. . . . And I also had many other patients—Arabs, Somalis, rich and poor, from the city and from the countryside. It was very interesting.

During this first stay in Djibouti, she met the future Emperor Haile Selassie—then called Ras Tafari—at a reception in the office of the governor of French Somaliland. In 1916, Zauditu—the daughter of Menelik II—had been confirmed as Empress, but many of the nobles disliked her and insisted that Ras Tafari at age twenty-five be recognized as the crown prince with the title "Supreme Regent and Heir Apparent." This made him in actuality the de facto ruler of Ethiopia, though the empress resented him. Ras Tafari was on his way to Europe for a visit. And being uncertain of just what other local rulers might be up to while he was gone, he took them with him.

Alexandra was invited by the governor to attend the reception. "I remember seeing Ras Tafari and the other rulers sitting cross-legged on a gold divan in the governor's house," Alexandra said. The royal baggage—with its many presents for the English King, French ministers, and others—was marked in green, Alexandra noticed. "It was easy to see. It would not get lost. I remembered that, and from then on all the corners of my luggage were painted green for easier identification."

In 1924 Herman Dabbert went from Djibouti to Addis Ababa looking for work with the government. And in June of that same year Alexandra also left Djibouti to move to Addis Ababa and make that their home.

The Franco-Ethiopian Railway proved very customer friendly. The train would stop at the sighting of wildlife to give first-class passengers an opportunity to try their hunting skills.

"Doctor Dabbert, how would you like your eggs cooked: soft-boiled or hard-boiled?" the fireman of the steam-powered locomotive[61] asked early in the morning while the train chugged along the Ethiopian savanna.

In his early days in Ethiopia, Herman was traveling by train and saw when it stopped at a station where mandarins were being harvested. It was his favorite fruit. He asked a man standing at the station if he could buy some. The man nodded and gave him a thaler, which disappeared with the man. Herman said:

> I waited for some time, but nothing happened. I thought I lost my money. The train started to move and suddenly a group of natives came racing with baskets on their heads, which they dumped through the open window. In no time, I was standing up to my waist in gorgeous mandarins! At that time, you could buy a hundred eggs or a whole live donkey for a dollar.

Addis Ababa

When we arrived in Addis Ababa, we saw a hilly city with abundant Eucalyptus trees everywhere. Their leaves' pleasant, fragrant aroma were used in a pot of hot water as an inhaler, good for bronchitis. At eight thousand feet altitude, the capital had a wonderful temperature year round. A healthy place, too high for malaria and many tropical diseases. The main street from the train station to the two Imperial palaces[62] had two parallel ditches on each side and had a cobblestone surface—good for horses, bad for cars. The rest of the streets had rough, dirt surfaces.

---

[61] This was the man whose job was to shovel coal into the fire that boiled the water that created the steam.

[62] For security purposes, nobody knew in which one of the palaces the ruler might spend the night.

The main street was so steep that what few cars there were sometimes had to back up the hill and the passengers had to walk. Most travel in Ethiopia—except for the railway between the capital and Djibouti—was by horse or mule back, however. Auto travel was difficult because of the poor roads. There was no electricity or telephones, and communication was by messengers on horseback.

Most houses had corrugated tin roofs that made a terrible noise when hard rains or hail would hit them. While the native "tukul" was round with a straw thatched roof and dirt floor, the typical one- or two-story houses had a redwood frame that would not rot— Eucalyptus for roof joists and beams held together by string. The frames of most of these houses were filled by mud and straw trodden by foot, plastered with a combination stucco, and usually painted white or left in a natural color. The wood floors were covered with Oriental rugs.

There were many lepers on the streets of Addis Ababa and other cities. Many were beggars that would threaten to spit if they did not receive alms.

One day I saw a leper woman on the street. She had a shawl wrapped around her head, so that only the face showed: but her face was gone—no lips, no nose, only teeth, blind. I wished to take her picture for one of my articles for German medical review, but she wrapped her scarf around her face. She thought that if someone took her picture, she would die. I thought, "Here she is without face, lips, nose, blind—and yet still she wished to live!"

Alexandra adapted without difficulty to the different culture and accepted the Ethiopian concept of time while also accommodating the Europeans who kept their own schedules.

For Ethiopians, the day starts at 6 A.M., which for them is one o'clock. Our midday or midnight is at six o'clock. It makes sense, since near the Equator there is not great variation in the timing between day and night, and you may as well start with one at dawn or dusk.

In March, is small rain time. June, July, August is heavy rain time. It ends exactly on 27th of September—the holy day of the cross, commemorating when Saint Helena and her son King Constantine went to Jerusalem and found the cross of Jesus Christ. It was an important date for festivities and bonfires and dances and lots of tetch and tala (local brews). It marked their New Year. The rest of the time was sunny and warm, never really hot.

No country could have attracted Alexandra more than this recluse Christian kingdom warped in time—primitive, beautiful, bountiful, cruel, scheming, and yet welcoming and gracious. She and Herman began settling into their adopted country.

There was a thriving "white colony" of missionaries, diplomats representing foreign countries accredited by the throne, traders, and educated expatriates held in high esteem by the native population that gave them the generic name of "Frenchi," or "Ferengi." There were about twenty-five Russians and their families. Most of them were refugees that had escaped from Communism. Most had a degree and a profession or were ex-military officers. Mr. Bartenef, a solidly built cavalry officer, had found a great job at the British Embassy. He was the official bouncer in charge of delivering gently any inebriated guests safely home. Among the Russians there were four doctors, five engineers, and an Orthodox priest.

After diplomatic relations with Communist Russia were stopped, the Imperial Russian Embassy was taken over by the Ethiopian Government. The property was leased to Monsieur Girard, the Belgian minister, and Ras Tafari, the future Emperor who decreed that the revenue be distributed among the Russian émigrés in Addis Ababa at the rate of twenty thalers per month (ten dollars). Alexandra and Herman had moved into a rented house at twenty thalers a month, so the stipend helped. Herman had become municipal engineer for the city of Addis Ababa at three hundred thirty thalers a month.

Dr. Alexandra Dabbert, Dentist in Addis Ababa

Alexandra always practiced out of her home. She was available at any time and acted as her own nurse, secretary, and accountant. She had no telephone. People made dental appointments by runner or by showing up and hoping for the best. Malpractice insurance did not yet exist, nor did antibiotics. Electricity was not available to the public, so drilling was done with a foot-powered dental drill hooked up to a foot treadle. Many patients preferred it and did not need anesthesia. It

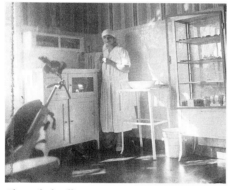

Alexandra's office

would be called "The Negus Machine" because it was acquired during the time of the Negus: the ruler of Ethiopia.

Fillings of cavities were made with silver and mercury amalgam before mercury was found to be poisonous at any concentration, although nobody felt the effects of such poisoning. There were no dental hygienists, and the dentist would clean the teeth and find cavities that many times were too small to be seen by X-rays. (It takes a thirty percent loss of bone before a cavity can be read on X-rays). The gum was rubbed with a local anesthetic made of cocaine paste that would numb the area before the Novocain injection. Alexandra was very conservative and tried all means to save the tooth before deciding that extraction was necessary.

Dentistry is an ideal profession for women. They are by nature careful and exact. But it is not so easy. Much diplomacy is necessary in dealing with patients of all sorts. And believe me, I had luck too. When I left Russia at age twenty, I already knew three languages (Russian, German, and French). I also read a great deal in French.

She had also studied Amharic in Dire Daua. There were two dentists in Addis Ababa when she arrived—one Greek and one Armenian. Because of Alexandra's fluency with languages and her upbringing in the Smolni Institute, which had made her feel comfortable within society's highest ranks, she soon attracted a prestigious clientele.

> My dental practice was interesting, fun, lively, and wide. It included all foreign embassies, all "foreign colony," from 1924 until I left Ethiopia.

Some of her patients, like Dr. Manuel Sorenson—an Adventist missionary who first came to her in 1924—would become lifelong friends. The most unique experiences began in 1924 when she became the official dentist to the royal court.

The Royals

One of her early patients for the royals was the "chief of meat" at Ras Tafari's palace. The position was a large and important post. Some one hundred head of cattle were slaughtered every day to feed the royalty and soldiers quartered there, "Perhaps a thousand soldiers," according to Alexandra. The chief of meat, a young man called simply "Lij," son of a baron, had to arrange for the continual importation of the necessary cattle from the provinces of the kingdom.

Alexandra had made for him two gold crowns, but he insisted that they be removable. He approached her one day on muleback, with three or four retainers accompanying him on foot. "A mule," Alexandra explained, "was much more elegant than a horse, and was much admired for its sure-footedness. A good mule could cost up to three times the price of a horse."

Lij saluted her. "Doctor, I lost my crowns. Can I come for new teeth? They must be removable like the old ones."

Her technician in Addis Ababa was an Armenian émigré from Turkey, escaping the Armenian holocaust, and one of many who had come to Ethiopia, especially at the time of the first World War. His name was Terzian. "He was very good technician. He made beautiful crowns for me."

She found out that Lij wanted his gold crowns removable so that he might not appear too proud and affluent when he appeared before Ras Tafari in his duties as chief of meat. Dealing with the court proved to be complicated because of various intrigues, security, and the royals' concept of fiscal responsibility.

One of the royalty of Ethiopia who came to Alexandra for dental work was the sister of Ras[63] Hailu of Godjam. Alexandra had been told that the well-to-do Ethiopians often did not pay their bills. It was the same attitude of entitlement on the part of "the nobility" she encountered in other countries. They preferred to reciprocate with gifts or favors, or not pay.

The woman came to her office accompanied by thirty or more khaki-clad soldiers with rifles, and with the traditional white cotton kutta or shama thrown over their shoulders, somewhat like a Roman toga. The exact drape of the kutta varied according to the occasion. Knowing of the difficulty of collecting for dental work done to the royalty, Alexandra cleaned only one side of the woman's mouth, hoping to complete the other half when the patient paid the first part of her bill. She never did.

Still she was so sufficiently pleased with the work that her brother Ras Hailu became a patient, too.

Ras Hailu

While on the trip to Europe with Ras Tafari, Ras Hailu had contracted with two Europeans to come to his kingdom—one a surveyor, the other a Russian engineer who became a friend of Alexandra: Nikolai

---

[63] "Ras" is a title often translated as meaning "duke." Since Ras Hailu was considered a regional king, it designated those who were a step below the title of "emperor."

Voronovsky. Voronovsky told her that in Paris, Ras Hailu visited a small store that specialized in watches.

"How much it cost?" he asked the owner.

"Which one are you interested in?"

"All of them," said Ras Hailu. And he bought every watch in the store.

He was fascinated by the bell cord in his hotel in Paris. One pull summoned a young man to his room; two pulls, a young woman. After one day, the hotel was forced to send a man along with the woman because Ras Hailu misinterpreted the meaning of her sudden appearances in his room.

Like all the provincial kings, Ras Hailu kept a palace in Addis Ababa. There were perhaps twenty-five buildings in his compound. The principal room where he presided was some forty-five by fifty feet in area, with floors of polished wood. All the walls were to be covered by mirrors four to six feet tall, in memory of the Hall of Mirrors at Versailles, which had impressed him. In the center of the wooden floor was a raised dais on which the Ras had his throne, which was—of all things—a dental chair.

On his return to Djibouti from Europe with Voronovsky in an elegant French ship bound for Indo-China, they stopped at Port Said where the Ras got into an earnest discussion with some Greek ship builders. He wanted them to build for him a steamship on which he could travel on his large lake Tana, source of the Nile. They were about to seal the contract when Voronovsky intervened.

"How do you propose to get the steamship from Djibouti to the lake?" he asked the Ras.

"We will ship it on the railway first."

"Excellency," Voronovsky replied, "even if the railway had a car big enough to carry such a ship, there are tunnels on the line which are too small for the ship to pass through."

The Ras pondered a moment. "Then I will send one thousand soldiers and they will carry it on their shoulders."

"But it is too heavy, even for a thousand soldiers." And so Ras Hailu's fantasy went unrealized.

One day after she had treated the Ras, Alexandra noticed that her smock was dirty, and she pointed this out to her boy.

"It is Ras Hailu," the boy said. "He uses charcoal on his hair to make it black."

Prince Asfa Wossen

The oldest son of Ras Tafari was named Asfa Wossen. He was born in 1916 and was a child of eight or nine when he came to Alexandra in 1924. His father did not love him because, according to a palace rumor, his mother (the future Empress Menen) had conceived him by a lover, not by the emperor. But this rumor was, in Alexandra's words, "pure fantasy"—which may have been motivated by a desire to cast doubts on his wife since she had publicly cast doubt on him.

Stone Child

Eleven months after Ras Tafari married Woisero[64] Menen, Woisero Romane Work—who was Ras Tafari's mistress—gave birth to a child. Woisero Menen was furious and shut him out of their bedroom, saying, "He is not true to me; I will not be his wife." It was a crisis in the court.

Ras Tafari was eager to mollify his wife and prove that he had been faithful to her. So, he called together the "Schmageles"—a council of old men—and asked them if it was possible to be born after an eleven-month pregnancy. They were uncertain and decided to ask the opinion of a Greek physician in the Capital, whose name was Doctor Jacob Zervos.

When the "Schmageles" had explained the situation to Doctor Zervos, he replied after a few moments, "Yes, it can happen. It is

---

[64] Woisero means lady, grand dame, or even countess.

possible that some children will not come to term until after eleven months have expired, instead of the usual nine. Such a baby is called a 'stone child', because it is slow to appear."

The "Schmageles" took this piece of information back to Ras Tafari, who sent word to Woisero Menen. She was so relieved to learn of her husband's fidelity that the child was received into the court and raised there and called "the stone child" from that time on. Doctor Jacob Zervos, a man with great diplomatic as well as medical skills, was soon made physician of the court—a post that he occupied for the remainder of his life.

Practicing inside the Palace

"From 1924 on, I became the official Dentist to the court of the (future) Emperor Haile Selassie," Alexandra said. "I took care of all of his children's dental needs." At the beginning of her time as a dentist to the Imperial family, Alexandra went to the palace to do her work.

Prince Asfa-Wossen had a full-time tutor, a "wonderful person" named Ato (Mr.) Abatku, a man of about forty who had a long beard. Ato Abatku had astonishing knowledge of the prince. When Asfa-Wossen first became Alexandra's patient, she went to the palace to clean his teeth and make needed fillings. The tutor told her exactly where

"By special permission of his majesty, it has been authorized that Alexandra Dabbert, a long-time resident of Addis Ababa, be known as a Dentist of the Imperial Family."

fillings were needed, even for very small cavities, which Alexandra was able to discover only with her instruments. "How did he know?" she asked herself.

At nine years old, the little prince already spoke fluent French and some German too. His life at court reminded Alexandra of the Russian court before Peter the Great, which she had read about. For example, when Asfa Wossen's two young sisters entered the room where he was, they went to him at once and kissed his hands. Already they were being taught to recognize the future emperor of Ethiopia. In later years the prince would come to her office for dental work instead of Alexandra coming to the palace. Ras Tafari had another son at that time. The second son was Lij (child) Makonnen, who was much loved by the regent. "He was a spoiled boy," Alexandra explained.

Other Expatriates and the Royals

Several former employees of the Russian Imperial Embassy stayed behind in Addis Ababa after the Revolution. When the ambassador and his aides were recalled to Russia, they left all their property and staff behind, thinking they would return. Some of the aides, perhaps more prescient, chose to stay in Ethiopia.

Efim, the former Ethiopian embassy chef, remained behind and became one of Alexandra's patients. In his sixties, he was a tall, beardless man with a sad face—never satisfied for long with any job. He had cooked for some wealthier private individuals and for most of the restaurants in Addis Ababa. There were not many of these. Most were simply large rooms in family homes featuring the cuisine of the family's native country, Italian or German, for example. Efim also cooked for a time for Ras Tafari and his large family. But he stayed only for a month and a half before quitting. Alexandra asked him why he had not stayed longer.

"To the devil with the court," he growled. "Every day I have to prepare for lunch four gangs (courses)—usually meat, soup, fish, and dessert. And these had to be large courses because at least fifteen persons dined with the Negus. I prepared the food in the kitchen, which was in a kind of basement a long way from the dining room. When my meals were ready, I had to cover each dish with a glass lid, then put a pillow on top of the lid—and not just any pillow, but it had to be a bright red pillow, because they believed that red was an antidote to evil spirits."

Once the food was ready, Efim had to walk with the slaves who carried the dishes all the way to the imperial dining room to make certain that no enemy of the Negus added poison to the food along the way.

At four in the afternoon, Chef Efim had to prepare the royal tea, which involved four kinds of cookies and sweets, and then accompany the procession—complete with glass lids and red pillows—back to the royal dining room. Finally at six came the evening meal, which required four courses to be prepared and then processed, all be glassed and pillowed for the long trek from kitchen to imperial presence. It was the trekking more than anything else that drove Efim to seek another post and be replaced by a Swiss and French chef.

Efim found work as chef for a Russian engineer named Sidensner, whose wife was regarded (or who regarded herself) as a most elegant socialite of impeccable taste. She had been a student at Alexandra's cherished Smolni Institute, which she believed was further indication of her high social distinction. One day Efim came to Alexandra to have a rotten tooth removed. She had heard of his new job with the Sidensners and asked him how things were going along.

He replied, "Barin dusha tcheloweck. The boss is a good soul. But as for the lady—" He snorted.

Grand Duke Alexander Comes to Tea

In 1925, the uncle of the last tsar, Grand Duke Alexander, came to Addis Ababa trying to sell to Ethiopian interests (this was before Ras Tafari became Negus) five churches that Imperial Russia owned in Jerusalem. Proceeds of the sale were to be used in support of Russian emigrants. His party numbered six and included not only his mistress, who was the niece of the Queen of Italy, but her husband too—a sculptor of international repute. The sculptor lodged in what was formerly the Russian embassy, rented to the Belgian ambassador, whose rent also was used to support the Russian colony in Addis Ababa.

The duke and his mistress, with other members of their party, stayed in a hotel in Addis Ababa. They asked Alexandra, who at this time lived in a rented house in the capital, to be hostess of a great tea for the duke. She was honored with the request.

There was only one samovar in the entire Russian colony, and it belonged to Doctor Gabrielov and his wife. It was necessary for Alexandra to send her boys to the doctor so that they might carry back to her his samovar for the great tea. Since her own houseboys were not trained for elegant affairs, she hired an Ethiopian who had been a waiter in the former Russian embassy. He possessed two medals from this service there. One commemorated Russia's victory over Napoleon Bonaparte retreating from Moscow. The other had been struck on the occasion of the three hundredth anniversary of the Romanov dynasty. For the grand tea, the waiter wore both medals on his white jacket— one on the left and one on the right. "For symmetry," Alexandra said.

The tea went off without incident, but when her boys carried the samovar back to Doctor Gabrielov, they lost the "key" which controls the flow of liquid out of the urn. The physician was certain the key had fallen into the long grass in front of his house, so he had the grass mowed. "The story had happy ending," Alexandra said. "They found the key in the grass where it had fallen."

Dental Bills

It wasn't just the African nobility that disdained fiscal responsibility. The Russian nobility in Addis Ababa, like the other wealthy and famous folks around the world—especially the aristocracy—disdained repayment of debts. After Alexandra had sent a bill to one Russian nobleman in exile, he sent his wife back to her on a day in October.

Alexandra on her lady's saddle

"My husband," she said to Alexandra, "is very angry to receive now a bill."

"But why?" Alexandra asked in confusion.

"Because he is accustomed to pay only in January and August."[65]

Other people came up with lame excuses. The Swedish Lutheran missionary and his wife were her patients in Addis Ababa. They always paid, though slowly. One time in 1924 when the missionary's wife was pregnant, she asked Alexandra to exercise her horse since she herself could not ride. Alexandra sent her boy to bring the horse to her. When she later sent the horse back by the same boy, she sent along with him a bill for their latest dental work.

The boy returned with the following message: "When your boy was bringing my horse back, he fell and bit his lip (the horse, that is). As soon as the horse's lip heals, you will receive your money."

For some months in her early years in Ethiopia, Alexandra earned extra money by giving German lessons to the daughter of the Italian

---

[65] This man was still living in Florida in December, 1987, when Alexandra told me this story.

ambassador to Ethiopia. When at the end of the month she would present her bill to the daughter, she would say, "Oh, put it on our dental bill." Puzzled, Alexandra did so.

It was not until later when Alexandra discovered that the Italian government paid all the dental bills of its ambassadors and their families, but did not pay for German lessons.

Traveling Practice

Alexandra tried to increase the family's earnings, and always strived to mix her professional work and pleasure. She decided to occasionally travel to other areas and offer dental services. Beginning in 1925, she went to the city of Harar to do dental work. Ras Makonnen, the father of Ras Tafari, had taken the city back from Egypt.

At right angles to the railroad, a winding mountain road—unpaved of course—led to the more salubrious highland walled town of Harar with its long history of wars for supremacy between Muslims and Ethiopians. It was a lifesaving destination for those who had contracted malaria in the hot lowlands. There in the higher, cooler elevations—too high for malaria-breeding mosquitos—they could breathe fresher air and enjoy the best coffee in the world. It was still rather primitive: water came from wells; sanitation was provided nightly by hyenas; and local kitchens used wood from Eucalyptus groves for fuel. It was a great place for horseback riding and finding trails through groves of eucalyptus and prickly pear. Alexandra loved it.

On her first visit she stayed for three or four weeks, working in a room provided by the French hospital.[66] One of her first patients in Harar was an elderly Franciscan missionary priest with an abundant white beard. She asked him what sort of work he did, and he replied that he had worked in the leprosarium for twenty years.

"But," he added with a smile, "it's not contagious. As you see, I have caught nothing, even in my beard."

---

[66]   In the ensuing twenty years she returned three or four times.

Franciscan nuns who worked in the leprosarium were also among her patients. She did not charge them any fee, and so in gratitude they would offer her simple gifts. One of these gifts was a typical Ethiopian handicraft: a small table of tightly woven straw, shaped like an hourglass. The top opened to provide a place to keep food warm.

"Our female lepers made this table for you," they told her.

She hoped the woven material, like the priest's beard, had acquired an immunity from contagion.

"One day, I was called to the wife of Dedjasmach[67] Emru, governor of Harar, to do dental work on his wife. As I entered her room, a young eunuch maybe twenty-five years old was helping her put on her black silk stockings.

Herman and the Stairways

Herman Dabbert had some unusual professional challenges as well, and as a result took some unusual projects in Addis Ababa. Around 1925 Frau Wilder hired a local architect to design and supervise construction of a five-room two-story wooden house on a lot not far from the Dabbert house. It was called "Pension Wider" and was "an economical house."

The workmen had erected scaffolding all around the framework so that they could haul supplies and materials up for work on the upper story. Upon completion of the upper story, they removed the scaffolding and Frau Wider discovered that the architect had forgotten to put a stairway in the plan so that she could reach the second floor.

She came to Herman. "How do we get a stairway in?"

His success in adding on a stairway must have spread his reputation because a year or so later a rich Armenian named Kevorcow built a large marble building on the main street of the capital facing the main plaza of the town. Called the Tabac Monopol, it contained offices,

---

[67] *Dejasmatch* is a title that means governor.

storerooms, and a shop on the ground floor for Kevorcow's[68] tobacco business. When it came time for the opening of the building, they discovered that the architect (not the Greek who had designed Frau Wider's house) had forgotten to provide a stairway to the second floor. Once more Herman was summoned to solve the problem.

Herman Works for the Empress

Ten underground Coptic churches, each one carved out of sandstone, lay in a barely-remembered area of historical interest near the town of Lalibela. The Empress Zauditu[69], daughter of the late Emperor Menelik, was the titular head of state, though Ras Tafari as regent held the real power. Yet the empress commissioned Herman to investigate and survey these churches.[70] The trip required a twenty-one-day mule ride to Lalibela, about a hundred-eighty miles due north of the capital.

The churches there are subterranean, their roofs level with the ground. Steps carved out of the rock lead some twenty meters down to their interiors. A Portuguese monk mentioned them in the 1500s and they were alluded to in the early 1800s. The monolithic cloisters were built in the thirteenth century by Ethiopian emperors that dreamed of diverting the flow of the Blue Nile and in the process built several churches hewn out of the rocks. Herman wrote:

---

[68] Mrs. Kevorcow used to invite twenty to thirty ladies of the town to tea every Thursday afternoon. Her Saint Bernard dog lay in the doorway leading out of her rooms, and whenever one of the ladies attempted to leave, the dog growled and bristled, thus ensuring a full complement at the tea until such time as Mrs. Kevorcow herself, deciding that the tea was ended, led the dog away. Then the ladies could leave.

[69] Also spelled "Szadituh" and "Zewditu."

[70] The rediscovered temples were written up by Herman and used as a doctoral thesis, published as a book in 1938 and dedicated to Alexandra. The Lalibela Churches have since then become one of the major tourist attractions in Ethiopia.

Riding up from the plains, you could not see them until you were standing on the top of a gaping hole containing this complex of beautiful structures. One hundred fifty Ethiopian soldiers, ordered by the Empress, accompanied my expedition. I was glad that they were with me as the priests and the people that lived there had stoned a number of intruders into the sanctuary.

Twelve

Alexandra Buys a Slave

Slavery in Ethiopia

When Ras Tafari, not yet crowned Haile Selassie, returned from his first state visit to Europe in 1924, he made some changes. He'd been to Paris and then to Geneva, where his land was admitted to the League of Nations on condition that he abolish slavery from Ethiopia. By royal ukase, upon his return, he had forbidden slavery and slave trading under the penalty of death by hanging. This did not end the practice, however. Such edicts took a while before they percolated down to the people.

Slaves had always been taken in the south of the country, around the rive Baro. They had features that contrasted with the Semitic looks of the Ethiopians. They were tall, strong, black, with large lips and they were pagan-animists. As non-Christians, that made it "permissible" to seize and keep them as slaves.

One day an elderly English gentleman came to see Alexandra.

"I come to you not for my teeth, but my niece, Mrs. Benting. She is curious: Are there still slaves Ethiopia?" Mrs. Benting was the wife of the British Ambassador to Ethiopia and she was Alexandra's patient.

"It is true," she answered, "There is still slavery. I will show you. Tomorrow morning we will go, and I will show you the slaves."

Next morning there came a cavalcade on horseback: the old gentleman—Mrs. Benting's brother-in-law, who was the military attaché—and two Indian Sikh soldiers in khaki turbans.

"Few Europeans had nice horses as we did. The German embassy had white horses. Their black soldiers in khaki uniform had white turbans, and the French wore red turbans," Alexandra said. They left at seven in the morning and rode some two miles toward the Entoto Mountains, to the northeast of Addis Ababa. There lived the Ethiopian "grand seignoures," each with a large property, but their houses were not so large.

They rode up to the first property and to the outer buildings, where there were many blacks squatting in the doorways—young and old, men and women and children sitting in the sunshine. "These slaves had interesting ears with lobes distended down in a loop for decoration," she said.

The old gentleman, a lord, went up to them and through an interpreter asked, "Who are you?"

They replied that they were the "barria," or slaves of so and so. The English lord went to several other houses, asked the same questions, and got the same answer. Ethiopians liked to have many slaves: in the kitchen, in the garden, in the stables, in the farms, in the house. They never paid the slaves, but the slaves received food, shelter, and some clothing, maybe once a year.

"Could they not escape?"

"How and where and why?"

Alexandra believed it was close to impossible to escape, and that many preferred the entitlements of the sheltered life of a paternalistic Christian environment.

The Hanging

One Sunday morning in 1925 or '26, Alexandra in her riding habit prepared to go out. Her neighbor—an Englishman named de Halpert, counselor of Ras Tafari (Haile Selassie)—saw her preparations and hurried over.

"Don't go to Gulale today," he cautioned her.

Gulale was a sort of suburb of the capital, and there were five principal roads out of Addis Ababa.

"Why not?" she asked.

"Because," said de Halpert, "they have just executed twenty-five criminals and there are five of them hanging at each road out of the city."

Alexandra rode out in spite of de Halpert's warning, curious to see the events.

> The corpses were hanging very high, perhaps thirty meters in the air, suspended from the branches of eucalyptus trees, each corpse wrapped in a clean sheet so that only the head and the legs from the shins down showed.

The law required that the body hang for three days from its gibbet, and only then could the victim's family remove it for burial. She had seen hangings before, of course, for the hanging tree stood near the marketplace in town. From its branches at least one criminal was hanged on Saturday mornings. There were other sentences less severe.

A butcher in Addis Ababa was convicted of selling donkey meat as beef to his customers. His sentence to have his right hand cut off at the wrist was carried out on the plaza in front of the post office stairs. For years Alexandra had a photograph of the maimed hand.

The butcher's family was on hand with a basin of boiling water mixed with butter. As soon as the hand was chopped off, they plunged the bleeding stump into the boiling butter mixture to stanch the flow of blood and—it was hoped—save the man's life. (Sometimes the shock was enough to kill them.)[72]

---

[72] In 1987 Alexandra read of Afghans who cut off both hands of captured or wounded Russian soldiers. Many of these men died of shock, loss of blood, and infection. Many who survived and were released to the Russians did not

Severe as Ethiopian justice was, Alexandra herself would soon purchase a slave.

The Servant Who Loved a Slave

Pavel Buliguin, the ex-Guards officer and Russian poet, had recommended Gabri to Alexandra.

"He will be an excellent horse boy for you," he said. "I was riding one day and Gabri was following me on another horse, holding a bottle of Vodka in his hand. His horse, called Chaika ("seagull" in Russian) was frightened by something, bolted, and jumped over a fence. Gabri was thrown off the horse holding the bottle of Vodka high, and it did not break. It shows that he is a good horse servant."

She hired him.

She was living with Herman in a house they rented in Addis Ababa. Her horseboy, Gabri (rhymes with Fabray), rode to the post office to pick up their mail since they had no home deliveries. Later in the day, Alexandra saw her black horse returning to the house, but a strange boy, not Gabri, was riding it.

"Where is Gabri?" she asked the stranger.

"He is arrested."

"Why? What has he done?"

"He has stolen a slave."

"Who is this slave he has stolen?"

"It is the woman Mulenesh, Gabri's woman."

"Who does Mulenesh belong to?"

"She is the slave of Ato Ilma Nacary."

Ato Ilma Nacary was the interpreter at the Italian embassy. Alexandra went to call on the Ethiopian Minister of Commerce, whose wife was Italian, to discover what sort of "diplomacy" was called for in

---

return to Russia but were taken by the Communists to East Germany for treatment. The government of the USSR did not want the Russian people to see these victims of the Afghan war.

this circumstance. She explained the matter to the Minister, then asked what would happen to Gabri.

"He will receive five hundred lashes if he does not return the woman. Of course he will die. No one can support more than one hundred lashes."

"Perhaps," suggested Alexandra, "I can buy this woman. Would that be correct?"

"Yes," the Minister told her, "that can be done."

"And what would be the correct price to pay for her?"

The minister mused a bit. "The normal price for a woman slave is perhaps fifty thalers. But I think you can pay more, perhaps one hundred-fifty thalers, because in such circumstances the owner of the woman will ask more for her."

Alexandra Buys a Slave

Alexandra communicated her desire to buy Mulenesh to Ato Ilma Nacary, and he invited her to his house for dinner and some preliminary dickering. She took along as companion Mrs. Veliashev, an elegant lady who had been a movie actress in Italy. While they dined, Gabri squatted near the table in chains, staring plaintively at Alexandra all the while.

Toward the end of the dinner, Alexandra brought up the matter of Mulenesh and the price Ato Ilma Nacary would require for her. Ato Ilma smiled and said, "Perhaps tomorrow I will have lunch at your house and we can come to an agreement."

It was all part of the diplomacy needed in such a case.

For this lunch Alexandra invited Pavel Buliguin, who had originally recommended hiring Gabri and who now counseled her on how to minister to Ato Ilma.

"First," Pavel said, "you must have plenty of two things: vodka and beer. They work together very strongly, and together they will do the job."

"What job is that?" asked Alexandra.

"Getting Ato Ilma drunk."

Alexandra did as Pavel suggested, and Ato Ilma attempted to match Pavel Buliguin drink for drink. And in the process, Ato Ilma got very drunk and agreed to sell Mulenesh, not for a hundred-fifty but for seventy-two thalers.

Ato Ilma was so drunk that he could not mount his mule. He could get one arm over the mule's back, but being a very large man could not pull the rest of his body up into the saddle. Finally he gave up the effort and staggered away, leading the mule behind him.

A day or two later a happy procession arrived at Alexandra's house, consisting of Gabri (unflogged), Mulenesh, and Mulenesh's mother—an old slave woman with long loops in her ears from wearing wooden ornaments. She was from the "slave tribe" called Shancala that lived in the southern part of Ethiopia. The Ethiopians used to steal Shancala children for slaves.

Ato Ilma Nacary was in the procession, of course, accompanied by six old men who were to act as witnesses, with thumbprints to document the sale. Alexandra did not know where they came from. When the document was signed and sealed and the proper sum paid, Ato Ilma gave her the document. And so in 1926, she bought a slave.

Alexandra, in turn, gave the document to Gabri. She wondered where she would put the two of them. Since Gabri could no longer sleep with the other boys, Alexandra gave him money and sent him to the market to buy wood with which to build a room adjacent to the house for himself and Mulenesh. He built it directly under the treatment room where she had her practice. The room was just large enough for a bed and a place to cook, and there Gabri and Mulenesh began their life together.

For three years, Gabri paid me two thalers each month until he had paid me the cost of Mulenesh's freedom. There was no guarantee, no contract. But Gabri was very honest, a man of his word. And he was very good with horses.

A New Home

The House in Addis Ababa

As the family prospered, the next step was the building of a house large enough for Herman, the designer of the house, and Alexandra to house her parents who were still in Germany, and to plan for the eventuality of a child. For his and Alexandra's new home, Herman varied the local practice of binding beams with string by using wire bought at Mohammed Ali, the main Indian store that had everything from hardware to cloths, saddles, medicines, firearms, delicacies, and toiletries—a pre-supermarket.

"My home in Addis Ababa was built in part of steel rails, about seventeen of them, which my husband Herman obtained for nothing from the railway company," Alexandra explained. The photos of this house under construction show its wood and steel rail frame over which wood lathing was attached. Natural mud and stucco was applied over the lathing, then whitewashed.[73]

The interior of the house was comfortable with Persian rugs covering the floors. One of the sofas was covered with the hides of forty-five black-and-white Golobus monkeys called "Gureyza" by the natives.

---

[73] It was so solidly built that when Taffara visited the site in 1968, the house and stables, though in disrepair, still stood intact. (See photo, page.)

Herman's drawing of his house design

House in Addis Ababa under construction

The ceilings were of canvas stretched tight against a wooden framework and painted white. This was their dream house.

The house had no running water, except for the well. Under the gutters, big steel drums collected rainwater. All hot water had to be heated in the kitchen, except on Saturdays when a caravan of donkeys brought hot water for the bath ritual[74] to the house from the hot mineral spa, some two miles away.

Ethiopian Plumbing

Open drainage ditches didn't exist simply to carry off rainwater; they were a part of the feeble sanitation system in Addis Ababa. There was, of course, no indoor plumbing. The arrangement of one of Alexandra's neighbors is illustrative of the way things worked. This neighbor had a two-story house. The bathroom was on the second floor in a room that projected a few feet over the street. From the floor of this room a pipe projected down, perhaps two feet below floor level. Whatever came through this pipe (from the toilet convenience on the other end) dropped directly on the road to the ditch beneath. It was a fairly busy road with the bank just across from the neighbor's house. Sometimes

[74] Described later.

when a person was doing business at the bank he would glance across at the house and its pipe and see someone doing business there too.

Herman's sketch of the doorway

The street dogs took care of these falling materials and so kept the road fairly clean. Paper they did not eat, nor of course cans. Nobody cleaned the streets, except the dogs and the hyenas at night. The daily afternoon storms during the rainy season helped to clean out the city.

The Gurague were from a very poor tribe that had come to Addis Ababa looking for work. They were everywhere on the streets. A group of perhaps twenty Gurague was put to work one day on one of the sewage/drainage ditches. After some days they were subsequently hired to carry bags of thalers from one bank to another in lieu of armored car service. They came down the road with canvas bags of the silver coins slung over their shoulders. When they reached the bridge spanning the drainage ditch they had been digging so recently—and therefore knew better than anyone else—one of them leaped into the ditch and ran off with perhaps two thousand thalers ($1,000.00)—a big fortune—bumping against his back. Alexandra never heard if he was caught.

Greek Builder of Outhouses

Herman and Alexandra didn't want the primitive system employed by their neighbor. There was a Greek contractor who built many outhouses. Next to the building, he dug two holes and lined them with cement. On the roof of the outhouses, a barrel kept full of rainwater. The waste from the toilet was carried by the water to the first cement hole and filtered into the second hole, which when built was filled with skins of recently slaughtered sheep that the Greek left in the open to fill with maggots.[75] The maggots remained and continued to keep the waste clean, so there was no odor.

> The water from the second hole is clean enough for watering my garden.
> We did not have toilet paper. It was not sold in my time. We used newspapers, magazines that sometimes were too slippery. It was a place to read and get enriching information from magazines like Istoricheski Vestnik, the Russian Historical Herald. It was a source of interesting old articles, as the source of the publication was from before the Russian Revolution of 1918 when the Russian Embassy in Ethiopia was still active.

The Stable, the Shipwreck, Smuggling and the Mule

The horses and mules were kept in a stable built at the lower end of the property. A portion of the roof on the stable was a special Portland cement roofing material that Alexandra bought in Djibouti around that time. It was part of the cargo of a French ship, the Fontainebleau, which caught fire en route to French Indo-China. It just managed to reach port in Djibouti before it foundered and capsized.

Herman's sketch of the stable

This roofing material was on its way to Indo-China where it was to be the roof of a Buddhist temple. It cost me six francs per piece, very cheap. The Franco-Ethiopian railway shipped it to Addis Ababa for me for nothing since I was doing dental work for the railroad for two months each year.

---

[75] Interestingly, the Johns Hopkins team of military surgeons during World War I developed a highly effective way to clean wounds, particularly in open fractures, by using maggots. The practice persisted into the forties.

Also In Djibouti, Alexandra bought a Belgian-made hunting rifle from the Belgian company Fabrique Nationale, which also sold Browning rifles. She bought an enormous three-barreled machine, a pair of sixteen-gauge barrels on top and a cartridge-firing barrel slung underneath. Abte was with her at this time and helped her do a little smuggling.

I smuggled my Belgian-made hunting rifle into Ethiopia. First I took it apart, then I placed the parts in a box, well-wrapped in cloth. On top of the parts I placed two layers of ripe tomatoes. Across the top of the box my boy Abte nailed several slats, just far enough apart to show the tomatoes underneath. This box was among my belongings when I came back on the train from Djibouti to Addis Ababa. At Customs the officials said to me, "Leave all your boxes here. We will examine them tomorrow, and then you can pick them up." I replied, "Good. That will do nicely." Then I paused and said, "But could you let me take only the tomatoes? They are very ripe and I am afraid they may go bad before tomorrow." They said to me, "Of course," and gave me the box.

After returning to Addis Ababa, Alexandra decided to sell her blunderbuss hunting rifle to some Ethiopians for a good mule and twenty silver thalers. Much discussion took place before this transaction was completed because the Ethiopians liked the gun so well.

"It is good," they said. "We can shoot out the lion's eyes with the two upper barrels, and then kill him with the other barrel."

"Baclusha was a dear little mule," she said. "It went with its two right legs and then its two left legs, just like a trotter." (Baclo is the Amharic word for mule, and baclusha is the Russian affectionate diminutive of that word.)

Domestics

Abte was the main aide who faithfully followed Alexandra, giving her advice and keeping her out of trouble. He and his wife were in her service for many years. There was always a cook and a helper. Abte Georgis and Seifu attended to the horses and accompanied Alexandra or Herman when they rode out. "Europeans never went out alone," Alexandra said. There was a houseboy, a cleaning lady, a laundry man, and a gardener: "He grew flowers—not vegetables—it was cheaper to buy them." And last there was the saintly Tasso whose face resembled a painting in a Coptic church.

"There was a big market, maybe two kilometers from where we lived. Of course, we rode on our horses to visit and buy," Alexandra said. There was a line of sellers— mostly women that came from their little farms to sell, buy, and barter eggs; fresh vegetables; and fruit. There were plenty of beautiful woven baskets—plain and in colors—spears, sabers, and pots and pans.

Mostly, the market came to the house. In the mornings on special days, one or several natives would announce themselves loudly at the gate to be let through, carrying on their heads their wares: fresh produce, seasonal fruit, chickens, and eggs. The cook would make the selections and have a big pan of water for the eggs. If they sank, they were fresh enough. If they floated, they were no good. Sometimes a fully-grown chick would be discovered. To tenderize the tough free-range chickens, they would be slaughtered and buried for three to five hours before the feathers were plucked.

Her progressive accomplishment in Addis Ababa didn't diminish her curiosity and passion to know more about the country, particularly if she could also help as a dentist. One of her patients, who was the owner of a distant coffee plantation in the heart of Ethiopia, invited her to visit and take care of his employees' aching teeth.

Fourteen

Caravan

*E*thiopia enjoyed two seasons: the dry season from October to June and the rainy season from June to September. Because there was less work in Addis Ababa during the rainy season, Alexandra often began traveling to patients in outlying areas in June. She and Abte boarded an overnight train in June of 1927 to a location by the Awash River, teeming with crocodiles. It was called "the most patriotic of rivers" as it originated in the Ethiopian highlands and petered out in the Ethiopian desert, never leaving the country of its origin. Alexandra's destination was the Golgocha coffee plantation in the province of Arussi. At the invitation of ten resident Europeans employed there, she would visit for a month to do dental work.

She did much traveling to her more distant patients in the comfort of a train, and then riding on muleback. The treasurer of the plantation met her at the Arussi station. He was in charge of the caravan of twenty to twenty-five mules carrying forty thousand silver thalers to the plantation to pay the five hundred workers. Each mule could carry perhaps two thousand thalers—a heavy load.

Mr. Pavlov, a bearded Bulgarian man in the caravan, was a big game hunter, and had a house full of trophies: skins of leopards, elephant

Mr. Pavlov, big game hunter

tusks, buffalo and antelope horns. He shot game for the caravan. "Not for sport, but for kitchen," Alexandra said.

Many caravans used the crossing. The mules swam, as did the cattle. "Mules are clever: When we must wade across unknown river, we always let the mule go first. The horses will follow." The natives swam, and those of them that could not swim took the cattle by the horns or by the tail. Alexandra went across in a dugout canoe manned by a Shancala tribesman. They were considered inferior, slave quality by the Ethiopians who were "much more elegant." She soon learned more about Ethiopian elegance. Pavlov warned Alexandra not to be surprised: "The boatman will be absolutely naked—with all hair out—it is considered elegance by them."

Alexandra changed from jodhpurs and boots into a dress for the crossing, because if the dugout capsized, she explains:

> It is easier to swim in a dress. I changed behind a tree. No one is interested there. There was a Greek in one of the caravans that was also crossing. He must have seen me (in the jodhpurs) before I changed. When he got close and saw me in a dress, he went to Abte and asked, "I see the lady here, but what happened to her husband?" We laughed. Abte was special.

She had forgotten that it was the time of the month for her menstruation, and when she realized it, Abte calmly and considerately handed her the necessary materials, which he had remembered to bring.

Crossing a second, narrower part of the river, "The water came up to my armpits." The current was not strong, but the mule carrying the boxes of Alexandra's dental tools floated down river. "We found him two hundred yards away downriver in the brush."

Once the caravan was across the Awash, some natives came to Alexandra with the skin of a boa constrictor for sale. It was perhaps two by six feet and was wrapped in a bundle, so heavy that she needed another mule to carry it. She bought it for two thalers.

One day, one of the mules carrying money wandered into the forest and rubbed off the pack on his back against the trunk of the tree, then wandered back to the group. They spent most of the day before they retrieved the missing two thousand thalers it had carried.

They rode their mules away from the Awash until the evening, when they came to another river.

"I am tired," Alexandra said. "Abte, please make me some tea."

Abte replied in Amharic, "Sorry, I can prepare only coffee. Water is too dirty for tea; it is good for coffee." At least, then, one could not see the dirt in it.

In the evening, they made campfires. "Abte called me to sit beside the fire. Because I was European, they wished me to sit in the firelight and it be seen that white persons were in the caravan." Ras Tafari as Negus severely punished bandits who attacked whites.

> While I sat there, they asked me different things. I remember the question, "If we dig deep, deep hole here, where will it come out?"
>
> I said, "First is the ground and water, then stones, then fire, then more ground again and then America. Do you know America?"
>
> They said, "No."
>
> I said, "You have seen missionaries from America?"
>
> "Yes, we have seen," was their answer.

Only Alexandra and Mr. Pavlov slept in tents. He had killed a warthog—a feast for everybody. She had suspended from her tent the animal's liver for the next day. During the night, there was great commotion. It felt like an earthquake was going to flatten the tent. In the morning, the liver was gone. "Only footprints of hyenas remained."

The trip took nine days and nine nights.

Caravan to Arussi coffee plantation, drawn by Herman Dabbert

The plantation belonged to a Belgian millionaire named Browers, a man who'd grown a full, golden beard. Mr. Hollander, a Dutchman from Java, administered the property. Coffee got its name from the Ethiopian region of Kaffa that produced the best coffee in the world.

The wife of the plantation manager was expecting any day, and a call went out for the doctor who was visiting at a nearby plantation. Pavlov went out for him.

On their way back to the plantation, they came to a river that was swollen by a mountain rainstorm. There was only a narrow, swinging footbridge. Below them the water of the river swirled and roared. The doctor refused to cross. He would wait for the waters to recede and told Pavlov how to deliver the baby. Pavlov, who had three daughters of his own, crossed the bridge, went on ahead, and delivered the child. When finally the doctor arrived, the baby was already successfully delivered.

On the trip home, Alexandra came upon some Danakil nomads camped by the river. A young woman was carrying a two- to three-month-old baby. She came to Alexandra and offered me the child. I asked Abte what she wished.

"She offers you her child as your slave," he told her.

They were very poor and there was drought that year. Many animals died. The woman knew the Europeans would take care of her child.

She said to Abte, "We will take."

"No, no," he told her. "You can not take."

"Why?"

"Because when you go back to the capital, people will see you with the baby and they will say, 'She ran off to Arussy to give birth to this black child.'"

Abte was five years older than Alexandra. "He was wise in these things and I followed his advice," she said.

When she returned to Addis Ababa, she took the skin of the boa constrictor to the taxidermist and sent it to Germany to Herman's mother and three sisters. They had shoes and handbags made for each of them, and gave the remainder of the skin to the shoemaker as a payment. Such skins were in demand and rare.[77]

But such gifts kept the connection alive to homeland and family. It said: We remember you; please don't forget us.

---

[77] Herman's nephew Eberhard would write: "I had the memory of this uncle in a fabulous country with strange artifacts, some of which he and Aunt Alexandra sent us. We had lion skins, spears and shields as well as robes and all kinds of things nobody where I lived had ever seen. I remember one Christmas when our school put on the nativity scene. I was one of the shepherds, watching the holy family. I was a little chap, still in kindergarten, and mother had dressed me up in skimpy bathing pants . . . with a leopard skin draped around me. In my hand I had a real African spear, and in the other an African shield. When the curtain went up, I was so embarrassed to stand in full light in this apparel that I shrank behind the holy family."

Fifteen

1927

Lev and Katerina Come to Africa

The Drosdovskys came from Germany to Djibouti in 1927 to live with Alexandra and Herman in Addis Ababa following Alexandra's long-standing determination to reunite with her parents. Her brother Roman was seventeen and stayed behind in Germany. Because of the arrangement with the Ethiopian government regarding the distribution of rent money from the old Russian embassy, Lev (and the rest of the small Russian colony) received his monthly "pension." Former General Lev Antonovitch Drosdovsky became a surveyor in and around the municipality of Addis Ababa, one of the requirements for all landowners being to have their property lines officially surveyed.

As a surveyor, Papa spent all day on his job and sent out word that he would eat only canned sardines, eggs, bananas, and yogurt, because it is clean. No meat, because it was not cooked enough or raw—a sure way to get tapeworm.

One time, Papa was staying with a family of rich Ethiopians. The maid of the house came with the yogurt in a night pot. It had still not been used by the family. They had bought it but did not know what it was for.

 When Papa first rode into town on Baclusha, the mule did not want to go across the bridge on the main street leading into town. It was necessary for Papa to go down the bank into the water and wade across the river. Later Papa brought Baclusha across the bridge with the horses, and so he (the mule) learned to cross the bridge. Baclusha was very individual. He did what he wanted to do.

A photograph from these days shows Katerina Drosdovsky coming down the path from the German church—"The Russian church was too far away," according to Alexandra—where she had just attended services. She was wearing a broad trimmed white hat and long white dress. A few yards behind her walked one of the boys in native dress carrying her handbag and a parasol in case of a sudden rainstorm.

One day Katerina complained to her daughter that she was "only a poor refugee." Alexandra replied, "What do you mean? You have always with you a boy who carries your handbag and umbrella."

Katarina and Alexandra on train

Katerina had purchased an ostrich egg at a railway stop in Ethiopia. As an Easter gift from the Drosdovskys, Alexandra painted the shell with an Easter motif and sent it to the exiled Queen Olga of Greece—formerly a Russian princess, aunt of Nicholas II—who had stayed in Lindau-am-Bodensee in Bavaria when Alexandra's parents were there.

Dentist As Artiste

Even as a busy young dentist, Alexandra found time for her artistry. She painted a portrait of "Nicholas the II," a copy of the famous artist Serov's painting. Both Alexandra and Herman loved drawing and painting. Herman was especially adept at capturing the grace and proportions of horses as well as other animals and birds.[79]

Pere Serafim[80] was a French Franciscan missionary. He came to see Alexandra and said, "I founded a school for young people and I wish a big painting of Saint George. Ethiopians like Saint George."

So, Herman painted the horse and she painted Saint George. It was a big painting, larger than a door. "We charged him only for the cost of materials and frame. It came to sixteen thalers. He paid me with a golden finger ring." Ethiopian gold was frequently made into spaghetti-like strings and then bent into ring forms that could easily be used as multiple continuous bands, depending on the length of the gold wire.

Alexandra found an interesting and profitable way to combine her dental practice and her art.

> In Africa, I never saw snow, only hail. I had nostalgia for snow, so I
> painted copies of old masters with snow scenes. I always put a price in
> the back of painting and sold many that way, but many remained in the
> house. I had copies of Titian, Rembrandt, Velasquez, and my originals in
> oil, watercolors.

One of her patients, a Mr. Romberg, was interested in a German lady, Mrs. Hall, who owned the boarding house in Harar where Alexandra stayed when she traveled there to tend to patients in that area. Mrs. Hall was also the tutor of the royal children.

She said to him one day, "For Christmas, do you wish to make two lady friends happy?"

He looked surprised. "Which ladies?"

"One is myself; second lady is Mrs. Hall."

"How can I do this?"

---

[79] See photo section.

[80] During the war with the Italians, he was taken prisoner by the Ethiopians for being white. See page 205ff.

Dentiste as Artiste

"Mrs. Hall was here yesterday, and she liked very much my painting." It was a two by three foot fall scene copied from a museum painting.

"How much will it cost?"

"Thirty-five thalers." She needed that much to finish the iron gate to her compound—the house, yard, stables, all of which were surrounded by a high wall with fragments of broken glass cemented on the top to make it safe.

"Good," he said, "I will send my boy this afternoon to pick it up."

Since Alexandra roamed many parts of Ethiopia to expand her practice—and frequented Djibouti and Dire Daua because of her railroad contract—she met many interesting people, one of whom became a painting companion. One day, a patient in Djibouti—an Englishman who was the British consul there—came with a young lady and an old lady.

I thought, "It is his wife and their daughter." But the daughter turned out to be his wife and the older woman was his mother-in-law. He was perhaps fifty years old, his wife only thirty. She used to go out painting with me sometimes. She was also a landscape painter, as I was, painting to re-member with.

With the new home, Herman and Alexandra both working success-fully, her parents with her, and even time to enjoy painting, life seemed ideal to Alexandra, but she had lost people and places worth remem-bering. She did not know what had happened to her homeland, her relatives. In Soviet Russia, Lenin had died and a new man named Stalin had taken over.

Sixteen

The New Plan

*B*efore his death in Communist Russia, Lenin had mandated a plan called NEP, New Economic Plan, in 1922. During this time, the regime had relaxed some of its despotic measures to offset some of the devastation of the Civil War. Writing letters to other countries was permitted, and a correspondence had resumed between Katerina and some of the family still in Russia. Zina, Alexandra's cousin and the sister of her composer cousin Boris Liatoshinsky, was living in Moscow with her husband Appollinaire, a professor of agriculture at the Moscow agronomy school. In 1928, Stalin ended NEP officially, claiming that progress wasn't fast enough. He instituted five-year plans and cracked down on dissidents.

In one of her 1928 letters, Zina told Katerina that Katerina's niece Mila (Ludmilla), whose husband had been shot by the regime, had been exiled to Kazakhstan in Siberia for five years, along with her nineteen-year-old daughter Irina. Her crime was simply being the widow of an army captain "executed" by the regime. Katerina told Zina to sell all the Persian carpets and send the proceeds of the sale to Mila and Irina.

Zina managed to find a buyer for the carpets, none other than her brother the composer, "who had money." He was still living at No. 5

Theater Street in Kiev.[82] Boris put the carpets not on the floors, but on the ceilings of his apartment, in order to muffle the sound of his playing at night on one or the other of his two grand pianos. His neighbors on the floor above had complained of this late-night music. Now, thanks to Captain Lev Drosdovsky's rug purchases in Baku and Katerina's practical heart, the composer could play in peace without remonstrance from the people upstairs, and help her exiled family at the same time.

Visitors from Europe

Roman Drosdovsky, Alexandra's brother, visited the family in Ethiopia. He'd studied in Germany where he became an electrical engineer with Bosh Industries in Stuttgart. He, along with most post-war Germans, exiled Russians and other Europeans considered Bolsheviks and their style of communism as the single most powerful threat to Western civilization. Yet he adjusted to loss of homeland and was an avid mountain climber, along with his future wife Dora, a German citizen. Other than the broken leg he suffered during his visit, he enjoyed the reunion and Ethiopia.

Herman's mother pays a surprise visit

Herman's mother, Selchen Dabbert, also came for a visit to Addis Ababa. She attended a party there and after a discussion with the English consul, she bet him she could beat him back to the house on horseback while he drove a car. Herman had no idea his mother had made such a bet until he saw both of them departing, the consul in an open cabriolet and she on horseback. Herman had acquired a car and tried to follow the two. His mother knew that the road made a long circumnavigation of the field. Herman couldn't follow her when she left the road and headed

---

[82] He would continue to live there until his death.

straight across the field to win the race. When he caught up with her, Herman told his mother not to do that again because the fields were full of tunnel holes made by animals and a horse could easily get a hoof caught in one, causing a dangerous fall.

More Affairs of State

In dealing with Ethiopian royalty, Alexandra could closely watch the political scene. Plots had unfolded in the effort to sabotage Ras Tafari. On one such occasion, his wife had to send guards to rescue him. To clear herself from implication of involvement in this attempt against Ras Tafari, Empress Zauditu in November of 1928 proclaimed Ras Tafari the official Negus of Ethiopia—a title previously used only locally and unused with respect to the ruler of the whole country.

Another event late in 1928 was a move against Ras Tafari by a governor loyal to Empress Zauditu. He was a dejasmach (governor) of Oromo. At a formal event, Saffo and his captains were openly disrespectful to the regent, but while they were encouraged to drink more and more, Ras Hailu—loyal to Ras Tafari—approached the rebel army of the dejasmach with money in one hand and whips in the other. The men were told to take the money and go home or stay there and see what happens. When the dejasmach went out to rally his troops, they had utterly disappeared, and he fled.

The dissatisfaction didn't end there, but Ras Tafari proceeded with his sweeping reforms and modernization, which further alienated the more conservative elements within the country. But life in the royal family went on as if nothing had happened.

Shash-Werk, the Niece

Alexandra first met Ras Hailu's niece Woisero Shash-Werk in 1928. A friend came in an auto to Alexandra's office and said, "Come, Shash-Werk needs you."

Alexandra began to assemble her dental tools, but the Woisero stopped her.

"No, no. She needs you for something else. Bring your deck of cards."

Alexandra had acquired some measure of celebrity in the capital for her ability to read the future in the cards. Shash-Werk had heard of her prowess and wanted to make use of it. She lived in a round tower three stories tall. Like most of the buildings in Addis Ababa, it was of mud-stucco and wood-frame construction. On the first floor were perhaps fifty armed soldiers, Shash-Werk's guards, lounging about smoking, drinking, and talking. The second floor contained the kitchen and dining room. On the third floor was Shash-Werk's bedroom, the floors and walls covered with very fine Persian carpets, those on the floor being very dirty. A low table had been set up with chairs around it.

"Do you have your cards with you?" asked Shash-Werk, anxious to get the proceedings underway. "Then go open the cards for me, please." She dismissed her servant girls, saying, "Go prepare cafe."

Alexandra said, "I am going to tell you just what I see in the cards, whether it is good or bad. Exactly what I see."

"Yes, yes, please," said Shash-Werk eagerly.

"I see," Alexandra said, "that there is a young man, and the heart suit tells me he is not very black. You think about him."

"Yes, yes," said Shash-Werk with excitement.

"And you are going to travel," Alexandra continued. ("Clubs," she revealed, "are the travel suit.") "And the young man will go with you."

"Ah," said Shash-Werk, with a sigh.

As it happened, Shash-Werk—who was at this time in her mid-thirties—was married to old Ras (Duke) Kuksa of Tigré.

It was common knowledge that she did not love him. She had applied to the Ras Tafari as Regent, not long before Alexandra's visit, for permission to travel from Addis Ababa to her home in Tigré via Djibouti. This involved a three-day train ride to Djibouti, four days from there to Massawa by ship, and two days by auto to Tigré. She had asked the Emperor to permit her "protector," the "not so dark young man" Alexandra had seen in the cards, to accompany her on the journey. Just a few days after Alexandra's visit to the tower room, Ras Tafari gave Shash-Werk permission to make the trip as she wished, just as Alexandra had predicted when she "opened the cards."

Adventurer/Author

The railway continued to accommodate Alexandra on her yearly trips. When she traveled to Djibouti or Dire Daua, the railway usually added a special railcar to the train to carry her horses and mules so that she could indulge in her favorite pastime—riding Rurik. She loved to explore new terrain followed by her groom on horse or muleback.

Herman's painting of Rurik, Alexandra's favorite horse

In about 1928, French adventurer Henri de Monfreid, one of Alexandra's patients and acquaintances from these annual trips to Dire Daua and Djibouti, faced a life in prison. On many occasions, he had shared his knowledge of Africa with Alexandra and also had a sense of humor.

Henri de Monfreid, who wrote many books about his travels and owned perhaps the first automobile in Dire Daua, was one of my patients. One day, when he had just bought the automobile, he found some natives squatting by it silently, staring at its undercarriage. He asked them what they were looking at. One of them replied, "We know that it eats and drinks, for we have seen it being filled. And we know it has children. (This was a reference to toy autos they had seen in local stores.) But we are unable to tell what sex it is."

Among de Monfreid's adventures was a trip from Greece to Suez with a load of hashish.[83] He owned a flourmill in Dire Daua and was also, so the rumor went, smuggling arms on the side.[84] At some time in the late 1920s, an informer told the police that de Monfreid was smuggling arms into Ethiopia. He was arrested in Djibouti, but there was at once a big problem: Where would they imprison him? They had no prison for whites in the blacks' prison. The police settled the contretemps by putting him in a padded cell in the insane asylum. "Whites never went to prison," Alexandra explained.

He was in his padded cell for about a week and then was mysteriously released. No doubt there was some question of payment. In any case, shortly after de Monfreid got out of jail, the Somali who had denounced him disappeared and was not seen again. His mother made a big fuss. She said, "He came one evening to the house of Mr. De Monfreid, and he never came back. It is a fact."

The police made a big investigation. They went so far as to pull up to the floorboards of Monsieur de Monfreid's house, all of them. The house was only a couple of blocks from the sea. They found nothing in the house. Many Somalis liked de Monfreid. His wife was German. I knew all the family well.[85]

Gebir

Because Alexandra knew so many people, and the foreign community of the area was a world unto itself, Alexandra's social obligations extended far beyond her practice. Yet she fully participated in the strange customs of a world so vastly different from those of her beloved Russia.

---

[83] The story is related in one of his books, *Hashish, Adventures of a Red Sea Smuggler in the Twenties* (New York: Penguin, 1985).

[84] His grandson became an architect in Paris and corresponded with Alexandra.

[85] De Monfreid became a Muslim and an inveterate sailor. He owned a sailing ship and witnessed many licit and illicit adventures.

Saints Boris and Gleb of Russia

The Saint of Lalibela and Ras Desta Damtu (an original
painting by Alexandra Dabbert of the Ethiopian hero
executed by the Italians for his guerilla activities)

Saint Nicholas, Patron of Russian children and sailors

Hippocrates, "The Father of Medicine"

Alexandra's original ikon of the Imperial Family as martyrs of the Russian Revolution

Fishers of Man

Madonna and Child

Baptism of Jesus

Her patient and friend, Mr. Babitchev, had been a cavalry lieutenant in Russia. He married an Ethiopian wife and had four children. "He had a big farm from his wife. Her family was rich." He received the title of general in the Ethiopian army, and so was known as Fitawrari (General) Babitchev.[86]

Mr. Babitchev's Ethiopian wife had died on the farm and was duly buried.

Alexandra and her horseman Abte Georgis were on the train, returning to Addis Ababa from a trip to buy cheap horse food. On her way home, she met Mr. Babitchev's secretary.

"Please, Dr. Dabbert, you must come with me to the plantation because tomorrow will be forty days since Mrs. Babitchev died. There will be a 'gebir'—a celebration for her soul. Four bulls have already been slaughtered. Our mules are ready."

She accepted and went with her horseman to the farm. Babitchev was delighted to see her, "another white face, and Russian like him, at that." She was given a good room with a European bed and asked when to awaken in the morning.

"Don't worry, you will hear. The birds at your window will tell you when to get up," Babitchev said.

At six o'clock the next morning, "four or five of the dead lady's servants came to my room and took the pillows and blankets I had used the night before," Alexandra said. "I realized then that I had slept in her bed. There was a big procession."

Four or five Coptic Ethiopian priests at the head of the line walked, chanting and burning incense. Then came the dead lady's mule with the empty saddle. Some servants carried her dresses, pillows, and blankets, and one boy carried a pillow, which Alexandra had used the night before, with all the dead woman's jewelry on it. The service was very long, and then came the *gebir*.

---

[86] His granddaughter was imprisoned by the Communists in 1974 revolution, when Haile Selassie was deposed. She hanged herself while in prison.

Everyone was invited to the gebir. Neighbors, friends, family. "AND BEGGARS. Many of them live by going from gebir to the next rich person's gebir." Lepers formed a large percentage of the beggar population.

When everyone was seated, the servants of the dead person brought one leg of beef at a time from each guest to the next. Ethiopians, carrying their "inseparable" daggers, would slice themselves a piece. Raw beef was considered a delicacy. The slightly alcoholic *talla* and *tetch* flowed. *Injera* (a wide and spongy pita bread made out of a minute Ethiopian grain called teff) and wott (sort of fiery hot stew) with different condiments and meats, and chickens with lots of *berbere* (hot peppers) were presented to everybody's fill.

"The party lasted more than a day, but I left next day," Alexandra said.

Seventeen

The Expatriates

When people left their homelands behind to live and settle in Ethiopia, many were escaping horrors worse than loss of home, family, friends, and culture. Some pined for all they'd lost, while others seized the day. Sometimes the fresh start worked, but sometimes it failed and the expatriates paid a heavy price. Some exiles felt freed by the distance from former social constraints. Others brought their ethics and philosophies with them. Alexandra saw it all. Most of them were her patients, and because of their small numbers relative to the native population, the foreigners' world in Africa was as well observed and judged as it had been in the home countries.

The Pass

Monsieur Girard, the Belgian ambassador who leased the former Russian embassy, was among those who had prospered in Ethiopia.

> The Belgian minister was very rich, and in his living room that was bigger than a house, he had a large carpet made of skins of hundreds of Colobus monkeys with large white and black spots like panda bears. He lived alone.

One day he sent his horse boy to me, bringing a big box of chocolates and an invitation to come to see him. I sent back the chocolate box with my horse boy and a letter that began: "Cher Monsieur, you have the wrong address for your chocolates."

It was not a proper thing to do, unless he was thanking me as a patient for my work.

Then, maybe one year later, the French doctor Renault came to see me—there were no telephones then—and told me that Mr. Girard had a terrible toothache. Would I go to the Embassy and treat him there?

I said, "With pleasure, Doctor Renault, I will go," and I went to the embassy with my horse boy Gabri carrying my instruments.

For Some, Things Went Terribly Wrong

Captain Knobloch, a retired Austrian Cavalry officer, came to Ethiopia hoping to become rich easily. He was wrong; it was not easy. He was single, very kind, very clean. He participated in the carousel described elsewhere. Then, he decided to return to Austria, where he committed suicide with a pistol: He wore white gloves so as not to get blood on his hands. He was very neat.

Mr. Nicolas Voronovsky—the Russian engineer who had arrived in Addis Ababa with Ras Tafari, back from his trip to Europe with Ras Hailu and other Ethiopian Kings—had shared many stories about the royals with Alexandra. Yet he also possessed a talent that raised certain existential questions: Did living in exile exacerbate existing problems and deficiencies? Were certain tragedies predestined? Could an ominous refusal to reveal a prophesied destiny provoke the very thing that was predicted?

Since we had mutual friends from Russia, he (Nicolas Voronovsky) came to see me. While he was visiting, Ivan, the nineteen-year-old son of General

Sveshnikoff, came to the house to deliver sour cream, cottage cheese, and other dairy products from his father's farm on his weekly rounds.

While we chatted, Nicolas remarked that he could read palms. He read my palm first and then took Ivan's hand, looked at it, but did not read it.

He only said, "You are too young, I don't like to tell your future." He seemed upset.

After Ivan left, Nicolas said to me, "That man has the palm of a suicide."

Next day, Ivan asked his brother to go to the kitchen and make him some tea. He took a small caliber pistol and shot himself in the breast—it only wounded him. He called then to his brother Alexander from the kitchen and asked him to bring a mirror. Apparently, the brother had not heard the shot. With the mirror, Ivan aimed his pistol into the mouth and shot himself.

He did not die immediately and was taken to the American Methodist Hospital, where he was in agony for three days . . . .

When Mama and I went to visit him, we met his father, the general.

"I am praying," he said, "that he dies soon—it is a terrible agony."

Why did he shoot himself? He had fallen passionately in love with Sophie, the wife of the Russian doctor Gabrielov, and had taken her some flowers. She had told him to "go to hell." She was not interested.

There was a big funeral. The whole Russian colony was there marching to the Ethiopian Orthodox cemetery. We had our horses and mule with us, but we were walking. There were only four cars in Addis Ababa at the time. Of the two cars following the funeral path, one belonged to the Empress and the other one belonged to the Methodist hospital, where Ivan had died.

There was a tradition in Ethiopia that on such occasions someone was delegated to give money to the beggars. There were some thirty beggars looking for the alms and they were told to accost a Russian ex-air-force colonel, but he had no money. He could only go to Alexandra's father.

Papa replied, "I have only two thalers. It is all my wife gave me. Take them."

Here was a general and a colonel and only one U.S. dollar between them.

Another sad outcome was that of Mr. Browers. Still with his golden beard "like a hero from Wagner's operas," he was the wealthy owner of the coffee plantation that Alexandra visited in Arussi—famous for the quality of coffee.

I was in Djibouti at the time, and he came to see me. He was my patient and I made a plaster impression of his teeth. The plaster of Paris got stuck to his mustaches and beard, and I had to carefully use my scissors to trim the hair off the cast. He did not mind.

He had brought to Djibouti the coffins of his two little sons that had died at the same time of dysentery at the plantation. He could not get passage for them on a French ship because they were not allowed to take corpses, and he wanted to have them buried in his hometown, so he was waiting for the Austrian freighter to get himself and the two sons back to Belgium.

Frauline Pitchke was the German governess of the daughter of the Italian ambassador to the court of Haile Selassie.

She came to me as a patient and seemed to be so happy. She was cleaning her future house and preparing to marry Mr. Ferrago, an officer in the Hungarian army, with an appointment at his embassy. Then I heard that she died.

She had lived in the Italian embassy. The ambassador's wife, my friend and patient, told me that Fraulein Pitchke took an overdose of morphine and was found dead in the morning.

She had become despondent when Mr. Farrago told her that he was still waiting for his government's permission to marry her. She thought that he had changed his mind and took the morphine. She had stolen the drug from the ambassador, who was an addict.

By next mail came the permission, but it was too late.

It seemed that most suicides at the time were the result of affairs of passion, and such was the case in the next story in which Alexandra's fine dental work worsened the tragedy. There was a Maltese gentleman at the British Embassy, Zafiro, fluent in Arabic and Amharic. He was in his fifties and married to a pretty woman—half Italian, half Maltese—some twenty years younger. They had three children. Like several of Alexandra's well-to-do patients, he wanted his porcelain false teeth mounted on a solid gold plate.

> It was heavy, but fitted well. Now, Zafiro was very jealous of his young wife. He probably had reasons to be….One day he took a pistol, put it into his mouth, and pulled the trigger. But he did not remove his false teeth, and the bullet shattered the gold plate, but did not penetrate the skull. It took him four days to die in great agony.

And Then There Were the Happier Endings

One day, traveling in a first-class railway car, Alexandra and others observed a prosperous looking gentleman in the car as they entered. Her mother asked her in Russian, "Who is this gentleman?"

Alexandra replied, "This is the 'intestine king.'" It was the title that friends had bestowed on him. He smiled and asked the two ladies to join him. He spoke fluent Russian. He was a German and exported sausage casings to Europe and had spent some time in Russia.

Dimitri Sidov was one of the exiled patients. Formerly employed by the Russian embassy as a waiter, he managed to create in Ethiopia a bit of heaven on earth. He was married and had one daughter.[88] In addition to his home in the capital, Sidov also owned a flourmill located on the railroad line between Addis and Djibouti, about three hours

---

[88] She died in the early 1980s in France.

distant from the capital. The railway train that carried Sidov and his guests back and forth from the mill to Addis Ababa stopped not just at the stations along the line, but also at individual farmhouses. If one wished to stop at the mill, he simply told the conductor.

Sidov had constructed three or four thatched native huts in his garden of banana trees, a sort of primitive motel and favorite place for people to visit on weekend trips. There were lots of chickens scrabbling among the banana trees and the ubiquitous gigras, wild guinea fowl that were eagerly hunted for their delicious flesh.

There was also a waterfall over which flowed the water that drove the millstones. On a bridge over the river, downstream from the waterfall, Sidov had constructed a one-hole outhouse. Waste fell directly into the water and was carried swiftly and cleanly away. On ledges inside the privy were placed copies of well-known Russian magazines of considerable cultural value, along with other books, all of which Sidov had taken from the Russian embassy after the ambassador was recalled. He kept these valuable works in the outhouse for their value as toilet paper.

"This is the barbarism of the twentieth century," Alexandra commented. "Sometimes, after I had been gone for perhaps half an hour to the facility, Herman would come calling for me. 'Alex, where are you?' I would be engrossed in one fine Russian historical work or perhaps reading the cultural magazine."

And then there was the exiled French version of a happy ending, the French ambassador defending French interests. One day a French woman pianist came to Addis Ababa to entertain the European colony with a series of recitals. During her visit, a French gentleman called Street courted her, and she became pregnant. But Street was married.

Word reached the French Ambassador De Refis. When he learned of the pianist's embarrassment, he summoned to his office three members of the French local colony, all bachelors. One, named Faussier, was Alexandra's patient who lived with an Ethiopian woman by whom he had a son called Napolean, about eight years old. The second was Mr.

La Riviere, also living with an Abyssinian woman. He had a twelve-year-old daughter for whom he had provided a good education. The third was Monsieur Le Baron. He also lived with an Ethiopian woman by whom he had had perhaps six children, all well and all helping him on his nice farm, some ten miles from the capital. He raised strawberries, grapes, and other produce. To these men, De Refis said, "You are not married and, as you see, this young lady has a problem. One of you should marry the pianist."

After some consultation, Le Baron agreed to marry the pianist. The Ethiopian mother of six and her children continued at the farm, working and helping. The pianist became an expert manager of the farm and even established a good restaurant with a swimming pool, to which Alexandra and family sometimes went for meals and recreation. "A happy ending without Puritan strain."

And there was a Russian version of a happy ending. An ex-Russian Navy officer, Kolia (for Nicholas) Benklevski, worked in the administration of the Belgian alcohol factory in Addis Ababa. Alexandra told this story:

> He was a very fine, distinguished person. His wife was in Washington, dancing with a Spanish troupe, and he was living with an Ethiopian woman called Atada, a very good women who was my patient.
>
> When he became rich, he bought her one mule and one saddle, so she did not have to walk. She was only unhappy, she told me, that she had no child with him. She had lived with him maybe three or four years.
>
> When his wife Mary broke her leg, she was unable any longer to dance and had to leave her lover and dance group. She was very pretty, daughter of a Russian navy doctor. She heard that her husband Kolia had good position in Addis Ababa, so she wrote that she was on her way to join him.
>
> Benklevsky paid Atada money to live in the Hotel de France, in front of my house, but he was unhappy because Atada was better wife

than Mary. When Mary took up residence, she redecorated the house, filling it with pictures of herself as dancer. It was painful for him.

Into this scenario stepped a construction man from Montenegro called Baikilovich who lived in Addis Ababa. Madame Benklevsky divorced her husband and married Baikilovich in a civil ceremony. Benklevsky, much relieved, went back to Atada very happy. Baikilovich died some time later, however, and Mary started a small but successful hat store.

There was in Addis Ababa a member of a very noble Russian family, Count Tatischev. His uncle had been murdered in Siberia with Tsar Nicholas. Count Tatischev was forty-five years old and had been married to a Swedish countess with whom he had a daughter. The countess did not care to live in Ethiopia, however, and returned to Sweden. Count Tatischev married widow Baikilovich, formerly Madame Benklevsky, the milliner. It was a happy end.

Kolia Benklevsky continued living with Atada near an area in Addis Ababa called Cabana, after the River Cabana that ran along it. It was an elegant area where the German, Russian, and Italian embassies were located. Behind Cabana was Entoto Mountain where several other immigrant Russian officers, elegant men of Aristocratic families, lived in native tukuls (round huts with straw roofs) because it was cheaper. That area was also the source of Christmas trees during the Season.

There, Benklevsky had a large pet monkey named Mulugeta or Mr. Mulu in Ethiopian. One day, Mulugeta invaded the German embassy and was discovered sitting on the ambassador's desk, where he had already upset the inkpot. The natives were scared because he was so large. Eventually, with food, he was persuaded to leave the embassy and became a celebrity.

Another day Mulugeta stole a native woman's baby while she was working in the garden. Mulugeta seized the baby and gently hauled it under one arm, forty feet up a large Eucalyptus tree. He sat there with the screaming child until at last he was enticed with food to come down out of the tree. He didn't drop the baby.

Alexandra loved animals and awakening to the crows of roosters, and the sounds of hoofs and neighing as the horses were taken out of the stables for their morning grooming. She was especially amused at Doctor Gabrielov's story of a happy ending for the monkeys.

Doctor Gabrielov, whose samovar had served the Grand Duke, had two monkeys as pets in his house. The doctor and his wife Sophie tired of these pets and their antics, and one day they rode out on horseback to Mangasha Mountain, half a day away, accompanied by two grooms, each one carrying a monkey. They reached a big forest, released the monkeys, and headed back home. But the monkeys didn't like the forest and followed the horses, sending out such pitiful laments that the doctor and his wife decided to take them back. The monkeys preferred more secure entitlements.

Eighteen

The Coronation

Carousel

In January of 1930, there occurred a great event in the social life of Addis Ababa. Called the Carousel, this event was performed in historical costumes at the racetrack before the horse races. A large crowd filled the stands, including Empress Zauditu and Ras Tafari, Negus.

A group of eighteen Europeans, nine men and nine women, took part on horseback, each pair riding the same color horse. Alexandra rode her Rurik and Herman rode Hans, both brown. The men were clad in blue velvet coats, and the women in green velvet jackets, with long white skirts. All wore eighteenth cen-tury tricorner hats over their white perukes, which had been ordered from England by Mary Barton, the daughter of the British ambassador. When the wigs arrived, a bewildered employee of the embassy wanted to know if the Empress now wished to introduce a new style, that of people calling at her court arriving in white wigs.

The carousel

At the coronation of Haile Selassie

The municipal band played martial music, and all watched the mounted horsemen parading before the stands in their finery. Each of them would receive from the Empress a gold coin to commemorate the event with the Empress's head embossed on it. Alexandra would keep it all her life.

Coronation

Empress Zauditu's increasing resentment of Ras Tafari's growing popularity caused her to send her husband Ras Gugsa with an army into battle. Gugsa's forces battled the government's more technologically advanced army on the Anchiem Plain on March 31, 1930. The rebel army was crushed and Ras Gugsa was killed. Two days later on April 2, Empress Zauditu died. The official reason was listed as being caused by her diabetic condition, but theories ranged from "shock and a broken heart" to her strange folk remedies to outright poison.

After a period of mourning, the official coronation of Ras Tafari took place on November second.

Katrina returning from church

There were many white reporters. I was pregnant, but it did not show, using my robe. The coachman was a Hungarian, wearing seventeenthcentury clothing, except that he could not find a white wig. The guests of the white colony were invited to the left, the Ethiopians to the right. I enjoyed the apples and pears that had come by ship from Europe and were otherwise unavailable.

At the right corner was the orchestra. The bandleader, Monsieur Edward Garibaldi, was an Armenian with an Italian name and my wonderful dental technician who made crowns and plates. He had learned to be a conductor in Constantinople.

Ras Tafari's father Makonen was believed to be a direct descendant of King Solomon of biblical times, and therefore, also the son. Ras Tafari adopted a throne name and was proclaimed "Haile

Selassie I, Elect of God, Conquering Lion of Judah, Negusnegheste," King of Kings, emperor of Ethiopia. His wife was also crowned Empress Menen of Ethiopia and his children held the titles of Princes and Princess. His coronation marked the end of feudalism for Ethiopia. This event made the European newspapers, Evelyn Waugh being one of the reporters.

In 1930, the first airplane flew in the Ethiopian skies. This French military airplanehad been bought by the Negus Haile Selassie, and had been used in the defeat of Ras Gugsa.

One Sunday, Katerina walked to church for services, accompanied—as was always the way for ladies—by one of the boys. On the way, the airplane flew over, and they watched till it was out of sight.

The boy then asked, "When this thing flies high, high, high, will he come to God?"

Katerina thought for a minute and then replied, "Yes, I think it will come to God, if he flies high enough."

Nineteen

Olik

In December of 1930, Lev went out to survey the property of one of his daughter's wealthy Ethiopian patients. He was accompanied, as usual, by a judge and the judge's secretary. The latter dignitary, who wrote up the proceedings, was usually a deacon in the Coptic Church and, as such, poorly paid. Since each Coptic parish had from fifty to one hundred priests to serve it, depending on how rich the parish, payment for their services was not large.

When Lev had completed his survey, the lady said to him, "I understand your daughter is carrying a child. I shall give her a cow. Then she can have fresh milk for her child. And she can have the first calf too."

The Cow

Next morning Alexandra's head man Abte said, "Madame, they have brought you a cow."

"Good," she replied. "Put the cow in the mule's place in the stable, and put the mule somewhere else."

She thought no more of the cow. Two days later Abte came to her again. "Madame, we cannot have this cow."

"But why not?"

"Because she has made hole in the wall with her horns."

"I will go see."

The barn walls were built of tree limbs covered with adobe, much like the house itself, though on a more modest scale.

"I think the cow is wild," Abte said, "from the mountains, and it is not accustomed to being penned up indoors. Besides, she is very big; she is more like a bull."

Alexandra examined the hole and then the cow, which was, as Abte had said, very large—not the usual Abyssinian cow.

"You are right," she said, "it is impossible to have such a cow. We will sell it."

"But who will want to buy such a cow?"

"We will see."

One of Alexandra's patients, a Dane named Rasmussen, asked her a few days later how much she wanted for the big cow.

"I don't know," she said, "perhaps thirty-five thalers ($17.50)."

"Good. When you are finished, we'll go look at your famous cow."

He went to the cow and lifted up its tail, making a close examination, then said, "Ah, I see she's already had two or three calves. But it is a good cow. I'll buy it."

The cow, however, didn't want to leave. She'd grown fond of her place in the barn and would not be budged. It took two men pulling with ropes from the front and two more pushing from the rear to get her out of the barn. Rasmussen tied her to his mule, and she obediently followed him to her new home.

Riding into Motherhood

Alexandra traveled on horseback, even after she had become pregnant. Several people, her mother in particular, advised her not to ride. Katerina even pleaded with Alexandra's doctor to so advise her. He said only, "She knows how she feels, and if she feels that she can go, she can go."

Three years before this time, an Englishwoman from the British embassy had come to Alexandra for dental work when she was far along in pregnancy. And she came on horseback.

"Aren't you afraid to ride in your condition?" Alexandra asked.

"No," she replied, "my horse is a stallion. He understands my condition and so goes softly."

Alexandra remembered this comment.

Later when I was carrying Olik, my horse Rurik is a stallion, and he knew how to go just as the English lady said. The German embassy sent me a mule named Liza to use at this time. They thought it would be a better and more sure-footed mount for me.

Unfortunately, Liza was not used to city life and shied at bits of flying paper, so I returned it to the embassy. My horse is better. I rode horseback until two weeks before Olik was born. The birth was a very easy one, lasting from two until five p.m. I think perhaps the horseback riding helped the muscles, and so made it easy for me.

The midwife to the royal family—Frau Hertel, a German lady from Berlin—was a "grand dame" in the capital, having assisted the empress in her births. She is the one that put Alexandra on a strict diet of peach compote for the last month of gestation, so that Olik was born weighing just under five pounds for easier delivery.

Olgard, her son born on January 23, 1931 and nicknamed Olik, got his name in an unusual way. One of her friends had read in the tealeaves that Alexandra would certainly have a girl.[87] Alexandra was all the more ready to believe this prophecy since she wanted a girl. "It is easier for a woman to stay close to a daughter than to a son," she

---

[87] In those times, obstetricians—when asked the sex of the baby during pregnancy—tended to tell the mother, "It will be a girl." If it was a girl, the prediction was correct. If it was a boy, all was forgiven.

reasoned, "because a girl is much closer to her mother than a son and not as likely to be alienated from the mother after marriage."

She preferred the name "Olga," and arranged for all her baby things to be decorated with the letter "O." She began to search for a boy's name beginning with "O," and finally settled on Olgard after an ancient Lithuanian prince. To ease the requests of her patient clergy, Olgard was also baptized with the

"I rode horseback until two weeks before Olik was born"

Ethiopian name Tesfay (Hope) by a Coptic; Vadim, by the Russian Orthodox; and Horst, by the Lutheran priests.

Herman sent word to Germany about the birth of his son. A five-year-old nephew—Eberhard, called Eb—believing all babies born in Africa were black, happily spread the word that his uncle had fathered a black child, and that he had a black cousin. In kindergarten, he still believed that children were delivered by God, not a stork, but white babies were born in Germany—and in Africa, all babies were born black.

"I announced at school," he wrote, "that I had a black cousin and was immediately admired by everyone because nobody could claim a black cousin, and I felt special. Unfortunately, it did not last long because at the next school meeting, my teacher 'congratulated' my mother on the little accident my uncle had with a black maiden. When my mother looked in astonishment, he told her that I had announced that I had a black cousin. This was soon clarified and my exalted status in the class diminished."

Birke and Olik

The following Christmas, Herman was still out in the wilderness surveying, and looked forward to returning home for the holidays. A train passed through the area only every two weeks. He had been riding with an askari (a trained guard) because the area wasn't safe. When he reached a hill from where they could see the station, Herman watched the train pull in. Even if he whipped his horse to a frenzied gallop, he knew he wouldn't make it in time. He dismounted and sat down, close to tears, head buried in his hands. At a touch to his shoulder, he looked up.

His askari said, "Why are you crying, Massa'? Next train leaves in fourteen days."[88]

Shortly after Olik's birth, Alexandra hired nanny Birke, who soon became inseparable from Olik. She was so close that Alexandra was known among the natives as "the mother of Birke's child."

Having a baby didn't keep Alexandra from her practice, and with the help of Birke and her mother, Alexandra was soon back at work.

Underpinnings

For the strangest of reasons, Alexandra was privy to the underpinnings of royal activities and politics. One time, the Minister of Foreign Affairs made an appointment and was invited for tea. He asked to look at an atlas.

"The Emperor is sending me on an official visit to Japan, and on the way he wants to stop in Yugoslavia!" (This was before air travel.)

---

[88] Herman would later think of this moment when listening to people in Berlin complain about missing a subway connection.

Frau Hertel, between the Queen and the Princess

Before major functions and celebrations, Ethiopian officials that had been abroad and received medals from other countries knew that Lev had been a general for the Czar and would come to see him and ask where to wear the decorations.

One day, Frau Hertel, the German sophisticated midwife to the court, came to the house to ask if she could borrow from Mama (who was a bit on the heavy side) a large corset, as next day the Empress had to attend a reception without her usual Ethiopian attire. Later she got her own corsets.

Frau Hertel mounted her horse, assisted by a new boy. This particular servant, anxious to do his work well, took hold of her boot and lifted her up to the saddle with such energy that she was propelled right over it and fell on the ground on the other side. In April or May of 1931, she had helped deliver a third son to the empress, a sickly boy named Sahle Selassie.[89]

Later a Swiss lady gynecologist would be called to the court of Haile Selassie to assist the emperor's daughter in childbirth, but would later cancel her contract with the Emperor. "All women here give birth like dogs, on all fours, and nothing I say has any effect."

Since Frau Hertel had been the court's midwife for thirty years, she would not be unhappy to see the lady doctor go. She found that such posture gave Ethiopian women, including royalty, easier delivery. "Maybe they could contract and push harder that way," Alexandra said. "I never heard of Ethiopian women needing Cesarean section."

Dental problems could interfere with the politics and high finance.

---

[89] He died sometime before World War II.

I had many ambassadors and other diplomats as my patients. Sometimes, by "pure coincidence," two would come at the same time and ask me to leave them alone in the waiting room so they could speak in full privacy. As long as they had teeth problems, I was glad to cooperate.

Mr. Zervos came to me with a swollen jaw. He had an audience next day with the Emperor. He was a very rich man, the brother of the Greek consul. Another brother, Dr. Jacob Zervos, was the family doctor of Haile Selassie.

I told him, "All night long apply hot pack to the jaw." It is interesting what people use for hot packs. Germans use boiled potatoes in a cloth. Italians use polenta in poultice. Peruvians use sweet potatoes, very cheap there. The French use boiled flaxseeds in a cloth.

I don't know what Zervos used, but in the early morning he came and the abscess was ripe to be cut. I cut and tell him to suck and spit. He was all right for the audience.

Doctor Jacob Zervos, the man's brother, is the one that told Alexandra to taste all the medicines herself before giving them to members of the court and royal family to show it wasn't poison.

One day Haile Selassie's son, Prince Asfau Wosen, came to see me for inflamed gums. I gave him a prescription for a solution of zinc oxide. He sent one of his servants to the German pharmacy to fill the prescription. I put the medicine on my wrist and tasted it, to show that it was not poison.

The experience reminded Alexandra of Russia, before the revolution. The governor of a province was advised to take castor oil.

. . .which tastes terrible and smells terrible. He was playing cards with his secretary at the time. The secretary said, "Excellency, I will take the medicine first to give you courage," but the secretary could not help but gag when he swallowed the oil. His Excellency the Governor refused to take the oil.

Twenty

Gifts

*A*lexandra had already learned that those in power, especially those considered "royal," had figured out a way to avoid paying bills. They preferred gifts of their choosing to the crassness of useful cash. But others in power had also crafted a mentality that allowed the flow of cash and gifts to work to their advantage. She learned that there are two words in Amharic for "gift." *Goursha* means "a gift afterwards"—for example, as in a thank you. The other word, *gubo*, means "a gift before."

The Gubo Way

The owner of a French restaurant in Addis Ababa remarked one day to Alexandra that the Minister of Public Works, one Ato (Mr.) Fasseka, had entertained a French engineer newly arrived in the capital. The minister, who had been educated in France and therefore spoke excellent French, had invited the new man to dinner with him. They had a sumptuous meal, which included several bottles of the best champagne the restaurateur had in his cellars. When the owner brought the bill for the evening's repast, he presented it to the French engineer, who in private protested.

"But he invited me!"

"Ah," said the restaurateur, "you are new. You will discover our ways. You will learn that when Minister Fasseka asks you to dinner, you must pay."

"But why?"

"It is his way," was the Greek owner's explanation. "It is the custom here that when an important Ethiopian invites you out, you are the one to pay for the honor."

Alexandra on Rurik, under a bridge near her home

In 1930, Alexandra was on her way by horseback to the home of Monsieur De Robillard, the owner and editor of *Le Courrier d'Ethiopie* daily paper. She always announced her return to work after being absent. She saw then by his house at the roadside a Ford auto belonging to Ato Fasseka, the Minister of Works of Ethiopia that the Greek restaurant owner had already warned her about.

She also saw distinctly that a chain had been passed between the spokes of one wheel and had been wrapped around the telegraph pole and secured with a padlock. Monsieur De Robillard explained the situation.

"I have arrested Ato Fasseka's car because he is two years behind in the payment of his subscription of Le Courrier. Until he pays, we have taken his car hostage."

Alexandra reported a more personal instance of debt evasion by officials. The cashier (treasurer) of Addis Ababa, Ato Kabada, was apparently very familiar with the gubo way.

Because of (Ato Kabada's) neglect, Papa had not been paid for four months. Something had to be done. I had three pistols. I took one of my

Browning pistols and gave it to the cashier. "Please," I said, "my father needs his pay." Next day he was paid.

About three years later, the priests of Saint George's Coptic Church became upset and wanted to make a petition to stop the soap factory near the church. It made very bad smell. They asked me for help.

This time, Alexandra obliged. She helped to write a petition in French to the Emperor.

> In civilized countries it is never allowed to build a smelly soap factory to be built in the center of the city, next to the Cathedral of Saint George. It is a crime against humanity.

Next day, Ato Kabada was fired and forced to leave Addis Ababa for six years. He had been stealing from the municipality and accepting too much gubo to give permission to the soap factory to be built by the cathedral.

Herman and Gubo

In the very early 1930's, Herman began to despair of getting a contract with the Ethiopian government for surveying the border between English Somaliland and Ethiopia. The new job would pay one thousand thalers ($500) a month—three times more than his present job as municipal engineer for the city of Addis Ababa. He had an infant son to support, so he was eager to get Ato Fasseka's signature on the contract. Moreover, the border survey required living in tents in the outback and shooting game for meals, all of which appealed to Herman.

Alexandra understood Ato Fasseka and knew what to do. She'd been given an English saddle worth a hundred thaler by a German woman who had no use for it.

She said to Herman, "Let's take this saddle to Ato Fasseka. You do not understand local diplomacy, but I do. We will make a gift of it to him."

Next afternoon she and Herman and their groom, carrying the saddle, rode the considerable distance to Minister Fasseka's house far outside the city. En route Alexandra explained to Herman the two words in Amharic for "gift." "Goursha," a gift afterwards, and "gubo," a gift before.

When the trio reached Ato Fasseka's home, they greeted him cordially, and Alexandra said, "We have come to bring you gubo." And Herman presented him with the saddle. Fasseka noted the use of the word.

"How can I serve you?" he replied in his elegant French.

"For several weeks," Alexandra said, "my husband has been trying to get signed the contract for surveying the Somali border. But he has not had success."

"Ah," said Fasseka, "I did not know. I will look into it. Come to my office tomorrow, Monsieur Dabbert."

Herman did as Ato Fasseka suggested, and the contract was signed and presented, thanks to the gubo.

Surveyor in the Wild

Herman spent four years surveying the Somali border between Ethiopia and "British Somaliland."[90] He lived in the wilderness, in tents, shooting his own game. The head of a large kudu adorned the entrance to their stable in Addis Ababa, but the rest of the carcass had been served for food for the workers of the surveying party.

Many years later, Herman, commented that those years in the bush surveying the border had been "the best of my life." When he took the job in 1931, he worked under Emil Beitz who was also a German. Beitz's wife was with him.

One day, Beitz did not return. His body was finally found with thirty-six dagger stab wounds, and his sex organs had been cut off. This latter fact threw suspicion on a French Somali as the killer, as they

---

[90] Fifty years later, the area was to explode in a savage war between the two sovereign nations: Ethiopia and Somalia, alternatively assisted by the U.S.A. and the U.S.S.R., who were engaged in the Cold War.

Herman, near the Somali border

were known to consider a victim's sex organs as a trophy that earned the attention of their future brides.

Not long afterward, a French Somali was arrested still wearing Beitz's ring. This ring with a Lapis stone had been purchased in Kabul, Afghanistan, bought on Emil's previous job. Alexandra theorized:

Probably his death was related to French concerns that better communications between Ethiopia and Berbera—the British Somaliland harbour on the Red Sea—would affect negatively the business of the Franco-Ethiopian railway.

Beitz was my patient, and I saw that ring many times.

After the murder, the Ethiopian Government gave to the widow Beitz the remainder of her husband's due salary for two years. The sum came to thirty-five thousand thalers (about $17,000). She returned to Germany. Herman succeeded Beitz as chief of the surveying party. When he applied for increase of his salary because of his added responsibilities, he was told, "We have already paid out the chief's salary to Mrs. Beitz for the remainder of the contract."

This medieval way of doing things irritated Herman, who forever remained deeply European. He loved the wilderness, but he detested Ethiopian business ethics, while Alexandra was more attuned to local customs, and frequent separation didn't help their relationship.

Twenty-one

Djibouti and Dire Daua

$\mathscr{A}$lexandra continued her practice for the railroad. She worked in January and February—first in Djibouti and then in Dire Daua— because it was cooler. The train went from Djibouti to Addis Ababa only two times a week on Sundays and Thursdays. She wrote:

> ## Madame H. Dabbert
> *chir. dentiste*
> DENTISTE PARTICULIÈRE DE LA MAISON IMPÉRIALE ÉTHIOPIENNE
> ATTACHÉE AU SERVICE MÉDICAL DE LA Cie DU C.F.E.
> sera de retour à AddisAbeba le 21 août
> et recevra les malades des dents à partir
> de ce jour, à son domicile, comme pré-
> cédemment, de 9 heures à midi, et de 3
> à 4 heures.

"Madame H. Dabbert, dental surgeon—private dentist of the Imperial Ethiopian House and attached to the medical services of the Franco-Ethiopian Railway, will return to Addis Ababa on August 21 and will resume her practice at her home as before, from 9 to 12, and from 3 to 4 PM"

There were always many fascinating people waiting to travel. And many of them came to me for their teeth. There were ambassadors, tradesmen, writers, engineers—many of them British. I had there the most interesting patients, from many countries and of many vocations.

Practice in Djibouti

In Djibouti, Alexandra preferred to stay in the Continental hotel because she could serve patients who weren't railroad employees there, and also because it was more convenient than a private dwelling would have been. The hotel had a huge restaurant on the ground floor, which was used sometimes for showing movies.

"I remember seeing Greta Garbo there. But most of the films were French, Djibouti being a French colony," she said.

In the hotel she took two rooms, one for sleeping and one as an office for her practice. Other arrangements were made for Abte. The doors of the hotel were never locked, day or night. Windows and doors were simply closed with non-locking shutters. A veranda extended around the second floor, and her patients used it as a waiting room. At the other end of this veranda, perhaps half a city block away, there was the shower room. In the morning, Alexandra had to walk to and from this shower in her bathrobe.

In Djibouti one day, Alexandra saw a new patient. Mr. Martin Louis was the director of the local salt factory by the Red Sea.

She looked into his mouth and said, "You have nice fillings. They look like those done by my French professor in dental school in Kiev."

"And what was the name of the professor?" he asked.

"Henry Martin," she told him.

"But that is extraordinaire! He made these fillings for me in Paris!"

When Mr. Lewis went back to Paris, he contacted Professor Martin and visited his office, saw on a wall a photograph of a group of his Russian students, and Alexandra was one of them.

In many ways, Djibouti—a port on the Red Sea—was a crossroads mixing people, cultures, and experiences. In 1930, Alexandra was practicing when a large French yacht came sailing into the harbor with the family, including three children aboard and the children's tutor, who had a very bad toothache.

"The tooth is so painful," she told Alexandra, "I don't know how I would have stood it if it had not been for the cook who gave me some garlic. Every night I packed garlic around the aching tooth and pain went away."

It worked. She wondered if it was the arsenic in the garlic.

On days when a liner put into port, en route between France and Indo-China, people from all around the area would come to Djibouti and make a holiday of it. On board ship they could buy things tax-free from the hairdresser on the ship. They were much cheaper that way. I myself bought perfume and blouses from the hairdresser.

These ships then sailed from Djibouti to Aden. Some of the wealthy women in Djibouti boarded ship there and spent the entire night in the hair salon getting a permanent wave. This was the kind of permanent wave that was done with a hot iron and took several hours. The hairdresser would stay up all night to perform this service. In the morning, when the ship pulled into Aden, these socialites would come ashore in their new permanent waves and take a local vessel back to Djibouti. They were older ladies with money. I call them coquettes. Such a permanent wave was good for six to eight months, after which they would sail again for Aden.

Whether businessmen, royalty, missionaries or native tribes people, Alexandra treated them all. A Danakil man came to Alexandra's office in Djibouti one day with a painful tooth; he needed a root canal treatment. At the time, under local anesthesia, Alexandra handled it by drilling a little hole in the affected tooth and extracting the nerve with a little coil of wire. She pushed the nerve extractor into the hole in the tooth, twirled the extractor, winding the nerve and the vessel around it, and gently drew it out.

The patient was very impressed. "Give me this worm," he said.

Intestinal parasites were quite common. The tapeworm was particularly frequent, because Ethiopians liked to eat raw meat. (Some overweight ladies, particularly Italian women Alexandra knew, actually welcomed such infestation, as they thought they could then better control their obesity and eat what they wanted.)

Alexandra gave the man his "worm." Half an hour later he was back with his friend, another Danakil from the inhospitable hot wilderness of the French colony. He said, "Take out the worm for him, too." He had the same problem and received the same treatment. They visualized "the worm" as a small parasite causing the pain. They would not return for regular treatment, though, and eventually there would be an infection of the tooth and the victim or a friend would pull the tooth out.

One of her patients in Djibouti was a pretty young Somali girl who wore colonial dresses. Her lighter skin suggested mixed parentage. Alexandra wondered who she was. The Greek who owned the Continental hotel told her she worked for a Belgian company, the Fabrique Nationale. Alexandra knew this company well because she'd bought her three-barreled rifle there, which she subsequently traded for her good mule Baclusha.

"And what does she do for the company?" Alexandra asked the hotel owner.

"She services the male employees," he said. "In that way they will not go to the marketplace and perhaps get diseases. She is reserved for Fabrique Nationale workers."

Alexandra also visited with the friends she'd made in Djibouti. The Sorenson Seventh Day Adventist missionary family members were all patients and dear friends as well. Jean Spear, the daughter of Doctor Manuel Sorenson, liked to tell the time when her father and Alexandra, followed by Abte, went to see the city's red light district. They saw on each side of the road houses with many women's faces by the windows.

Suddenly there was a commotion, and four or five women ran out, grabbed Dr. Sorensen, and joyfully dragged him into one of the houses. It took Abte's presence of mind to run into the house and free Dr. Sorensen by insisting that he was a white Saint and was not interested in sex.

Dire Daua

The Franco-Ethiopian Railway provided Alexandra with a cottage when she worked in Dire Daua, one occupied by employees who were then on vacation in France. When Alexandra worked her designated month there, she—along with her parents and Olik—stayed there and especially enjoyed the garden, which was full of fig trees, papayas, oleanders, and pomegranates. She worked mostly in the early morning and late afternoon hours when the temperature was more tolerable.

Pan Vazek, the Czech who worked in the local bank and also bought wild animals from the natives to sell to German zoos, had many baboons

Olik with Lev

with prominent red rear ends. Just outside of town, he had built a little house with a small door. He would spread a corn trail from the nearby bush to the little house. Monkeys would follow the corn into the house, and when there were five or six monkeys inside, the natives would release the trap door.

> I visited the little house one day and I see a male baboon sitting with much self importance, while a female was picking lice off him. It reminded me of the time when I was talking with one of Dire Daua's chief city officers,

Balambaraz Bayene, a Catholic who spoke flawless French. While we talked, he would comb his hair and gently deposit the lice that he caught to the ground unharmed. I was scared I would be assaulted by these lice.

There were many giraffes in Ethiopia, but transportation to European zoos proved difficult because of their long necks, and also because giraffes would go uphill, yet would refuse to go down between slopes because they are afraid of heights.

Wildlife, hunting, and riding seem to have been the main benefit to the stay in Dire Daua for Alexandra and her family—although she never hunted for sport, only for "kitchen" or for taxidermy.

Alexandra and her parents in Dira Daua

Superstitions and Folk Remedies

Mrs. Hall, the tutor to the royal family, once traveled by train from Addis Ababa in third class. This in itself was unusual: only natives traveled third class. She had her parakeet with her in a cage. After Mrs. Hall seated herself, the parakeet suddenly piped up, "Madame, Madame." The natives thought there was a spirit in the coach and ran out. She traveled the rest of the time in an almost empty car.

Mrs. Hall owned the boarding house in Harar where Alexandra often stayed. She spent a month there with Olik and Birke while Olik recovered from whooping cough. Mrs. Hall's parakeet soon learned to imitate Alexandra calling nurse Birke. Now and then, the parakeet would call, "Birke," who would reply, "I am coming," before realizing that the caller was the bird.

Alexandra favored a popular folk remedy, although it isn't known whether she tried this for Olik's whooping cough. "When we had a cold with coughing, we put cups on the chest. Maybe four, five, or six on the chest," she said. A burning cotton swab soaked in a little alcohol was introduced inside a sturdy glass cup "to burn out the oxygen" and immediately applied to the skin on the chest. The French missionaries called the process "la ventouse" and used it extensively. The vacuum this created would suck the skin into the cup. It was left on for about five minutes. The skin drawn into the glass would become red and purple—and to remove the cup, one would put a gentle pressure with a fingertip between the skin and the glass to let air into the glass in order to detach it from the skin. "It gave good, inexpensive relief."

She also used "la ventouse" to drain mature "furuncles" or skin abscesses as soon after they had been incised—a condition that happened more often to white men, mostly on their backs and legs. "I did not see it in blacks. I understand it happens frequently in diabetics."

Alexandra didn't incorporate all folk remedies. She once had a terrible sore throat complete with pus, pain, swelling, and difficulty swallowing. The Ethiopian cure for such a severe sore throat concerned the uvula. They believed that the swollen and red uvula was the cause of the disease and that it must be removed. They used a horsetail hair and made a noose, looping it around to snare the uvula. "I decided that it was not for me," she said.

Makonnen, the second and favored son of Emperor Haile Selassie, was treated in this way and almost died, though managed to survive. Some traditional remedies were dangerous.

Father Leopold told me this story on the train to Dire Daua. Natives have a custom: When somebody is very sick and near death, they push mint in the nose to keep out evil spirits, and bread in the mouth, so that if he or she dies, there will be something to eat on the way to the next world. Once he removed the stuffing in a sick person gasping for air. The patient survived without the stuffing and lived many more years. An assisted suicide?[91]

---

[91] Father Leopold started a printing business and had discovered a deposit of limestone that could be used in concrete as building material. It brought steady income to his community.

Twenty-two

1935

Taffara

In 1935 when Olik was four years old, Alexandra arranged for a companion, a seven-year-old Ethiopian boy called Taffara. He was the stepson of Abte Georgis, the groom, and lived with Alexandra's family. He played and surreptitiously brought comic books to share with Olik, as Alexandra disapproved of "literature that made children stupid." He applied himself diligently to reading, writing, and arithmetic.

Before the Italian invasion, the roads for cars were bad. Cars having become more available, Alexandra acquired a Citroen. At least once a month, usually on Saturday, the horses and Olik's mule were sent with one or two servants to one of the missions located on the periphery of Addis Ababa, and the family would then drive there by car and spend the night in a guest room. Early in the morning, they would ride their horses, Olik and Taffara on the mule, to some attractive area by the river or some forests and stop for a picnic. The horses were taken to the water hole and unleashed to enjoy the grass.

A photo from those times reveals Olik in a white pith helmet, sitting on Baclusha with Taffara mounted behind.

The servants would unfold a big printed cotton sheet for the food, tea, coffee, and wine. There was always Russian salad (a mixture of small cut boiled potatoes, red beets, pickles, cucumbers, vinaigrette, and mayonnaise), hard-boiled eggs, and tins of sardines and meats—enough for everybody, including last-minute guests. A siesta or an exploration of the nearby area followed. They would return home at dusk by car, and the servants would ride the horses and mule back to the stable at their own pace.

Olik and Taffara on Baclusha

Like the picnics, grooming and hygiene were also something of a group project. "Every month the Indian barber would come and cut our hair in our yard," Alexandra explained.

Bathing wasn't entirely private, as on Saturdays there was a ritual: the order of the bath. During Herman's long period of work on the Somali border, the entire family used to have the weekly bath. Over a mile away, at a popular sulfur spring, the procedure went like this: Abte-Giorgis was in charge of delivering to the house five-gallon gas cans filled with thermal hot water carried on the backs of a caravan of donkeys. The trip to the mineral spring, which bubbled with boiling water, took half an hour. "I know it was boiling," Alexandra said, "because one time the container leaked, and the mule was left with blisters on its back. We could not load it for several weeks." They brought the water back to the house and poured it into a metal bathing tub.

Once it had cooled to the point that one could safely enter it, the bathing began. First little Olik had his bath, then Alexandra, then Katerina, then Lev, then Birke, and finally, last of all, Taffara.

At the time, this seemed like the natural pecking order. Strange how the order of the bath revealed a whole cultural value system. So much has changed since then.

More Royals

Eventually the royals began coming to Alexandra's home rather than her going to the palace, and Olik had to sit first in the dental chair to re-assure the apprehensive children. When the Empress had an appoint-

ment to come for treatment, it was an event by itself. From early morning the police would reinforce their road-blocks of the nearby streets and cor-ners. The queen—always accompa-nied by her eunuch, Ato Ipsa— fre-quently came with her children and retinue. Entering the waiting room and seeing the portrait Alexandra had copied of the Russian Emperor Nich-olas II, Empress Menen would re-spectfully bow to his memory.

Alexandra, traveling by horseback to the royal palace

On one such day, while Alexandra was having lunch with the princesses and the tutor, the princess said, "Yesterday, after your treatment, Papa called us and asked us to open our mouths so that he could see what you had done."

"I had made several filings for them," Alexandra explained, "and the Emperor wished to see what kind of work I had done. I have never seen a European or American father who wished to look into his children's mouths to examine the dental work. The Emperor was a good father."

Ras Hailu's niece Woisero Shash-Werk went to Bad Homburg in Germany in 1934 for treatment of her syphilis, a very common disease. Her father was Ato Ilma, a brother of Haile Selassie. An Ethiopian woman named Gennete Heruis, the daughter of the Ethiopian state secretary and a friend of Alexandra's, accompanied her on her trip. Like her uncle, Shash-Werk misinterpreted the meaning of the young man's appearance when she pulled the bell cord in her hotel room. To the shame of the more educated Gennete, Shash-Werk flirted shame-lessly with the hotel employees.

When Shash-Werk's father Ilma died, he left a widow, a "very, very large Woisero." She too came to Alexandra as a patient. One day, when Alexandra went to the waiting room to summon her to the dental chair, the Woisero said, "No, I wish first to go to the bathroom."

"Very well," said Alexandra. "I'll call Birke and she can show you the way."

"No," replied the woisero, "I have my pot."

Her lady in waiting produced a small chamber pot. Alexandra returned to her practice room, waited a few discreet minutes while the Woisero took care of her needs, then returned to the waiting room. The widow had finished and left in the middle of the room a dark ring, just the size of the too-small pot provided for the occasion. Alex called her reliable Abte and showed him the spot.

"Look," she said, "your princess made a spot. Please clean it up."

He grumbled in Amharic, "She is a pig," and went off to get cleaning implements.

A Woisero from the district of Wollo came to Alexandra's office with inflamed gums, a common complaint among the Ethiopians, perhaps owing to their predilection for extremely hot pepper. As a treatment, Alexandra first put powdered cocaine on the gums. "No prescription was needed for the cocaine," she explained. Then she cau-terized the gums with a benzine-powered burning tool—the same tool she used later to decorate the frames of some of her icons.

In two or three days the Woisero's gums were healed. In perhaps another week, an aristocratic-looking gentleman with a little beard and wearing the long white Ethiopian dress came to her office. She could tell by his lighter complexion that he was probably an aristocrat. She asked him what she could do for him.

He replied in Amharic, "Several days ago my sister came to you seek-ing relief for her swollen gums. You ironed her gums and it helped her very much. Now I am asking if you would please iron my gums too."

Alexandra was always amused at modern interpretations of dentistry.

Finally, after years of largely unrewarded service, Alexandra learned that she was to be given a watch by the Emperor Haile Selassie. Frau Hertel, the German royal midwife, said to Alexandra, "You must ask for a man's watch. They are better than woman's watch."

So Alexandra did that. "I wish a watch for my son," she told the proper official at the court.

"It was a very good watch," she said later, "an Omega gold pocket watch. I gave it to Herman." It was yet another instance of recognition from the royal family, and greatly appreciated. "It was considered an honor to be appointed to the court. Instead, they gave presents."

The Trip

The previous September on the 29th in 1934, Mussolini had affirmed Italy's friendship with Ethiopia, and no one had any inkling that the affirmation was a lie. Hitler had become chancellor in Germany and things were changing quickly. Germany had no love for Communist Russia, archenemy of the Drosdowskys and Dabberts. So when Alexandra's family traveled to Germany in 1935, they thought their world a reasonably stable place, and that Hitler would continue to provide order and prosperity. At the time Europe seemed so normal and appealing, especially to expatriates.

Alexandra had claimed for the first and only time the annual passage to Europe for her family as offered by her railway employers. The family sailed on the Itoury, a German ship that had come from Indochina. It carried many wild animals for the Hamburg zoo. The snakes were kept in bags. One morning, one of the bags was found untied and empty. Olik and his nurse Birke became recluses in their cabin for the rest of the trip. The snake was never found. There were oversized boxes for the giraffes and cages for the monkeys. One male monkey killed two of his wives, so the sailors called him Bluebeard.

Olik and Birke

Herman, Alexandra, Olik, and Birke stayed at Herman's parent's home in Bernburg, Germany.[92] Other members of Herman's family gathered as well, including Herman's nephew Eberhard Zeidler who was five years older than Olik. Eberhard remembered drawing pictures of animals at the time and that his Uncle Herman was a master at it and helped him greatly.

Eberhard also admired his Aunt Alex's interpretation of a German saying in a game of charades. Alexandra held a piece of golden jewelry in her mouth, "smiling at the ceiling. Nobody could guess what it was, and she announced, *Morgen stund hat gold im mund*. This translated as, "The morning hour has gold in its mouth," an equivalent of, "The early bird gets the worm."

Eberhard reported that no one in Bernburg had ever seen a black person and that Birke was a "sensation" there. He wrote, "When she would go out with Olik and me for a walk, all the neighborhood children would creep along twenty feet behind us to see this apparition."

Birke opened the door of the Dabbert home one day. She was surprised to see another black man standing in front of her. He was equally amazed to see a black woman staring at him. He was the chimneysweeper.

One day, Birke came running, her dark skin somehow pale. "The devils are clinging to my feet."

---

[92] After the second World War, the home became a residence for the Soviet occupation forces. Later, when Herman's nephew Eberhard, who in the meantime had become a famous Canadian architect, visited the place and took a picture of the ancestral house, he was arrested as a spy. Thanks to the intervention of the Canadian Embassy, he was eventually released.

Alexandra went to see what the problem was. Birke had been ironing with an electric iron, and the cement floor was wet, so that the electrical charge was passing up her legs.

Herman had brought the gold watch along that Alexandra had given him. He gave it to his sister who lived in East Germany. At this point, Herman stayed behind in Germany to look for work in what he imagined to be an orderly, businesslike world. Though he'd loved the freedom of the African wilderness, he was fed up with their way of doing things. Alexandra's parents were still in Ethiopia, and she loved life there. She chose to return to her beloved African Eden. It would prove to be a far-reaching decision.

Alexandra, Olik, and Birke did a bit of touring on this trip, including a Paris visit to her old professor, Dr. Henry Martin, who'd done such distinctive fillings. He took them to an elegant restaurant. She ordered frog legs "to try something new. I ate them, they tasted like young chicken, but I was ashamed to tell in Addis Ababa about them. Civilized people did not eat them there."

Back in Germany, Herman's family had gathered for the death of Herman's father. In the aftermath of settling family affairs, Herman had problems returning to Africa. Hitler wanted to keep him in Germany to have someone who knew the African situation and help develop German colonies in Africa again. Herman objected and then received a letter signed by Hitler that Herman could either work in the Colonial Amt (section) or be sent to a concentration camp. For years, his family remained unaware of this situation.

Twenty-three

The Dance of Elephants

When the elephants dance, the grass gets crumpled.
— African Proverb

In 1871, Rome had become the capital of a reunited Italian state. Expectations arose of following the European powers' colonial expansion. Prime Minister Francesco Crispi was the architect of the Italian plans in North and East Africa that resulted in the acquisition of Eritrea and a portion of Somalia at the cost of an upset at the battle of Dogali and the loss of six thousand in the disastrous defeat at Adowa in 1896. The memories of this humiliation in a backward country persisted. Revenge had to wait until Mussolini revived and ignited the Italian will to restore the former glory of Rome. They invaded Ethiopia in 1936 and proclaimed Victor Emanuel the Third, Emperor of Ethiopia.

War in Ethiopia

Alexandra hadn't been back in Addis Ababa long before Mussolini ordered the invasion of Ethiopia on October 2, 1935 after a border dispute. Italy had bored many wells just inside the Ethiopian border. When an Ethiopian military unit protested Italian presence on Ethiopian land, the Italians had responded with force, proclaiming that they had just cause. Haile Selassie had great faith in the League of Nations and registered his protest with them. Mussolini also pressed his case and awaited the outcome. When the League of Nations exonerated both parties and suggested a resolution, Mussolini rejected it and began the attack. The League of Nations declared him the aggressor, but did nothing. The way was clear to use not only his modern army, but also poison gas. No one except Haile Selassie would try to stop him.

Alexandra's patient, Prince Asfau-Wossen, now a young man of twenty years, went to the Front with his father in the northern part of the country. He was then sent back to Addis Ababa to take his father's place in directing the operations of the government there. Though already married, his marriage, like all royal marriages, was made for reasons of State. His wife, four or five years older than he, was divorced with a boy of about six.

Asfau-Wossen 'Forgives' a Hospital Bill

Initially, life in the capital didn't change drastically. The war in the North hadn't yet affected most Ethiopians. Asfau-Wossen stood in for his father in the capital and, regardless of war, little boys still contracted pneumonia. Olik and Taffara both had to be hospitalized. The bill came to six hundred thalers ($300.00), a very large sum at the time. Alexandra's friend, Frau Hertel, suggested that she take the bill to the prince and ask if he would reduce it for her.

She drove to the Lidji Yassu Guibby[93] (palace) in her Citroen. Alexandra's automobile licence plate with its red numerals on a white background—the ordinary plate had black numerals—won her immediate admission to the palace grounds. She parked and went to the *aderash* or main reception room. A large number of petitioners and

---

[93] This palace got its name from Lidji Yassu, a pro-Turkish and pro-German Ethiopian who was imprisoned by Haile Selassie at the time of the First World War, and who remained in prison during all the time that Alexandra was in Ethiopia. Haile Selassie sequestered the palace and made it his own.

officials stood about the room, but Alexandra was the only European. Asfau-Wossen, in khaki drill, was seated at the only table in the room.

He greeted her in faultless French. She showed him the hospital bill and explained how difficult it was for her at that time to pay all of it.

"Give me the bill," he said and called his secretary, a young man also dressed in khaki, and said to him, "Pay this bill for Madame Dabbert." Then, to Alexandra, "We cannot reduce the bill, but we can pay it for you."

One day toward the end of the Italian war, Alexandra was in the emperor's small palace, working on the teeth of one of his young daughters. This particular palais was called the Italian house because it had been built by the Italians of very good wood from the jungle, the kind of multicolored wood used to make pianos. It was situated in a grassy park. Alexandra glanced out the window as she worked and saw a figure in khaki riding slowly toward the palais on a mule, "a very fine mule," she observed. When the figure was very near the palais she recognized Asfau-Wossen.

Next day she learned what had happened to the prince. On his return from the Front to Addis Ababa, he camped for the night in the district of Wollo with some of his father's relatives. In the course of the evening, he saw some members of the ruling family of Wollo, accompanied by their servants, approaching his tent with their sabers drawn. Asfau-Wossen seized a kerosene lamp and hurled it into his tent. In the darkness and confusion of the ensuing fire, he ran off, found himself the fine mule that Alexandra had seen next day, and rode off into the night.

"No one knows this story," Alexandra said, "except for two or three of the prince's relatives, who were also my patients, and the person who told the story to me."

Italians Encroaching from the North

The Ethiopians put up a valiant struggle despite poisonous gas and air strikes for which they had no real defenses, along with defectors acting on previous grievances—such as the Tigré forces—the people of the region governed by Shash-Werk's unloved husband—and the Muslim Oromos.

The Italians moved closer, but the European expatriates didn't feel particularly threatened by the invaders. Alexandra decided to remain in Addis Abba and continued her practice. However, she had to do some improvising. All Italians previously living in Ethiopia had been expelled. That included Mr. Garibaldi, Alexandra's dental technician who was an Armenian from Constantinople, but with an Italian name. "He was a good technician; he did perfect work for me."

Alexandra and her faithful Abte had to design a working centrifuge. First, they put a wax mold of the crown into liquid plaster of Paris mixed with fine river sand. Three wires protruded from the mold. Once the plaster had hardened, they pulled out the wires leaving three tiny orifices for the molten gold to follow. With a Bellows Foot operated, gasoline mixed with air, and the gold was heated to its melting point and poured into a centrifuge made from a can attached to three wires to a cane. Abte would swing the "centrifuge" round and round forcing the melted gold down the three orifices into the wax mold, replacing the wax and forming a gold crown. When it cooled, they broke open the plaster cast and voilá, there was the crown. It worked until the situation improved.

And the possibility of an approaching invasion didn't stop some patients from coming up with lame excuses to get out of paying bills. During that time, the same Swedish missionary's wife who wouldn't pay until the horse's lip was healed complained about the cost of an extraction for her ten-year-old son.

"But it's only five thaler," said Alexandra.

"But," the missionary's wife replied, "I have to pay the taxi fare both ways, and I must buy ice cream and a toy for my son."

The judicial adviser of Emperor Haile Selassie was the well-paid Mr. Auberson from Switzerland. His wife had long been one of Alexandra's patients and always paid her bill. She was very nice, Alex said.

Then one day Auberson himself came to her office. He wanted a gold bridge, a very expensive job. Once the job was done, Alex sent him a bill, then another bill—several bills, in fact. She learned then from her dressmaker that Auberson was going to return to Switzerland for good because of the instability. She hastily sent her servant to him with the bill for three hundred fifty thalers.

The servant returned later without money and said that the man told him he was going to Switzerland for only a few weeks and would pay the bill on his return. He lied. Nothing more was heard of him.

One day in 1936, when it was war against the Italians, I did not have telephone. Only telephone was from the Emperor to his important officials, his doctor, and few others. I received a message by man riding on horseback to come to the French Hospital. Doctor Mayenberger, a Swiss doctor, wanted to see me. An Ethiopian chief had been wounded in the war by a bullet that had broken his jaw. I had done such work in Kiev in 1916. We had at the Army hospital, when I was dental student, one Russian soldier with similar wound. The chief's teeth had to be wired in place and the patient was told to return in one month to have the wires removed. He did not come back for one year, and only because one wire had become broken. All was healed.

During the war with the Italians, the Ethiopians took Pere Serafim as a prisoner simply because he was white. He was the French Franciscan missionary who had commissioned Alexandra's icon painting of St. George. They held him captive for months, took his clothes away, and gave him a native outfit. They summoned him every morning and said, "Now we are going to kill you," but someone else would start arguing and they would say, "Not now, tomorrow."

"I was ready to die," he said.

Alexandra insured her house in Addis Ababa with Lloyds of London for two thousand English pounds to cover damage to the house including damage incurred during wartime. They began to see wounded streaming in from the Front. Each time they saw or heard an Italian airplane, they hid with their gasmasks on in the cellar.

Count Tatishtchev—the man from the famous noble family married happily to the former dancer turned milliner—had become the secretary of the Ethiopian Red Cross during the war against the Italians. Ethiopian provincial chiefs donated to the Red Cross, but they never had any money, so instead they gave beautiful rugs. These rugs were available from Moslem pilgrims that had gone to Mecca for Hadj, a once-in-a-lifetime Islamic tradition to visit the site of the birth of their faith.

"I heard that he had at least eight Oriental rugs," Alexandra said. "When the Italians came, I heard he left with the rugs and went to Italy." He sold the rugs, and with the proceeds bought a small hotel in the center of Rome. It wasn't the first time a rich noble proved dishonest and chose to forget his debts.

The Italians Are Coming

There was a period of four or five days just before the advancing Italians occupied Addis Ababa. After seven months of war, the Ethiopian government collapsed. Law and order broke down completely, and the capital city was in chaos with robberies, looting, smoke, gunfire, and murders everywhere throughout the city.

The German embassy among others had sent round a note, which each person who read it had to sign, telling them of the danger just ahead and recommending that they come to the embassy for safety, and to bring food and other supplies with them.

Alexandra had four rifles, which she gave to her servants. Even some of the men who had formerly worked for her returned to the house to help guard it during the unrest. For two or three days, she carried

Protective high walls surrounded the house

supplies to the German embassy in her Citroen automobile, including food, bedding, flour, clothes, condensed milk, sugar, and so on.[94]

"Those were dangerous days," she recalled. "The sky was red at night and one could smell smoke from the fires. Looting everywhere."

She had barbed wire strung atop the walls in front of her house bordering the road, and she had one of the servants attach one wire to the electric pole in the street to suggest to the natives that all the wires were "live" and would electrocute anyone who touched it.

The day before they moved to the embassy, Mr. Heilig—the vice director of the English bank, a Hungarian Jew—advised Alexandra that she should change all her paper money into silver coins at once because the paper would be worthless when the Ethiopians were defeated. "I can still see him hurrying to my house from the bank just up the next street. He had the three or four hundred thalers in his pockets, bulging them out and making it difficult for him to walk."

Carrying this much money would be a tremendous problem. Where in the car should she put the silver thalers for the trip to the

---

[94] The steamer trunk she used to pack these items in stayed with her all her life.

embassy? She decided to put them in the battery box of the car because she thought no one would think to look there if they were stopped. They began the drive to the embassy, but at once the horn of the car began to toot, toot, toot. It was the silver thalers. They were shorting out the horn and making it honk.

Alexandra felt that they were well organized before they moved. She drove to the German embassy in the loaded Citroen. Katerina, Lev, Olik, Olik's nurse Birke, and Taffara rode in the car with her. Behind them were Abte on a horse and his wife on a mule. The streets were so crowded she had to drive very slowly. She didn't want to draw attention to the little caravan.

They were just half a mile away from English embassy where one of Alexandra's good friends stayed.[95] The English had many Sikh Indians guarding the walls of their compound. "They were very good soldiers."

As Alexandra's household finally arrived and were admitted to the Embassy, Abte returned on his horse to the house to defend it with the other servants. All but the women and children lived in tents on the embassy grounds. Alexandra and Olik slept on mattresses on the floor of the embassy, down low because of occasional bullets that came flying through the windows. She removed the seat of her car for use in the tent outside. They spent about five days there.

On May 2nd, Haile Selassie fled Ethiopia into French Somaliland, and then on May 5th, the Italians reached Addis Ababa and began their occupation.

Gradually, calm returned. Alexandra returned to her house to find that her men had not only protected it well, they had also appropriated goods from the looters passing by. The household had acquired eleven more mattresses and much chocolate. She paid her people two hundred thalers ($100). "Later I wrote to Lloyds of London Insurance Company to say that I had spent two hundred thalers to protect my house, while so many other houses, unprotected, were destroyed by rioters. Lloyds are very honest: They sent me a check for two hundred thalers."

[95] In 1987 Alexandra was still receiving letters from this friend.

Ethiopia became an Italian colony called Abyssinia, also called "Africa Orientale Italiana, or A.O.I." It included Ethiopia, Eritrea, and Italian Somaliland. In June, General Rodolfo Graziani took command of Italian forces. Ras Desta Damtu, the son-in-law of Haile Selassie, had become the leader of the Ethiopian resistance. On June 30, Haile Selassie addressed the League of Nations in Geneva. His eloquent speech stirred world sympathy. He criticized League nations for not honoring their treaty and not providing for the collective security. "It is us today," he warned. "It will be you tomorrow."

Marshal Graziani

Soon after, a great festivity, which many Ethiopians were invited to, honored Graziani, now the Italian Viceroy of Ethiopia—the new ruler who became Marshal Graziani. But many Ethiopians had something else in mind for the occasion.

Graziani and his retinue stood in front of a large porte cochere at the palace. Standing at attention on each side were Somali soldiers in their long pantaloons and red vests, sabers at ready—and in the background, several dozen Italian officers in their gala uniforms. All, except the Somali honor guard, looked to the right at the approaching Ethiopians.

They moved closer, clad in white "shama," the flowing cotton white tunic over tight white pants, typical in Ethiopia. "The tighter the pants, the sheerer the shama, and the more elegant the person," Alexandra said. "I have seen men wrap newspaper around the feet when removing pants so they will slip off easier."[96]

Under the shama, one Ethiopian had concealed a hand grenade that a few minutes later was hurled at Viceroy Graziani and his staff.

Many in the photograph were killed and Graziani himself received twenty-six wounds, but recovered. The Italians reacted brutally and

---

[96] See photo of Alexandra in 1925 on horseback with Ethiopian guards around her, dressed in their shama (page).

many died that day. The Italians set fire at their houses and tukuls built of wood sticks, mud, and straw—and that night was red from the flames. As the fire started to burn the thatched straw roofs that had hidden cartridges, shells started exploding in all directions. Perhaps twenty percent of the city burned that night.

Ethiopian neighbors escaped to Alexandra's compound, and she harbored perhaps twenty families before quiet was restored five days

later. "Even Mrs. Gardner, an English lady whose husband was a lawyer and adviser of Haile Selassie and had departed with the fleeing Emperor, walked in during the night and came to stay. It was frightening." Thirty thousand people died. During the repression process that followed, the great Ethiopian patriot Ras Desta Damtu, seen in a photo taken minutes before his death, was executed.

Ras Desta Damtu shortly before the Italians executed him

Alexandra later painted one of her icons featuring the Saint of Lalibela riding alongside Ras Desta Damtu, both with halos.

Mushrooms

Later that year, after the rainy season, Olik looked for white mushrooms in the green fields on the outskirts of Addis Ababa. He saw at a distance what looked like two or three big white mushrooms. They proved to be human skulls that had been neatly cleaned by the ants and by the rains, victims of the Italian revenge against the "terrorists."

Olik took one of the skulls home as a trophy. Next morning 'Holly' Tasso came and asked me, "Madame, will you ask Olik to give me the skull. I would like to bury it in a dignified manner."

He is the one that gave a major portion of his salary to help the war refugee family that was invited to stay in his modest house.

Traditional Ethiopia came to an end and the "contemporary" Italian civilization took over.

Twenty-four

The Italian Occupation

In December of 1936, Alexandra set up an indoor créche. At the appearance of the "first star," the big front door opened. Right there in the living room, the guests and the children saw a live donkey munching straw on one side, a dry bed of hay with two or three live lambs, and some rabbits. Then, the three live horses made their entrance. The Madonna was Mrs. Marcacci, Olik's teacher, in a robe and veil who was supposed to be holding a doll for Jesus Christ. But there was a problem: The doll was late. It had been borrowed from the Ossents, a Swiss family that was participating in the occasion. Their two daughters were among the guests, Verena and Erica, Olik's close friends. Seifu, one of the grooms, was late in returning. Finally, he came galloping back with the doll. He'd been stopped by the police who suspected that the rider was kidnapping a child. Santa came and gave the gifts to a dozen children that had behaved, the Christmas tree was lit, and all then moved to the dining table. Straw remained under the

A visitor in the house

tablecloth in remembrance of the humble beginnings of Christianity and they had lots to eat and drink.

Ethiopia was still far from pacified. The Italians favored those factions like the Oromo and other Muslims who had collaborated to defeat Haile Selassie. The young, educated elite who had escaped reprisal from Graziani continued to work for the return of the emperor. Haile Selassie, exiled in Britain, kept trying to win the support of Western democracies.

Eight months after assumption of power, Graziani was replaced. A new governor, appointed in November of 1937, was instructed to be more flexible and begin large-scale public works, soon replacing Ethiopian subsistence economy. They feverishly started a building program that within the next three years would bring paved roads to Ethiopia, along with electricity, telephone service, hospitals, public health, and a modern infrastructure that had previously not existed.

The Practice Resumes

Alexandra's household depended on her income, especially with Lev now out of work. Over ten years of working in civil service, he'd completed one thousand two hundred surveys of properties. Now the Italians would hire one of their own. With Lev's small pension for Russian exiles also gone—and to avoid depleting her savings, her one hedge against disaster—Alexandra continued her practice and patients returned. She also returned to work for the French railroad.

> I always carried with me a pistol when I traveled between Djibouti and Addis Ababa. But when the Italians came, they forbade the possession of firearms. So I wrapped my pistol in a kerchief and put in the middle of my cosmetics case. The customs officials always looked only in the corners of the case, never in the center.
>
> Another time before the Italian invasion, I was returning to Addis, and at customs, I hid my revolver on the bottom of a basket, put some

seaweed and live crabs, and more seaweed on the top. The crabs had free claws.

One of the first patients in Addis Ababa after resuming practice was Ato (Mr.) Ipsa, Empress Mennen's eunuch, about fifty years old and "very big and fat." The Emperor and the Empress had escaped to Eng-

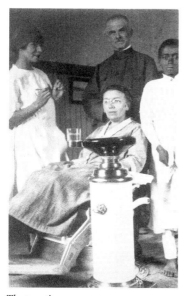

The practice resumes

land and had not taken Ato Ipsa with them. He was angry because he had been left behind.

"I am very offended that the Empress did not take me to foreign countries," he told Alexandra.

Her good friend the charismatic adventurer Henry De Monfreid wrote a book, *A la Pursuit des Merchants d'Esclaves*—following the steps of slave traders. He described how eunuchs were made from young boys. From the River Baro region, slave traders took them to the Red Sea to sell in Southern Arabia. Elegant Ethiopian ladies were proud of their eunuchs in their houses. De Monfried, who also wrote several books describing his exploits as a hashish trader in the Red Sea, explained that there were two kinds of eunuchs.

The first class had all cut away and a cork was used like for a wine bottle. These were very expensive. The second class had only testicles cut out. They were not as expensive. They appeared normal, only no beard, no mustaches, and the voice remained of a young boy.

The Italians had re-abolished slavery and declared miscegenation illegal, but failed miserably in their attempt at enforcing racial segregation. Love easily overcame racial distinctions, as evidenced by the lighter skin of the many newborn babies during that time.

> When Italians came, I was told, "Madame, you can not put in same waiting room soldiers and officers and blacks in same reception room. They will not like it." Waiting room became for officers and balcony for soldiers and natives. You must be diplomatic, go with the flow.

The Italians demanded that Alexandra have an Italian license to practice dentistry. She had a German diploma. Thanks to the close relationship of the forming "Axis" between Nazi Germany and Fascist Italy, Alexandra's license was recognized and accepted as valid, which allowed her to continue working as a dentist. They also abolished Ethiopian paper currency and instituted the lire.

> They were nice to us. I was terrified when I first heard that they were coming, but Frau Hertel, the midwife to the Empress, reassured me. "Don't worry," she said, "you have sixty patients now. Then, you will have six hundred." She was right. I became so busy that I had no time left for painting.

Ethiopian natives had few dental cavities. They were affected more by gum and periodontal disease, which Alexandra believed to be a hereditary advantage combined with the disadvantages of hot pepper consumption mentioned earlier. A new dental technician with more current tools arrived after the new Italian colony was proclaimed, and Alexandra soon prospered with the influx of Italians with aching teeth.

> In 1937 I had two patients, one German and one Italian. They both had operation for cancer of the palate. Doctors had removed the tumor and used skin graft obtained from chest. Hair that continued to grow, they trimmed with scissors. It made difficult to make impressions for dentures. The plaster would stick to the stubble.

Alexandra had always found that the worst patients were the rich and the aristocrats, of course. But with fascist rule, there was more political pressure to make payments, which Alexandra greatly appreciated. Plaintiffs did not have long waits to receive their dues in clear-cut cases. Still, the nobility—from whatever country they came—were slow to pay their dental bills, and sometimes didn't pay them at all. One Italian nobleman in particular believed that the honor of having him as a patient was all the payment Alexandra should desire. He was the Prince of Ischia and an officer in the Italian army. He had some minor work done by Alexandra—a small job, costing only three hundred fifty lire. She sent out two bills, but heard nothing from the prince. Two years later, while she was treating a captain in the Carabinieri, he asked her if she ever had trouble collecting her bills from his fellow officers. She said yes, there was one.

"Who is it?" he asked.

"It is the Prince of Ischia. But he is no longer here in the city."

"We'll find him," said the captain. "Don't worry."

In a week she had the money. The captain of Carabinieri had located the prince in Mogadishu, capital of Somalia, and the lire was sent post haste. The prince, however, told the captain that he had already paid the bulk of his bill, three thousand lire, and that the three hundred fifty lire was just the remainder.

Among the German nobility who came to her for treatment was the Graf (Count) von Huen, who worked as a journalist in Ethiopia for one of the Hamburg newspapers. He ran up a sizable bill and did not pay it. Alexandra finally wrote to his newspaper in Hamburg. They replied that he was not a member of their staff but only an "occasional journalist," and that they therefore could not be responsible for his debts. There were many others like that, including lawyers.

One day a count, a baron, and another man came to her office for dental work. When they identified themselves as being of the nobility, she paled.

"You must pay one half first," she said, "and the rest upon completion."

They were agreeable to this arrangement. It turned out that the count, who was very wealthy, had come to Addis Ababa to purchase the local brewery. His mother-in-law was with him and also came to Alexandra.

Continuing Unrest

Though life in the capital seemed to have returned to normal, the out-lying areas harbored forces that didn't accept Italian rule. In early 1938, fighting broke out in Godjam, Ras Hailu's territory. Educated young men, the survivors of Graziani's killing spree after the assassination attempt, had regrouped under the name "Committee of Unity and Collaboration." Haile Selassie continued pressing the Allies to oppose the Italian occupation.

Divorce and Remarriage

Just before the Italian invasion, a divorce was granted between Herman Dabbert and Alexandra. He remarried soon after. "I was happy that he married again," Alexandra said. "I was free. We continued to be friends." This was a family that believed in restraining emotions. Its dissolution was not discussed and may not have even been fully understood because of the situation with Hitler. Olik was told his father had left because of job opportunities in Germany, positions that would include a good and predictable salary and the assurance of a foreseeable retirement plan. In later years, the sheer irony of this would remind Alexandra of the Jewish joke: Do you want to make God laugh? Tell him your plans!

In 1938, a handsome Italian officer—one of Alexandra's patients, Captain Ferdinando Pozzi, who was in charge of a tank company—became a frequent visitor to Alexandra's house. He befriended Olik by teaching him to shoot. He gave him his first air gun and later a twenty-two caliber rifle. Seven-year-old Olik was delighted to go out hunting and to share the soldiers' and officers' mess—in that sequence. He even rode in a tank, trampling young trees and charging all kinds of terrain. Italian tanks in those times were not much bigger than a large station wagon.

Like Herman, Alexandra also chose to marry again. Captain Ferdinando Pozzi—Nando for short—became her second husband. They decided to visit Italy and meet his family in Menzago near the Swiss border. The family was very welcoming. Olik was surprised to see

Captain Ferdinando Pozzi, Alexandra, and Olik feeding pigeons in Piazza San Marco, Venice

children drinking red wine at meals. The family stored apples in the attic and the aroma often lured Olik. She used the opportunity to take a refresher dental education course in Germany. Olik went with them.

For the return to Ethiopia, they bought two Fiat cars and landed in Massau on the Red Sea. This unbelievably hot harbor had become the main channel of communication between Italy and Addis Ababa. The Italians had improved the long, dusty, gravel mountain road—still dangerous and still under construction. From the hot and steamy lowland through Asmara in the highlands, and Dessie to Addis Ababa, they covered the distance in five days.

Alexandra ran one of the cars and was the first woman in Ethiopia to drive by herself all the way from Massaua on the Red Sea to Addis Ababa. Frequently, she and Nando drove with a column of other vehicles for mutual protection against guerilla attacks. Olik commuted between Alexandra's and his stepfather's car—an extraordinary adventure—sharing the beauty of a pristine and unpolluted beautiful country.

Alexandra's Fiat developed a problem in Addis Ababa. It was so reluctant to start after it had been sitting idle that she parked it facing downhill so that it could be easily pushed. But one day, she parked it on a lower level than the street in front of her house. When her servants saw the hill they would have to push the car up, they ran into the street and shouted, "Gurague! Gurague!"

The impoverished Gurague were always on the streets, looking for work. They came running from every direction and helped push the car up the hill into the street for a few coins.

While some military became bored alcoholics in the new colony, Nando took advantage of new possibilities. From his knowledge of motor vehicles and tanks, Nando wanted eventually to start a business servicing cars and trucks. His military duties limited civilian work, however. In driving his military vehicle one day, he encountered a tree trunk that proved to be a python. He detoured around it as it slid off and disappeared in the tall grass.

Initially, the Italian occupation didn't stop Alexandra from traveling to Djibouti and working for the railroad company until 1939. She'd worked with them for fifteen years, but when World War II broke out with Hitler's invasion of Poland in September of that year, relations between France and Italy deteriorated to a point where the French had to surrender the railway. Travel by rail became drastically restricted.

Mussolini had described his alliance with Hitler as an "axis of blood and steel." Yet Italy was one of the poorest nations in Europe, and General Graziani—former military governor of Ethiopia, who was stationed elsewhere in Africa at the time—believed it would be several more years before Italy was ready to join Germany in combat. He was reported to have said that it wouldn't be the same as fighting Abyssinians.

By June of 1940, Rommel had reached the English Channel, and Mussolini thought the war was almost over, with Germany sure to be the winner. So on the tenth, he entered the war on the side of Germany. France shared this assessment and surrendered eleven days later.

Abte Georgis told Alexandra that because of the war, the Italians were expelling the English subject, called the "Coffee Arab," and he needed to sell two of his rugs. He was an Arab merchant who traded goods from his trips to Mecca. Like Alexandra, the man was a carpet lover. He asked her if she would like to see them.

"Ishi." She agreed in Ethiopian and rode on Rurik, already saddled. Abte Georgis rode Truvor, the white stallion. They went to a section behind the market, to the Arab "caravan people" in a small courtyard. The "Coffee Arab" accepted her offer of four thousand five hundred lire (forty-five British pounds) and they returned with two nice rugs. She believed that the Italians would win the war and that she and Nando and her family would all stay together in Ethiopia.

Great Britain wanted Haile Selassie's regrouping loyalist forces to join with them and fight to expel the Italians from Ethiopia. In August, the Italians seized British Somaliland, forcing the British to evacuate their garrison and escape to Aden. Italian forces began invading Sudan. From Khartoum, Haile Selassie worked with British headquarters to coordinate his resistance forces.

Alexandra knew all too well how unreliable paper money was in wartime. She worried that her bank account in lire might be at risk.

The Last Mail

World War II just started. One day at lunch, one of my guests—Captain Attilio Lelli, in charge of the bakery and provisions for the Italian military in Addis Ababa—was telling of a letter that one of his friends had received from his mother from Italy: It was going to be the last mail. Because of the war, Ethiopia became isolated from Italy. In the letter, Agnese Marini wrote him about a house in Pescara degli Abruzzi that was for sale: Would he like to buy it?

I listen and think. I remember from past experience that money goes down (inflation) but house goes up. It is investment. I ask: Will he buy the house? No, he did not need another house; he already had a seventeenth-century house by the church.

Then I asked, "How much for the house?"

"Two hundred thousand lire."

I had that sum in the bank. I said, "Can I send the money to his friend's mother?"

The answer was "yes," but only by telegraph; no more normal mail.

I went to the Italian bank and sent to the lady I had never seen two hundred thousand lire by telegraph to buy a house I had never seen in a town that was absolutely foreign to me.

Nando was off fighting, but it wouldn't be long before Italy's military inadequacies began to reveal themselves. A British naval attack severed Italy's supply lines. Infantry troops from India arrived on the scene and pushed the Italians out of Sudan. British troops moved up from Kenya, and Haile Selassie's guerilla forces joined them when they reached Ethiopia.

History was again about to collide with the well-ordered, happy life Alexandra had forged for herself and her family. It would begin with a smaller crash, however. In early 1941, ten-year-old Olik learned to use his bicycle, and one day was hit by a motorcycle on the street by his house. He was unconscious for a little while and started vomiting blood. They took him to the Italian hospital, and the doctor decided to operate. Fortunately, nothing very serious was found, but in those days, they kept abdominal patients fasting. No food or water for at least twenty-four hours. No intravenous fluids. No antibiotics.

Finally, after five days he was discharged. He was so hungry, that on the first day he ate five eggs. He felt a little sick after that.

Alexandra asked him, "What would you like after your ordeal?"

"I want to learn English," was his answer.

At the time, he already spoke Amharik, the language of Ethiopia, which he'd learned with the servants and their families; Russian, taught on a daily basis by Katerina; German through a German lady who came to the house weekly and brought fresh bread from her bakery; and French from a svelte Armenian lady who had come from Beirut, where French was spoken flawlessly. Olik fell in love. His French improved, but his feelings were not returned.

Olik wanted to learn the language of the newest conquerors who were so much taller than the Italians.

Within a few days, Addis Ababa fell to the combined advance of British, Indian, South African, and Ethiopian armies. On May 5th, Ethiopia was delivered back to Emperor Haile Selassie. Interestingly, one of the early results of the emperor's return was that many slaves went back to their former owners because they'd had easier lives as slaves.

After the Italians surrendered, the new Ethiopian government under British supervision issued severe sanctions, including imprisonment and execution for Italians found to possess firearms. That was followed by nightly robberies and murders. Alexandra had a flimsy excuse that her servants were Ethiopians and had the right to firearms. She hid a rifle up in the crawlspace on a ceiling beam. The ceiling was covered by canvas. One day, a storm blew through and shook things. Lev happened to glance upwards and became terrified to see the unmistakable silhouette of the rifle that had slid from the beam to the canvas. It was *immediately* repositioned and secured.

Nando had left behind a few hand grenades hidden between the leaves of the giant banana tree. After the thunderstorm during the rainy season, Alexandra looked out from her dental office and saw with horror that one of the grenades had slid out. It lay in plain view at the base of the plant. She immediately replaced it to its hiding place among the banana leaves.

Many Italians had brought Alexandra their valuables, knowing that her walled compound provided a safer place. Even the Italian hospital staff brought a trunk full of equipment from the operating room. It was later lost when transferred to the missionaries. Expecting scarcity before the Italian surrender, Alexandra and Lev buried in the garden two barrels full of provisions such as flour, sugar, and oil. These staples passed to the servants after the family left Addis Ababa.

News came that Captain Ferdinando Pozzi had been captured and sent to India as a prisoner of war.

Twenty-five

"Enemy Civilians"

*A*lexandra kept her emotions to herself, focusing instead on her relief that war in Ethiopia had come to an end. Nando had at least survived, and her family and property remained intact. Yet the new challenges of an uncertain future lay ahead.

Resident Italians wondered what the emperor would do with the "enemy civilian population." He decided to order out of Ethiopia all the foreign settlers of enemy nationality (Italians and Germans), including those who had lived in Ethiopia long before the Italian invasion. It was an easy move to "expropriate the enemy" and hand their belongings to the native population. While the Second World War was raging in North Africa, an agreement was reached and the Italian government provided several Red Cross passenger ships to "repatriate" the "enemy civilians" back to their country of origin.

The edict of expulsion included Alexandra and her family, as she had married an Italian officer, thereby dissolving any favor she might have expected from the royal court. In spite of gallant attempts by Alexandra to stay in Ethiopia—or for that matter, anywhere else in Africa—her efforts failed. Alexandra, her son, and parents were ordered to join the last five thousand Italians out of Addis Ababa and move to distant concentration camps, presumably on the way to one of the harbors on the Red Sea to embark for Italy. And nobody knew, in the midst of war, how long the captivity would last. About that same time, Haile Selassie also sent Henri de Monfreid out of the country. The Negus was against him. When he returned to France, he became a celebrated adventure writer. In addition to the book about smuggling hashish and slave trading, Secrets of the Sea and Sea Adventures are two of his other books.

Expulsion

One hundred pounds per person, the allotment to each exile. Twenty years of building a home and a life had to be condensed to one hundred pounds. Alexandra paid great attention to the rules and regulations that applied to her expulsion from her home into the unknown. She wondered if she should return to Italy, when, to which camps the family was going, for how long, and what were the priorities to be included in the allowed one hundred pounds.

- Minimum of dental equipment, for use anywhere
- Books and writing material for Olik's education
- Hiding places for additional photographs since only five per family were allowed
- Clothes for all weather conditions from desert heat to winter cold
- Hiding places

The Chianti wine bottle with a woven straw around it would be used for drinking water and provide space in the bottom for small jewelry. Alexandra also hid some of her diamonds in the bottom of a vermouth bottle, covered with melted waxlike "gutapercha" used for temporary fillings for cavities and wrapped the bottle in crocheted covering. It became Olik's water bottle.

What about the precious photographs and other documents: property, professional documents, passports? Alexandra told her problems to her patient, a young Italian soldier who had been a carpenter before the war.

"Don't worry," he said, "I can find a way. Do you have a large trunk that you will take with you?" he asked.

"Yes, of course."

"Good, I will build a false bottom, and nobody will find your papers."

"But they will look inside and maybe find it!" she protested.

"No," he said, smiling. "I will not put it inside, but on the outside."

It worked.

ꝑ

As if in dread of the coming upheaval, Baclusha the well-loved mule had died. Rurik and the other horses were given to the Ossent family. Alexandra left two motorcycles and several trunks with the American Methodist missionaries in Addis Ababa. She left some of her memorabilia, including the smaller of the two Persian rugs she'd bought from the "Coffee Arab" only two years earlier in two trunks with Major Steekpool, the British police chief who was a patient of Alexandra. He took it upon himself to save those trunks and deliver them to a friend, Mr. E. Blau in Nairobi, Kenya with the hope of eventually getting them to Alexandra after the war.

Abte and his wife, with eighteen years of service, had stayed with Alexandra's family right up to the end. Alexandra left Taffara, Olik's companion, in the charge of Seventh Day Adventist missionaries. Taffara, aged thirteen, and Abte Giorgis would be allowed to live in Alexandra's compound by the new occupiers appointed by the Ethiopian government. Both were unemployed, however. Taffara would soon go to work for the Singer Company, selling sewing machines, and sharing some of his earnings with Abte Giorgis.

At the first gathering point—the train station—Alexandra was granted a first-class compartment for her and her family, as she had been appointed medical officer responsible for the train. That trip lasted two nights.

The first concentration camp, in an abandoned Italian airport in Dire Daua, provided a huge hangar full of humanity and bed bugs. No one really knew whether this was a temporary stop of quarters for the duration of the war, but Alexandra took no chances. Within a week, she was allowed to move out of the camp and settle in the main Bololakos Hotel where she could resume her dental practice and thus finance her family's stay in much better surroundings in this hot desert town. The rattan chair her patients used was replaced when one of her Italian patients, an omnibus chauffeur, brought her a bus driver's seat. She was immediately busy attending to the needs of local civilians as well as military personnel.

It was not the first time Alexandra had visited the Bololakos, privately owned Greek hotel with a big courtyard, perfumed by acacia and other fragrant desert trees. "We all ate on the terrace overlooking the fairly large garden." The aroma of coffee beans freshly roasting always filled the air. A man named Abu was in charge of the roasting process. "He was a frail Muslim clergy that doubled as watchman at night. He would munch his greenish chad, a native stimulant, and make his rounds all night, reciting verses from the Koran."

Hungry flies covered the kitchen tables, however.

By the kitchen in the morning, some fifteen chickens had their heads chopped off and thrown in an empty barrel. Sometimes the beheaded chicken would fly out of the barrel and escape into the garden. The flies took care of the blood. We never saw a dead fly in the food!

The nighttime brought noise. The hotel bar was a loud evening gathering point of British army personnel in search of liquor and distraction.

In 1942, General De Gaule was in the French colony to organize his army to fight the Germans and General Petain. The British helped in the training. As a consequence, there were suddenly many more French and British military personnel in Dire Daua. Alexandra was authorized by the British authorities to treat them in her modest set-up at the Bololakos Hotel, making do with a straw armchair and her trusty foot-powered dental drill.

In the dust and heat of the desert, she always dressed in white and worked from early morning to late afternoon. As she stood standing on the balcony by her office room, French officers on the first floor thought she was a nurse.

"Is the doctor here?" they would call to her.

"Yes, I am the doctor," she would answer, and ask what they wanted.

They were surprised that she was a dentist and would ask, "Where did you study?"

Alexandra would reply, "In Germany."

"Oh good," they'd say and become her patients. They had respect for German schools and training and therefore trusted her.

The resettlement in Dire Daua lasted six months. In August, the word came that the rest of the "civilian enemies" should assemble for transportation to Berbera, a harbor on the coast of the Red Sea in what was then called British Somaliland. They were to board Italian Red Cross ships to take them to Italy. After three hot, dusty days, the column of old busses and trucks arrived at a holding camp near Mandeira some fifty miles from Berbera, and the "civilian enemies" were herded into tents and barracks that had previously been built by Italian prisoners of war awaiting transportation to their destination in India. Perhaps Nando had taken part in the construction.

No walls around the camp held prisoners inside. There was no sense in thinking of escape into endless wilderness. At night, one could hear the roar of lions. During the day children loved to wander dry creeks and wild desert tracts, and at night the stars were so numerous and bright.

Olik awoke one morning complaining of a severe headache, chills, and fever. To Alexandra's consternation, his urine had become ominously dark. Black fever. Olik was admitted to the field hospital. For lack of nurses, the Italian doctor allowed Alexandra to take care of her son and others in the big tent.

Next morning, the British commander showed up on rounds and noticed Alexandra in the tent. He demanded to know who had given permission for an unauthorized civilian to be on the premises and threatened to relieve the Italian doctor from duty for disobeying orders and ship him to India. Alexandra would never forget the defiant stand of the Italian doctor who stood by his decision, no matter what the consequences, for the good of his patient. "He was a good doctor!" she said.

The commander agreed for Alexandra to stay.

After a few weeks, a new convoy formed, including the two Italian Red Cross ships, the "Vulcania" and the "Saturnia," anchored off the Somali coast awaiting the final transportation.

On the way to the harbor where the prisoners were supposed to board the ships, Olik rode in an ambulance, still sick with malaria. He needed water. In another truck, riding with other civilian prisoners, Alexandra kept Olik's bottle, laden with diamonds. The vehicles halted and a British officer walked along inspecting.

With deliberate nonchalance, Alexandra asked him to pass the water bottle to Olik. The officer lifted it, not noticing anything unusual in the balance or thickness of the bottom, and passed it as requested. All Alexandra's preparations had paid off.

The cruise would be a long twenty-eight days, as the Suez Canal was out of bounds. The ships would have to circumnavigate the southern tip of Africa and cross the straights of Gibraltar before reaching Italy. However, the voyage was about to grow even longer. Out in the Atlantic, German submarines had engaged an Allied convoy. The Red Cross Ships then had to take an evasive course that took them almost to Brazil.

During the long days on board the ship, the constant conversation speculated on what kind of Italy awaited the new arrivals. Italy had been the center of the Roman Empire that controlled Europe,

Northern Africa, and the Middle East. From the Black Sea, to the Atlantic Ocean, Pax Romana reigned when Jesus Christ was born. Within four centuries it all collapsed into the Dark Ages. Christianity became the quiet standard bearer of the Western civilization, buffeted by unending invasions from all directions.

Contrary to forecasts of the end of the world, the Renaissance took off with unexpected vigor. But beginning in 1309, Pope Clement the Fifth (a Frenchman) moved the Papal Court from Rome to Avignon—"The Babylonian Captivity." During that time, Rome fell into anarchy.

The fragmentation of Italy persisted. New populist ideas of fraternity, liberty and equality claimed by the French Revolution and Napoleon Bonaparte spread the seed for a new social order to all of Europe. The social unrest that followed did not spare Italy. Patriotic figures as diverse as Giuseppe Mazzini, the ideologist; Camillo Cavour, the statesman; and Giuseppe Garibaldi, the warrior galvanized the peninsula in an irredentist fervor to unite the peninsula in a single sovereign reign. In July of 1871, Rome became the capital of the reborn Italian State. At the beginning of the twentieth century however, dreams converted into nightmares caused by the First World War. Mussolini had restored law, order, prosperity, and a new vision of grandeur—and the victory in Ethiopia had fueled that hope.

With the loss of Ethiopia, an Italian victory in World War II became more and more doubtful. The uncertainty of the future shook Alexandra's optimism.

☿

One rainy and cold fall day in 1942, the ships reached Bari and everybody gave thanks to Saint Nicholas, the Patron Saint of that city, for a safe trip. Rome became the first destination.

Twenty-six

Italy

Rome

Life was unpredictable in Rome. With a scarcity of food, people lived on meager food stamps. Alexandra and her family ate many frogs, not in the way they had eaten them in Paris, but because it was the time when there was no meat and people ate unusual things for sustenance. Anchovies and marinated eels were favorite supplements. At night, they would take refuge in cellars as soon as the air raid alarm would go off. Nobody knew where the bombs would rain nor realize that, in spite of ominous sounds of airplanes and explosions, Rome would eventually be spared from destruction.

Alexandra and family were directed to Pensione Nardizzi, a venerable boardinghouse across from the War Ministry and the King's Palace. Its central location made it within walking distance from just about anyplace. Alexandra had to obtain the necessary dental license to practice in Italy before moving to Pescara where she owned her unseen property that she had bought in Addis Ababa.

The family visited exiled Queen Olga's residence in Rome to honor her memory. Olga, formerly the Russian princess and aunt of Nicholas II, had died in 1935. At the villa, Olga's lady-in-waiting was the same woman who had been with Olga in her exile in Lindau-am-Bodensee.

Olik, Lev, Katrina, and Alexandra, exiles again, in Rome, 1943

She recognized the Drosdovskys and took them on a tour of the Roman villa. In the bedroom of the deceased queen, hanging on the wall near an icon, was the hand-painted ostrich egg Alexandra had painted in Ethiopia and sent to the exiled queen as an Easter gift.

Waiting for the Italian government's bureaucracy to validate Alexandra's license to practice dentistry in Italy, Alexandra and her parents decided her brother Roman and his wife could shelter Lev and Katerina more effectively than she could as a newly arrived immigrant. With hopes of weathering the war, her parents moved to a small town near Stuttgart.

During the next few months, Alexandra and Olik explored "The Eternal City," the Vatican Museum being a favorite. Raphael's Christ in a boat with his disciples on the lake became her favorite.

She attended a reception by Pope Pacelli with other wives of Italian officers who'd returned from Africa. The wife of the owner of the boardinghouse had loaned Alexandra a black veil, and in her own black dress, she was properly attired for the visit.

She decided then that she and Olik should become Catholics so that they could always count on the presence of the Church rather than searching for a Russian Orthodox place of worship that became less and less available. The Basilica of Santa Maria Maggiore became the unforgettable site that received two new converts into the Papal flock. It all seemed so majestic after Ethiopia. Rome was an inexhaustible source of historical attractions.

News from the eastern and southern battlefronts, however, killed any holiday spirit. During the bleak winter, photos of cadavers buried in mass graves made the headlines. The KGB had rounded up some thirteen thousand Polish officers and executed them. Occupying German soldiers discovered the burial site in Katyn in the Ukraine. Soviets tried unsuccessfully to blame the Nazis. This was also the sobering time when the Soviets destroyed the German and Italian troops at Stalingrad. By that time, the Italians were ready to give up. Many were fed-up with Mussolini, but others were determined to fight on as fascists on the side of Germany.

Still waiting for the license, Alexandra contacted Agnese, the mother of Captain Lelli's friend.

"How can I reach you?" She wrote.

Agnese soon answered, "Come by train to Pescara to see your house. I will meet you at the train station. I will be in black dress." She said the house needed much repair and was rented, but they had to leave in three months because the owner, an Italian refugee from Africa, was coming.

Pescara

Eventually, with the license to practice, Alexandra and Olik took the train one morning from Rome, heading east, and in late afternoon reached Pescara, the main harbor city of the Abruzzi region on the other side of the mountains from Rome on the Adriatic Sea. Not a particularly attractive city, Pescara was the home port of big fishing boats with enormous sails distinctively painted in bright designs to identify the vessels from afar when returning with their catch.

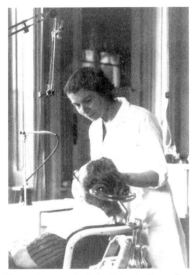

Alexandra practiced dentistry in time of war

Alexandra and Olik moved to her home. Agnese, who had helped Alexandra buy the house, warmly welcomed them. She introduced the newly arrived to the delicacies of the local cooking. The scarcities of food in Rome had disappeared and fish was plentiful.

Alexandra's house was a few minutes from the popular sandy beach. Life was peaceful. Her house had been refitted, and she soon was at work. With so many dental practitioners mobilized and moved away by the military, Alexandra soon became busy. The war was out of sight, out of mind.

Her parents returned from Germany, happy to be reunited, yet utterly disappointed with their experience. They would not elaborate, but were obviously distressed as they continued to shake their heads about their sojourn in Nazi Germany. Roman had by then joined the German Army fighting the Communists on the Eastern Front. As did many Russian émigrés, Alexandra and her family had hoped that Germany would defeat evil Communism and could not understand how Christian nations like England and America could have allied themselves with the devil. "For us, nobody was worse than Stalin," Alexandra said. The Communists had killed half her family. Though she had only an inkling of the full extent of Lenin's and Stalin's tyranny, by 1943 they had forced the starvation of millions in the Ukraine, executed millions in the Great Purge, and exiled millions more to gulag labor camps. Yet Hitler's Third Reich had completely disappointed Lev and Katerina, even though at the time the full extent of Nazi atrocities was completely unknown.

War Closes In

For Italians, the news of the war was not good. The Allied forces had landed in Sicily, and the Red Army was advancing in the East. One summer day, while having a sweet watermelon for lunch, they heard a deafening noise of airplanes, which appeared in formation like little stars. A terrifying vibrating din and bangs followed, and the earth quaked. Alexandra ordered everybody under the kitchen table, except for ex-general. Lev was the only one that stayed composed. Shortly thereafter, the air raid sirens sounded the alarm—alas, too late to warn anyone.

Before the distinct smell and dust of stirred earth had time to dissipate, the neighborhood had changed: smoke and ruins, moans and groans from every direction. Alexandra immediately opened the gates to the garden and started administering first aid for the hurt. Within minutes, there were more than twenty-five casualties being treated. Katerina started tearing bed sheets to make bandages.

Alexandra said, "I told Olik in Russian, so that they would not understand, to write down the names, especially of those who will die soon. It was a good preparation for a future surgeon."

The bombing had interrupted the water supply, but there was a well in the yard, and Lev drew water for drinking and washing. One woman had been nearly scalped. The skull was exposed, and her permanent-waved hair lay off to the side. She was conscious all the time that Alexandra washed the dirt away and put her permanent back.

The woman asked, "Where is my daughter?"

They found the six-year-old; she was also hurt. The woman's husband was also a prisoner of war held in India, as was Nando. Alexandra asked her how she felt.

"My head has no pain," the woman said, "but here . . ." She pressed her stomach and groaned.

She had internal injuries and died two days later.

Olik wrote all this down. "We must stop bleeding with pressure packs and improvise splints to protect fractures. We used window and door shutters as stretchers."

It took Alexandra several days to locate the shutters and get them back after the horsedrawn ambulance took the injured on the makeshift stretchers to the hospitals.

Later, a police report stated, "The family Pozzi-Dabbert-Drodovsky gave much help to the bombing casualties."

The house in Pescara was not badly damaged. Only a few roof tiles needed replacing.

"When will they bomb us again?" people wondered.

They started going to the beach early in the morning. It was safer to be in a little hole in the sand, rather than under crumbling buildings. One morning, somebody shouted "Airplanes!" and everybody ducked. It did not take long to realize that the "airplanes" were in reality peaceful pelicans.

Alexandra decided not to wait. On bicycles, with Olik, they found a big farmhouse a few miles north of town, rented two rooms, and the family moved there. After two weeks of peace and quiet, the family returned to their home.

Up to this time, King Victor Emanuel III had favored Mussolini, but with the loss of Libya and the Allied invasions of Sicily, a changed of government followed. In July of 1943, Mussolini was arrested and secretly sent to a lodge on the highest mountain in the Appenines. Victor Emanuel sued for a separate armistice.

On a drizzly gray morning, Alexandra and Olik took a morning walk. From a low hill, they saw the silhouette of a ship they recognized as a destroyer. Later they learned that the ship was commissioned to carry Victor Emanuel to safety in southern Italy. German soldiers filled the vacuum the demoralized Italian soldiers left after their surrender, and fighting continued.

That was when the second bombing air raid shattered tranquility. The farmhouse where the family had stayed was blown to pieces.

Pescara suddenly became deserted—only hungry cats and dogs rummaged for food. It became clear that the whole family should move somewhere else.

On September 20, war between Italy and the Allies officially ended. However, German rangers rescued Mussolini who then established a fascist socialist republic that attracted those who remained loyal to Il Duce. The fighting did not stop.

"Russicum," a Jesuit institute focused on converting Russians happened to be located some thirty miles north of Pescara, close to a little town called Rosetto. They offered the family a place of refuge, provided that Lev, who was knowledgeable in music, would help translate the Russian Orthodox hymns into the Catholic liturgy. A gypsy horsedriven cart transported the essentials to the convent, which became the family's new residence.

Yet even there it was not safe, as the north/south nightly military traffic would use the highway running between the monastery and the sea. The trucks were prime targets for the marauding "mosquito" British fighter planes. Noisy machine gun and antiaircraft exchanges took place between the nearby German gun battery as it fired at the fighter planes.

A walk to the hills took Alexandra and Olik to a nearby farmhouse. Its outlying stable became a shelter for the chickens and ducks trying to obtain cover during the gunfire and air raids. Alexandra reached an arrangement with the owner. The wine cellar became their bedroom at night and Alexandra's dental office during the day. The farmhouse family would receive free dental care. So that it would not attract attention of the planes or the Germans, farmers and inhabitants of Montepagano would discretely flock for dental treatment. The ancient hilltop village lay two miles southwest of the farmhouse.

The hilltop village of Montepagano had a very old church that had been there before the Christian era. In the shape of a temple, it had no windows except for an opening in the roof through which came rain, snow, and sunshine. Yellow, brown, and dark streaks on the village walls indicated where the antique restrooms were located—just outside the walls, so that the waste dropped to the ground into a pit as in Addis Ababa.

Alexandra visited the local doctor in Montepagano, who showed her his cellar. Dark and musty, it could have been a delicatessen full of hams, sausages, smoked venison, and wine bottles. He preferred to receive such items as payment for his work. It was better than money. That was long before credit cards and checks became available.

Yet currency was still essential, and Alexandra realized that she was low on cash. At the time, the nearest bank was ten miles away by bicycle and then another two hours by train into the interior. Alexandra and Olik decided to get into a boxcar to stay by the bicycles. It proved to be a wise decision as its sturdier roof seemed safer, and half an hour later two planes strafed the train, bringing it to a dead halt. Machine-gun fire had blown out the engine and steam billowed out of the holes.

This big commotion caused everybody to jump off the train and scatter into the fields. Olik would remember the din of the bullets hitting the roof of the boxcar, actually seeing the silver ribbon of bullets streaking less than two feet from his eyes, and then jumping train and running for his life away from the train. Somehow, in a strange detachment, he looked at a woman running just as fast with a shoe in her hand and realized it was Alexandra. A dead bicyclist lay in a pool of blood on the road. Those images would never leave him.

After minutes that felt like hours, the planes stopped firing at the running civilians. Alexandra and Olik returned to the boxcar. They finally reached Teramo in time to cash the money and have a well-deserved pasta meal before deciding to forget the train and returning through winding mountain paths on their bicycles, back to their farm in Rosetto.

෯

In the fall of 1943, at night one could hear the rumble of guns, sometimes for hours it seemed, with eerie flashes continuing along the southern horizon. The sound of the incoming bombs filled the air with the frightening metallic screech of the bomb fins' vibration as they fell ever closer. As a consequence of the war, firecrackers and fireworks would immediately evoke in Alexandra and Olik the memory of exploding cartridges and artillery anti-aircraft barrages.

As the battlefront approached Rosetto, Alexandra decided to visit the German command post to ask if anyone there could be of assistance. Would it be safer just to stay put, or to try to reach northern Italy and the home of her husband's parents? Nobody knew how fierce the battle for Rosetto might be. After explaining in her perfect German that Roman was in the German Army on the Eastern Front and her father had been a Russian Tsarist General who had acquired a German passport, the Germans offered to help. They would make available for Alexandra's family empty trucks returning to the North, providing that there was no furniture except for the dental equipment.

The move was done at night in stages using German military trucks, always in a hurry. One soldier sat on the hood, listening for approaching aircraft. Alexandra and Olik sat with the driver, Lev and Katrina behind checking that nothing was stolen in transit.

Once, for lack of accommodations, the truck stopped at the Canossa Convent in Verona, and Alexandra implored the nuns to let the family stay. Coincidentally, she had known nuns from this order in Ethiopia. The nuns must have been frightened to see a German military truck stopping at their front door, especially at ten at night.

Alexandra asked a nun through a huge iron door, "Please, accept us for the night. I am your dentist from the Ethiopian Mission."

There were nuns that had returned from Ethiopia and recognized Alexandra. They let the family stay in the room reserved for the padres with an entrance from the outside, but no entrance to the convent except for a small hole for confessions. That night, an air-raid alarm sounded, and the nuns let the whole family into the convent's cellar that held maybe ten casks of wine and a well for clear, sweet water that had been there for maybe five hundred years.

Alexandra told Olik, "Watch good, because you may never again be in a women's nunnery."

Finally, after nine days on the road, the family reached its destination. Nando, who still languished as a prisoner of war in India, was born and raised in Menzago, a village in Lombardy in the foothills of the Alps close to Albizzate, the nearest town on the thoroughfare halfway between Milan and Switzerland. Nando's sister's family lived in Albizzate where Alexandra's whole family of four barged in. Infrequent letters came from India, and Alexandra and Nando maintained minimal communication.

Soon, Alexandra was able to move to an apartment and start again her dental work. She began to notice a difference in her clientele. The Southern Italians, especially the Sicilians, "are good husbands and fathers of their children." When they wanted to use the services of a new and unknown dentist, Alex found that the father came first. If all went well, and he wasn't wracked with pain, and received good treatment, then he would bring in his entire family. The northern Italian, in trying out a new dentist, would first send in his mother-in-law and then the rest of the family. If by that time he found the dentist is good, he came in last of all. The northern Italians were comparable to the American Yankees, more industrious and business-minded than their southern counterparts who spoke different dialects and had a different concept of life. "Dolce far niente" meant "sweet do-nothing," which expressed a more placid and sensuous lifestyle.

The Northern cuisine—which included polenta (grits), risotto with wild mushrooms and hare, aromatic apples, and sweet grapes—was abundant, although among the long-eared pelts of rabbits, one could identify also short-eared ones that had belonged to cats, and one could get horse meat without the darn coupons. Lev and Katerina were the cooks and Olik started attending high school classes at the local parish with half a dozen other students.

They still hadn't completely escaped the war. At night, the deafening rumble of invisible waves of Allied bombers flying overhead on their way to their targets in Germany would last for half an hour. The fact that they had to fly over neutral Switzerland didn't deter them. Luckily, the family was spared from direct bombings. Some guerilla activity was present and became more common during the last months of the war.

The leftist guerilla fighters captured Mussolini and his group as he was fleeing to Switzerland and given assurances of safety. Despite these promises, they executed him, his mistress, and the whole group in Como, took them to Milan, and hanged them by their feet. That was the end of that.

Twenty-seven

The End of the War

T he end of the war was met with celebration by most, but it was also a time of sadness at the realization that so much had been lost and destroyed. Roman had lost his life on the Eastern Front. Uncle Alexander, Katerina's brother and the former admiral of the tsar's Black Sea fleet, was living in East Prussia but had perished in an air raid during the war.

Olik's father, Herman Dabbert, had been working in a section of the Nazi government called the Colonial Administration, which Hitler intended to activate after his victory in order to administer to the newly acquired German colonies. Herman had done other work during the war, but after the war the whole colonial section fell into Soviet hands. Everyone was arrested and many were condemned to death. Herman had never joined the Nazi party and still possessed the letter that Hitler had signed, offering a job with the German government or placement in a concentration camp. This letter not only saved him, it also allowed him to work as the head of the Department of Works in the new East German government for a time. Alexandra began sending Herman and his wife food packages. Herman's sister feared the Soviets above all, and when they came she and her family fled East Germany. To escape, they left all their possessions behind, including the gold watch Haile Sellasie had originally awarded Alexandra.

Shortages of supplies intensified for months after the war, during which time the bread became tasteless and rubbery. There was no gas. Inflation struck. Unemployment was a severe problem.

Young people particularly felt jubilant at the war's end. Forced recruitment by fascists or anti-fascists was over. However, the sudden appearance of men and women wearing red scarves intimidated many. Along with the bliss of knowing that the peril from bombings was over, came the sobering realization of a new set of realities. The menace of a Communist takeover threatened the fragile new democracy in Italy. There was already a Civil War in Greece. Tito's Yugoslavia was ready to give a hand to the Italian "Reds," and the Comintern (Communist International) was hard at work to unite the world under Stalin's umbrella. Political and economic unrest and the sudden surge of dozens of parties made some smart Italian say, "Era meglio quando era peggio"—it was better when it was worse.

Somehow life gradually improved and the village of Albizzate resumed its pace. Carletto, the Chaplinesque, flat-footed mailman, waddled to Alexandra, waving Nando's last letter, proudly announcing that Nando might be coming back soon, while at the same time munching freshly roasted chestnuts.

Olik, who had informally taken lessons in the parish school during the war, transferred to the state high school in Varese—an attractive small city eight miles away by train. During the cold winter, every student was required to bring a piece of firewood delivered with frozen fingers that would refuse to move.

Soon after the end of the war in 1945, Alexandra and Olik went back to Pescara to sell the house there. They traveled by truck, sitting on barrels full of caustic soda for four days. They even slept on the truck.

The house was standing, but all the furniture, the kitchen, and all the mirrors were stolen. Only her paintings on the walls and photograph albums were still there. She sold the house for one million two hundred thousand lire. Before the war, she had paid two hundred twenty

Only her paintings on the walls and photograph albums were still there

thousand lire. A farmer who had prospered during the war paid cash to buy the place. Black marketers did pretty well during the war.

Next day, with the check under her corset, she returned to Albizzate.

"God helped me," she said.

The parish priest, Alessandro Viscardi, said, "Why you not buy a villa?"

Alexandra said, "Because I have not so much money."

"You will have enough!" was his answer. He sent her to a man who needed capital for his business in Switzerland and sold the villa to her for one million three hundred thousand lire. Those diamonds from the Vermouth water bottle helped Alexandra to buy the second house in Italy.

During that time, she managed to reconnect with some of her Ethiopian possessions. Ato Tamrat Emanuel, a "Fellasha" Ethiopian Jewish rabbi who was a personal friend of Alexandra's and had previously translated some of her articles for his papers, finally returned one of

Dream villa in Albizzate

the trunks that contained the smaller Persian rug Alexandra had bought from "Coffee Arab." The other trunk was lost, however.

Alexandra learned that Abte became a jeweler skilled in making beautiful Coptic silver and gold crosses. Olik's companion Taffara Deguefe had excelled in his studies, pushed his way by selling Singer Sewing machines, and was employed by the State Bank of Ethiopia. By sheer intelligence, diligence, and integrity he had progressed.

Late in 1946, Nando returned from captivity a changed man. The dashing, proud officer had become passive, dependent, and had lost all initiative to resume a normal life. Alexandra and he tried for about a year and a half to make a home together in her villa, but the marriage could not last. There was no divorce in Italy, though, so they separated permanently. Her beautiful home had become meaningless, and the continued menace of the communist takeover appeared imminent.

She turned her sight in a different direction. The urge to leave Europe became an obsession. She tried to get an Ethiopian visa and return to her property with the intention of working there. She received no answer. "They don't like to give back properties." She wrote to Canada, but received negative results.

When she went to the Argentine consul, she was told, "You may enter but your parents will have to wait a year, till you have paid your taxes." She tried the consulate for South Africa and learned that she could enter, but would have to take a license examination in English, and that her parents were too old to come with her.

She finally went to Doctor L. of the Italian Foreign Ministry. "When I go, I take five gardenias with me for his wife. They are for a little attention. Not corruption, but attention," Alexandra said.

He asked her where Olik wanted to go.

"Which country is the farthest from Russia?"

"Chile," he told her. "Go to the West Coast; it is better than Argentina."

She told him that Olik wanted to become a doctor and asked where the best university was.

"Peru is the best," he said. "It has oldest University in America." He directed her to the Peruvian immigration office to see Mr. M. and said, "Be very kind to his secretary, because he is in love with her."

Alexandra went and "was nice to her and he gave me the visa. I said, 'Thank you very much. I will send you a souvenir.'"

She sent him the painting that she had made when she was very good with oils—a battle between sailing ships in an elegant antique gold frame. "It was one that I painted on a piece of airplane fabric from a crashed airplane. Good canvas was difficult to find then."

In 1948 Alexandra sold the villa for six million three hundred thousand lire, which amounted to $10,000. Relatives who saw the house commented, "You sacrificed this beautiful villa for your life in [South] America?"

"I had no regrets," Alexandra said.

Now, I had to change six million three hundred thousand lire for dollars and it was forbidden then to buy dollars in the bank. I had to buy on black market. A lady patient who worked in the bank gave me a telephone number in Milan. Her father was a general. It was from him that I got the idea for painting mosaics.[98] He himself had painted large mosaics that were hanging in his house.

I took the train to Milan and telephoned from dental store. A man told me to wait by a certain shop in Galleria del Duomo. When he

---

[98] See picture of Saint Nicholas.

arrived, I got in car and his son drove us while I explained how many dollars I needed. Black market man was very elegant and his car was new Ford. Six million lire is a mountain of paper money. He drove to Albizzate to make the exchange. When I found out I was short on money, I removed my gold chain of Ethiopian gold and put it down on top of the money to cover the deficit.

Alexandra gives a Communist a gun

First class tickets for the boat were $680.00 each, for a total of $2,720.00. They could have gone by plane for $720.00 each. It would have been much faster, of course, but a plane could not carry the family's fourteen boxes of luggage. So, they booked first-class passage on a ship. "When you go first class, you meet first-class people," Aexandra said.

Two days before they left Italy, there was an attempt on the life of Palmiro Togliatti, the head of the Communist party in Italy. This caused an immediate reaction and civil disorder broke out. It seemed that there would be no end to roadblocks, strikes, and blazes. Genoa, where Alexandra and family were supposed to board the ship to Peru, was more than a hundred miles away. They wondered how they could reach the port city.

A friendly gas station owner assured Alexandra that he could find a truck to transport the family and fourteen pieces of luggage, which included the dental equipment. "It's not hard to find Italian Communists who will work for some money. They will take you to your ship."

So, if you can't fight them, join them! In the night, Lev and Katerina sat in the front seat with a Communist driver, displaying an official red sign. Alexandra, Olik, one Communist, and fourteen pieces of suitcases, boxes, and bags—all of them with a corner painted green for easier identification—sat in the back. And so the Dabberts and Drosdovskys left Albizzate.

Through empty roads, the truck did not even have to stop at the numerous roadblocks and reached Genoa safely. Alexandra gave the driver her handgun for his good work. He was very thankful. The ship sailed the next day, August 2, 1948.

Twenty-eight

The New World

*A*board the "Sebastiano Caboto," the family spent some time learning about their new destination. On the west coast of South America, Peru had been a source of great wealth to Spain in colonial times. Spain had been exhausted from fighting the Moslems, but absorbing the wealth brought in by the American colonies reinvigorated it. Under the administration of Spanish Viceroys, there was an influx of Western European culture into Peru. To this day, the best Spanish is spoken in Mexico and Peru.

Four times the size of Texas, Peru includes the narrow Peruvian coastline, which spreads from Ecuador in the north to Chile in the south for about fourteen hundred miles, and from the cold Pacific Ocean to the Andes, "la Sierra."[99] To the east of the Andes, lies "la Selva," which forms two-thirds of Peru and is the least populated area, the wildest part of the Amazon rainforest. The majority of the population is concentrated in the barren region of the coast, brought to life by some thirty-five insignificant rivers that flow westward from the Andes to the Pacific Ocean. It seemed incredible that this bleak area had been inhabited for some twenty thousand years.

---

[99] The Andean "Sierra" is a high chain of mountains that initially taught the American space effort about the effects of high altitude physiology.

Peru seemed fifty years behind Europe in its class struggles. Peru had become an independent republic in 1821. Freedom from Spain did not end the trials and tribulations of the native population, however, and numerous revolutions shook the elusive quest for democracy. The conquistadors had named Peru "El Dorado," which meant "plunder and exploitation." Their legacy of several hundred years of diseases imported from the Old World, repression of the Indians, and the traditional use of coca leaves took its toll and contributed to the low level of self-reliance, entrepreneurship, and health of the Indian population.

The growing unrest between the "haves" and the "have-nots" and leftist teaching in the state schools and universities continued to cause attempts to overthrow the entrenched wealthy class. The following anarchy would be suppressed by the military, who would bring back a semblance of law and order at the expense of economic progress and human rights. Eventually, there would be elections for a democratic, civilian form of government, which in turn would succumb to a vicious circle of corruption and weakness. Then the cycle would start all over.

When Alexandra and her family arrived, the civilian government, elected in 1945, had just been overthrown by a military coup. General Manuel Odria took control, insured order, and began eight years of public works under harshly repressive social controls.

Olik thought the place looked like the pits—dirty, dusty, and gloomy. It rained only on rare occasions, but low clouds seemed to hide the sky forever. But the area was rich in archeological points of interest, and there were always fresh flowers. "They were so beautiful and cheap," Alexandra said. It would take a while for Lima to reveal her treasures.

When Alexandra arrived in Peru, neither she nor her other family members could speak Spanish, yet. This didn't stop them for long. Within two months she had bought a house in the nice neighborhood of San Isidro that served as office and living quarters for her family. The house had five bedrooms, five bathrooms, two rooms with a bath for the servants, and no central heating. Hot water had to be heated as

House in Lima

needed in the kitchen or in the tub with a special portable electric heater. Better that than the Ethiopian mules. Among the comforting furnishings shipped from Italy was the Persian carpet, reclaimed from Africa. And for added interest, the family lived a block away from a *huaca*, one of the many ancient burial mounds in the valley of Lima.

Jeronimo Yucra came from Cuzco—the Inca capital of Peru—to Lima, and the lucky star directed him to Alexandra, who hired him. "Since I came to work for Doctora Dabbert, I never again went to sleep hungry," he said.

From contacts aboard ship, she cultivated new connections and acquaintances and soon found that Lima was a kaleidoscope of fascinating people. She found an unexpected coincidence in running into Mr. Ossepov, a Russian émigré who had been a student of Lev's when he taught artillery at the military academy in St. Petersburg and an officer in the tsarist army, and with her usual curiosity, she soon learned their story.

Ossepov and his wife were an elderly couple, ex-estate holders in Russia, whose daughter had married a wealthy Peruvian landowner some two hundred fifty miles away in the mountains. Ossepov had grown a generous white beard. When he'd visited his son-in-law's hacienda, he was surprised by the deference received by the native Indians, who fell on their knees at his appearance. They thought he was Saint Peter.

Alexandra still had no license to practice, but she immediately let it be known through conversations, going to churches, and cultural events that her services would soon be available. Meeting expenses was not easy, initially, and the whole family contributed from the start, supplying a Swiss delicatessen with jams and preserves and marmalades.

Family settled in Peru

The family considered it an adventure to learn where to go to the dump to get the jars, sterilize them, and go to different markets to get the best and less expensive strawberries, oranges, tangerines, and kumquats.

In the meantime, Olik had successfully taken the examinations in Spanish, received his Peruvian high school diploma, and passed the entrance tests to start his premedical courses at the University of San Marcos in Lima, which was founded in 1551. It was the first in the Americas and to this day continues teaching and being a political irritant to the rules of the establishment.

Alexandra had to take five examinations at the University to obtain her license to practice dentistry—all in Spanish.

It was not so much for knowledge as for money. I wrote my thesis on the character, diseases, and gem fillings of teeth of the Peruvian mummies that I was given for study at the local wonderful Museum of Archeology. It was well received.

She was fifty years old, but there was still fear of competition. She had to be careful not to create barriers by those who might resent such competition. "You can give little gifts. It is only attention, not corruption. A little to drink, a little chocolate, some flowers for the lady of the house—and it is done."

In the waiting room of one of her examiners, five diplomas hung on the wall. When she examined them closely, however, two were for shooting flying doves and one was for belonging to a fishing club. With exams finished, this examiner asked her to a restaurant and offered her champagne. "It was courtesy," she said.

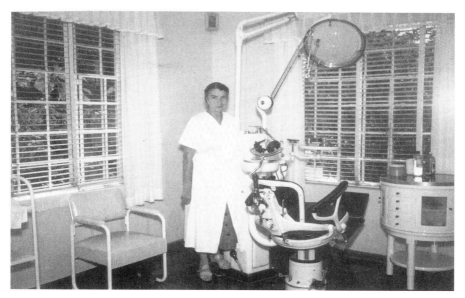

Alexandra's dental office at home in Peru

Later, one of her examiners said to her, "We've helped you because you told us that you will not work in the city, but in your house on your friends." Since "friend" and "patient" were so often synonymous with Alexandra, they may not have anticipated the eventual scope of her successful practice.

She needed a new foot-powered drill and purchased one in Peru. Many of her patients, including Olik and the Swedish Missionaries, preferred the foot-operated drill to the electrical drill. "It was less threatening," she said. Nevertheless, she soon bought an electric drill.

Alexandra didn't hesitate to promote her business. When she bought furniture for the new house, she suggested that the owner of the shop should send her patients so that she could make her payments. First she bought basic furniture, but a Peruvian friend suggested an extraordinary opportunity. The bishop's palace was liquidating some beautiful colonial furniture that ended up in Alexandra's living and dining rooms.

She had an account in a bank in Rotterdam, which opened before World War II. From Lima she wrote to the bank and asked them to send her the money. They replied that since she had been an "enemy," (carrying an Italian passport) during the war, she would have to wait fifteen years for her money, and that in the meantime they would pay two percent interest. She badly needed the money and so wrote directly to Queen Wilhelmina of the Netherlands. The Queen replied through an agent, "We cannot help."

In spite of her generally bad feelings toward the English government, Alexandra had a high regard for the English banks and insurance companies, especially as compared with the Dutch. She'd had an additional account at an English bank in Aden. She wrote that bank for her money as well and received it at once, "with no discussions about enemies or two percent. English banks are very honest."

When she bought a car, she told the dealer the same thing she'd said to the furniture salesman: Send patients so that the payments would be assured. Her first car in Lima was an English Standard Vanguard. "I bought it new and it was always broken."

To further help with finances, Alexandra rented one of the rooms to Ursula von Fircks, a German baroness and nurse. Katerina had known Ursula's great uncle. Ursula did not help Alexandra in her practice and did mostly private night duty for which she was well paid. Ursula became a drinker, however. One day, she fell and her face turned black and blue. Another day, upon returning home, Alexandra saw the bottle buyer with two bags full of empty bottles. He asked, "Why don't you sell me more bottles like your friend does?"

In Peru, Alexandra painted more watercolors, mostly flowers and landscapes. She also started painting icons in the mosaic style as suggested by the Italian general with black market connections. She used the image of Raphael's Christ in a boat with his disciples on the lake, a painting she remembered from the Vatican, as a motif for one of her favorite icons.[100] Every painting that she hooked on the walls of the reception room had a price tag on the back, and many were sold to patients.

---

[100] She would later sell this painting for $2,000.

She'd learned a lot about managing her money. In Peru, Alexandra always asked for some money down in order to avoid the previous difficulties of collecting from patients who tried to evade paying their bills. A new friend offered further advice. "Do not put in your books money that you receive in cash, only money paid with checks." She therefore recorded her cash money phonetically in Russian using Ethiopian characters—over three hundred fifty letters. "Not even Olik could read it," she said.

One night, the gardener came to see her after hours. He had been to a dentist downtown who had made an extraction. The man was still bleeding, and his mouth was full of clots. He came by bicycle a long way to see Alexandra since he couldn't reach his dentist.

> I opened my office and sewed his wound. I had watched an American nurse, Margaret Bergman of the Adventist mission in Addis Ababa, sew up a deep cut of the tongue of one of her patients. I used her technique and it worked. I told him, "Leave the bike here and go home by foot. Riding is harder and makes you bleed more. Return in three days, and I will take out the stitches."

This made her remember how in Addis Ababa Taffara had fallen off his bicycle, and Alexandra had stitched the cut on his head. Also in Addis Ababa, one of her horses had collided with a military truck, which was driving on the wrong side. (The British reversed lanes wherever they occupied territory.) She stitched the wound on his neck as well. Alexandra missed her horses and riding. She also missed friends and family, but she kept up a prodigious correspondence all her life with people all over the world.

Word came in 1949 of the death of Haile Selassie's beloved son Makonnen, the one Alexandra had considered spoiled. The public was told that he died in a road accident in his Volkswagen. But in reality, he was killed by the husband of a woman that he had an affair with. The husband, a general, warned Makonnen that if he came again to his wife, he would kill him. Makonnen ignored the warning. When the general found them together, he shot Makonnen in the back of the head.

"Haile Selassie was just," Alexandra said. "The general had warned Makonnen. (He said,) 'My son should not have gone back to this woman.' People tried to console him, but he said, 'I am sorry to lose a son, but I have sixteen million sons: my people.'"

Taffara Deguefe was doing very well. The management of the State Bank of Ethiopia recommended him to Emperor Haile Selassie, and Taffara was selected to be sent to Calgary, Canada.

As her practice grew, her patients came from all countries, and Alexandra could see what kind of work was done by dentists from around the world. "The best were the Swiss, then came the Germans." Mr. And Mrs. Wilhelmi were some of her German patients. So often in listening to her patients' stories, vivid memories of her own struggles of outrunning the forces of history returned to her. The Wilhelmis had lived in Peru, and were well traveled. He'd returned to Germany to enlist and wound up on the Eastern Front.

He had been captured in the battle of Stalingrad and was a prisoner of the Soviets. He was freed through a Red Cross Swedish Agency much sooner than others. While a prisoner, he had five operations for pleuritis. There was a greedy Russian doctor who coveted a ring that Mr. Wilhelmi had bought in Peru before returning to Germany to enlist in the army. He had bought this ring at the market in Huancayo. It had effigy of Viracocha, the Inca god. It was cheap and could be had for little money, but the Russian doctor liked it.

Wilhelmi said to me, "I know that you believe in the Madonna and you believe in Saints. I believe in Viracocha, because he saved my life."

He told the Russian doctor that he could have the ring if the doctor would help him escape. It was just the time when the Swedish Red Cross was helping the invalids to return home. In the ward with Wilhelmi were many other on the list to be freed. One of them died after he had already received permission to leave, and the Russian doctor gave Wilhelmi the dead man's name and put him in his place. The other patients kept silence. In exchange of freedom, the doctor received the ring, which was replaced as soon as Mr. Wilhelmi returned to Peru to become the director of a big textile factory.

One expatriate friend, Father Serafim, revived Alexandra's early memories of the Caucasus. She told his story. "Russian priest in Lima was my friend: Father Serafim Fetisosov. He was born in Northern Caucasus. His father was also priest; it ran in the family."[101]

When the Communists came, they killed his parents. The people of the village took him to a monastery for his education, but again the Communists came, closed the monastery, and sent the orphans to a state home. Serafim and two others escaped to the mountains and lived in the forest for five years. "For this he was good maker of picnic fires, he had much practice in the forests of Caucasus." The police found him, however, and he was arrested. They imprisoned him for two years in Tiflis. "Then Stalin's mother died and was amnesty and he was released from prison."

Serafim went to Rostov on the Don and became an underground priest. Then in World War II, the Germans came and gave him good treatment. During the retreat, they gave him a cart with two horses to escape from Russia to Romania, then Hungary, and then to Austria. "It was long walk." There were fifteen of them, with millions of others fleeing the advance of the Communist army. "He eventually went to Canada. Fell in love, had a baby. For this, he was sent to Peru."

He lived in a small church in a poor district. Every Saturday, Alexandra drove her parents to vespers. "There was a small but very good liturgical choir," she said.

Alexandra's circle of expatriate friends and patients widened from the Ossepovs and Wilhelmis and Father Serafim, to include a few couples and others. Doctor Karateev, a professor of geology and mining at

---

[101] Russian Orthodox priests had wives, but monks and the church hierarchy were supposed to be celibate.

the University, was a down-to-earth, irreverent Ukrainian—a benign atheist who had no scruples about taking communion whenever and wherever he felt like it. "How can it hurt me?" was his philosophy. His very formal British wife was also quite tiny.

Doctor Karateev told the story about their stay in the jungle. His wife had gone ahead on a trail, and as he was trying to catch up with her. He saw a huge anaconda snake cross the path and he felt in a quandary: "Should I kill this snake or not? What if my wife is in its belly? Might she still be alive?" Fortunately, the snake had not seen his wife.

Then there was Mr. Rostov who directed the Lima ballet. He was funny when on stage, dancing in a parody of the trio in "Swan Lake." Then, Mrs. Von Meck, a descendent of Tchaikovsky's patroness, was the sister of Mrs. Michailov who had been the lady in chamber of the last queen of Italy. Her husband was a typical depressed aristocrat who became furious when he was revived after he tried to commit suicide.

The Pospisils were a vital part of this circle. They had escaped from Czechoslovakia where they had owned several mines. The father had brought his two sons and an attractive daughter who became quite close to Olik and inspired many events that included performances, receptions, and presentations of literary, philosophical, artistic, historical, and archaeological subjects.

At least once a week, they had an established time to get together with these new friends and discussed the latest news, politics, personal reminiscences, experiences, personalities, and events. They decided beforehand which house would be next for the gathering that would extend from teatime to past dinnertime.

Frequently on Sundays, Alexandra and Olik—along with a few friends, sometimes in one car or with other cars—would drive down to the solitary beaches. Close to the coastline, the sea was very deep and the Humboldt Stream brought cold water to the surface. The fish were abundant and so were the pelicans, seagulls, and cormorants. An unpaved washboard trail through fields and banana tracts would lead to sandy beaches washed by enormous waves that made swimming hazardous.

Visiting the "locals" at a necropolis, with Olik and Toka, Alexandra's black King Charles spaniel

On each side of the beach rose barren rocky hills with remnants of ancient pre-Hispanic ruins and a necropolis that had been excavated by farmers who frequently used ancient pottery in their primitive kitchens, or they would sell some of the more decorated findings. Human bones were scattered everywhere, but were of interest mainly to young medical students. There never was any need to dig, and mother and son slowly collected two boxes of specimens and bones that showed pathological conditions for Olik's class of anatomy.

As Alexandra and Olik explored bits of the bleak area west of the Andes that had cradled some of the most advanced cultures in the ancient world, they marveled at the amazingly advanced irrigation systems, textiles, and ceramics. In the case of Paracas, a site two hundred miles south of Lima, numerous trephined skulls, many of them with signs of healing bone, showing that the patient had survived the radical operation, attested to advanced neurosurgical skills.

Alexandra and Olik walked among the bones of those whose civilizations had fallen prey to the Incas and then to the Spanish conquest of the overextended Inca Empire, stretching from Ecuador to Chile,

Bolivia and Argentina. Violence, Old World diseases, and exploitation had left their clues behind in the bones.

Lev had essentially retired in Peru. A former general and surveyor who didn't learn Spanish, he found solace in discussing political, historical, and philosophical issues with the European circle of friends. He died in 1951 at home in Lima of prostate cancer. It had been thirty years since he'd given away his cherished horse Barinia to an Austrian officer. Alexandra said, "We found in his billfold small white envelope, folded up. Inside is piece of Barinia's hair. He had not forgotten her."

Twenty-nine

Excursions

*I*n 1952, Olik graduated from the University of San Marcos and entered San Fernando Medical School, a branch of the venerable San Marcos University, to continue his studies. Taffara was in Ann Arbor, Michigan studying to become a lawyer.

In 1953, Alexandra read in the newspaper an account of a terrible flood in the Netherlands after the Zuider Zee broke its banks and covered a large portion of the country with great loss of property and life. Alexandra at once sat down and wrote to Queen Wilhelmia about her bank account, its funds still held by the Dutch banks. "I have read of your great suffering from floods," she wrote, "and I wish to donate ten percent of my money to the victims of the flood."

Alexandria believed they must have been ashamed, "because immediately they sent me all my money, in care of my cousin Oksana in New York City. It was not possible at that time to send the money directly to Peru."[102]

With the money from the Dutch bank, she bought a second car, a used 1951 Chevrolet. She bought it for $1,000.00 from Adventist missionaries. A patient of hers who was an auto mechanic looked it over and guaranteed that it was in good condition. "I had it for twelve years," she said. "It was wonderful car."

---

[102] Some of Oksana's story is told in the last chapter.

With Lev gone and Olik so intensely involved in his studies, Alexandra stayed busy with her practice. On Saturdays she still drove her mother with one or two of her friends to vespers with Father Serafim.

The wife of the director of a German bank came for treatment one day. She looked sad and Alexandra asked why.

"This morning my husband flew to Europe and did not take me with him," she answered. Alexandra did her treatment, and then the woman asked, "Please open me the cards!"

She'd known that Alexandra sometimes read cards, so Alexandra opened the cards and saw that the lady would be going on a long trip immediately.

"No, it is not possible. I must stay here. It is a fantasy."

That same afternoon she received a telegram from her husband to come to Germany at once. He had an accident resulting in a detached retina that required an immediate operation. He wanted her with him.

Three years later she stopped Alexandra in the bakery in downtown Lima. "I am just on my way to come to see you," she said.

Alexandra thought that she would come because of her teeth and said, "Come in half an hour. I will be home."

When she came, the lady said, "No, I come not for teeth, but for cards."

Alexandra said, "No, I open cards only for my patients."

She limited the reading of the cards to close friends and patients. When Ursula, the nurse who rented the extra room, went to her work at night, she would say, "Oh, doctor, please open me the cards. How will be this night?"

That afternoon, Alexandra opened the cards and saw death. Somebody would die.

Ursula said, "Oh, how sad. It is my very rich and nice Jewish patient. I am sorry if he will die." The next morning she told Alexandra, "My patient did not die, but his beloved Persian dog died, and all night we worked to put dog with candles and flowers in bathroom for funeral next day."

"Instead of patient, it was the dog that dies," Alexandra said. "I remember one evening a Russian lady asked me to open cards. I found only one half of cards." She called her cook and houseboy, Jeronimo, but nobody knew what happened to half of her cards. "I believe really that God does not like that I open cards, so I never opened them again." With a few exceptions.

Lev had been buried for several years when Alexandra had his remains exhumed and transferred to another cemetery for better "perpetual maintenance." The law required that the coffin be opened and the remains verified as being those of the deceased. A new casket was required, as it had deteriorated with time. Alexandra herself did not look, but asked Father Serafim to be the witness.

He did so, and then came up to Alexandra and asked her, "Why did you put such big shoes on the General?"

She replied, "They were the shoes he always wore."

So much had the body shrunk in the very dry climate of Lima, that the shoes dwarfed the general's feet and legs.

Sometimes dental knowledge bore grim responsibilities, but Alexandra accepted her role in being of use wherever necessary. One early morning, her friend and patient Mr. Wilhelmi and his eight-year-old son appeared pale, distraught, and sad. An airplane had crashed that morning near Lima and Mrs. Wilhelmi, who was a stewardess of Varig, a Brazilian airline, was killed with all the others. He needed his wife's dental chart for identification.

Another patient, a mining engineer, was found dead one morning and Alexandra was urged to come at once by the son.

"Can you put his teeth back in?" the young man asked. "He left them in salt water at his bedside. He looks so ugly with his teeth out."

She was there in half an hour. It was necessary to work quickly before the body stiffened. She put in his teeth and he became "normal-looking."

A grim medical responsibility fell on Olik while he was in medical school. In the anatomy department, Olik approached a cadaver—and recognized it. He knew a little of the life of the man whose corpse had become a science project. A banking institution had given free rooms to Russian singles. One of them was Mr. Kudriavzev, a mining engineer. The man's mother had inherited "Eliseev," what Alexandra called "the best food store in Saint Petersburg," but the family had lost all in the Revolution. When the man died in a traffic accident, nobody had come to claim him, and the police delivered his body to the Medical school.

Excursions

Alexandra and Olik were able to explore Peru on numerous trips and vacations before he graduated. Chiclin was a huge hacienda where sugar cane was grown for the nearby sugar factory. Its owners, the Larco family, had made a fortune a century earlier, when an ancestor gambled on news that came from a ship that had just anchored in Peruvian waters near Trujillo in the north. Because of the Crimean War between Russia and Great Britain, cotton was in short supply. The Larco man had galloped three hundred miles south to Lima, bought all the available cotton, and made a fortune in resale.

The Larcos had a marvelous archeological museum of the Mochica-Chimu cultures that had prospered where their land was located. Alexandra and Olik were invited there several times. On one occasion, they met Doctor Kinsey, who was at the time studying ancient Peruvian sexual practices, which he found depicted in the *huacos* (ceramics). It was also a great place for horse riding, something Alexandra hadn't been able to enjoy since her days in Ethiopia.

They also enjoyed their travel adventure to Huancayo, some one hundred fifty miles northeast of Lima and reached by a train that the British had built. It ascended to a high point of over fifteen thousand feet above sea level before descending to more comfortable altitudes and the main Indian city of Huancayo. Famous for the colorful Sunday market—with its distinctive ponchos, smells of roasting guinea pigs (a delicacy), and incense from the main church—surrounded by

Riding a Tennessee walking horse in Peru

eucalyptus groves. Peruvian cowboys called *chalanes* proudly rode Tennessee walking horses. This town was a must for anybody interested in Indian and Latin-American culture. It did require a day to get used to the altitude. It was also ideal for horseback riding, and Alexandra took full advantage.

There was a market for ponchos, in cotton or wool, with different designs and colors that identified the area of origin.

Cuzco and Macchu-Pichu, of course, were also the destinations for anybody that wanted to experience unexpected and wonderful views. Five days by car, or a little over one hour by plane, took Alexandra and Olik from Lima to visit these amazing places. It would provide infinite inspiration for Alexandra's watercolors.

Pukalpa, on the Ucayali—the main Peruvian branch of the Amazon—was also a worthy destination for a traveler wanting to discover a different world—one predominantly green with so many birds and butterflies of all sizes and colors. Alexandra had patients from the American religious linguistic mission, who were in the process of translating the Bible into native languages, converting the natives of the jungle to Christianity, and also assisting them with tools and medical aid. They moved mainly by planes equipped with floats for landing on rivers and lagoons.

When Alexandra and Olik joined them for lunch, nearly fifty people showed up in the dining hall, all cheerful and in high spirits. At the Pukalpa airport during that time, a big airplane had gotten stuck in the mud and had to be regularly serviced until the following dry season when the field would harden enough to let the plane take off and return to its home base.

The Young Man

At twenty-seven, Olik had graduated from medical school and had finished at the head of his class. His rotating internship was over. He could have started practicing, but he had won a one-year scholarship for post-graduate studies abroad.

Alexandra had started prodding him to become financially independent, and Olik lacked Alexandra's ability of self-promotion in an environment that was not friendly to beginners. Trying to make a living in Lima therefore didn't appeal to him. He had become interested in surgery in general—and orthopedics, in particular—and was anxious to improve his skills and chances. He'd been accepted for a surgical residency at the Bellevue Hospital in New York and had received an immigration visa for the U.S.A., made easier at the time because he qualified to enter the country on a limited quota reserved for Ethiopians. He left Lima in 1958.

Alexandra's Peruvian chapter needed a shift of perspective. Life had assumed a comfortable level of lifestyle "a holding pattern," as pilots sometimes announced to their passengers.

She took comfort in her faithful companion "Toka," the black King Charles, the adorable breed of Pekingese/cocker spaniel that loved Coca Cola. Yet even she was aging. Her friend and patient, Mr. Buckley, shared Alexandra's love of dogs and horses along with exploring the

Alexandra riding stylishly in Peru

nearby hills with their ancient arti-facts. He wanted a naked Peruvian dog, like a Chihuahua. "They are hard to find. I went with him to the outly-ing villages. He thought he could drive his big car." He reasoned that if a bus could go there, so could his car. "But he scraped the bottom of the car and left the muffler behind. We found a naked albino dog—ugly, like a rat!"

Alexandra continued her practice, her visits with friends, her reading of books and journals in French, Ger-man, and Spanish, and kept up with current affairs. She maintained her foreign correspondence. Herman Dabbert had escaped to West Berlin and became a professor at the Free University. Ferdinando Pozzi, her second husband, had died. Taffara had returned to Ethiopia, where he held numerous offices including that of director of the Ethio-pian Civil Aviation and the Governor of the National Ethiopian Bank. Alexandra learned that her cousin Boris Liatoshinsky, who was still a composer of distinction in Kiev, had received the Stalin prize for one of his compositions, an historical opera with a ballet. And, of course, she wrote weekly to Olik.

After a hectic year at Bellevue in New York, Olik was accepted in 1959 for training in orthopedic surgery at Duke University in North Carolina. He had passed the E.C.F.M.G., the medical examination that foreign graduates had to take to be able to train in the States. He had taken the State of Washington examination to obtain a license to prac-tice in that state—one of the very few that would grant that privilege to foreign graduates—and had in his hands the coveted license to prac-tice in that state. So he began a three-year residency in orthopedics at Duke, which included one year training at the Shriner's Hospital in Greenville, South Carolina. There he met Frances Thomason. They both loved horses, and she kept horses on her dad's farm. For the first time, Olik learned to brush horses before saddling, a job that had always been done by a groom. He and Frances became inseparable.

In one sad letter to Olik, Alexandra described Katerina. "Grandmother is getting more and more nervous, troubled, and confused. Her friends are gradually visiting her less and less. She gets agitated and has trouble sleeping and constantly asks me if I am there. I would like to travel, but I can not leave her."

For the last two years of her life, Katerina had suffered the mental deterioration associated with Alzheimer's. The stress of care giving, with the determination to keep her mother at home until the end, had been difficult for Alexandra, but her promise to stand by Katerina till the end was fulfilled. In 1961, Katerina died at home.

The death of his grandmother made Olik realize he had to start his professional life so that he could start planning for his mother to come to the U.S.A. to join him. After three years of orthopedic training, Olik passed the Orthopedic Board examination and was accepted by the Veterans Administration for a position as an orthopedic surgeon in Oakland, California. He then married Frances Thomason from Laurence, South Carolina in 1962. He became a naturalized American citizen, and passed the California medical license examination.

Alexandra had many comforts in her life, but especially dear to her was her new dog Koka, a cocker spaniel that had replaced Toka. Koka made her life less lonely and happily participated in outings, and especially loved trips to the beach. Alexandra wouldn't go anywhere with friends unless Koka could come along.

After her mother's death, Alexandra had to make some difficult decisions, probably the toughest in her life. In 1962 in Lima, one could sense trouble in the air. In her weekly letters (in Russian) to Olik, she seemed wary.

People are worried about the June elections. They are withdrawing money from the banks. Lots of uncertainty. A major cataclysm is predicted, but nobody knows what and when.

Faustino (her employee at the time) has been coughing for a month. I took him for x-rays, but they are being repaired—as usual.

I feel so tired, then the patients start coming, and I feel my morale goes up.

I have mixed feelings about what to do. Moving away from my home here. I am winding down my practice. Slowly there are fewer and fewer of our friends left. Many are leaving for Europe.

Major changes didn't happen at first. A free election returned civilian rule with centrist Fernando Belaunde Terry as President and things settled down a bit. The economy suffered with continued uncertainty, however. Worried about expropriation of their businesses if the country continued to drift to the left, many European and American investors left Peru, along with local landowners.

Another Moving Experience

Olik intensified his efforts to persuade Alexandra to leave Peru and join him in the States. She herself admitted that many of her friends and patients had left or died. Olik asked her to pull up roots again for what would be the fourth time in her life. In her sixties, she wondered if she could really endure another move and make another jump into an unfamiliar world, one where she knew only her son and didn't speak much of the language. Since requalifying for a dentist's license in English was not to be considered, and the move would mean she couldn't earn a living, she would need to be ready to retire. With the possibility of feeling like a refugee again, she dreaded the loss of her economy and independence.

Alexandra stayed on in Peru for several more increasingly lonely years, but in 1967, political struggles deteriorated into the kind of situation she had fled when she first left her homeland in Russia forty-five years earlier. The violent insurgency of the Maoist "Sendero Luminoso" or "the shining path" had begun. Ayacucho, home of the Ossepov's daughter who had married a wealthy Peruvian landowner in the mountains, became one of the most victimized areas during the Shining Path Maoist insurrection. Alexandra didn't want to stay for the probable election of the Marxist general, Juan Velasco Alvarado.

Olik had settled in San Diego where he had fallen in love with his occupation. He promised to contribute three hundred dollars a month if she would come to San Diego. Alexandra decided on another move.

Selling real estate for dollars became almost impossible, however. Peruvian soles, by law, could not be converted in dollars. After weeks without a prospect of a buyer, she finally asked Father Serafim to come to the house and bless it. He did so, every room and every icon. The very next day, a mining engineer who worked with the Americans came, checked the house, and bought if for $25,000.00. It amounted to one million three hundred thousand soles. When she bought the house, one dollar was worth twelve soles; when she sold it, it took fifty-two soles to buy a dollar!

With a mixture of optimism and sadness, she planned her next step. Sifting through all that had accumulated during the twenty years and deciding what to take was a formidable challenge. Of course, the dental equipment, including the foot-operated dental drill, would have to be included—Olik would be in need of dental care—and, of course, her Peruvian furniture that one time stood in Lima's bishop's palace was included. Of course, her Persian rug. And of course, Koka, her cocker spaniel, that had succeeded Toka.

The immigration process was lengthy, but since Olik had become an American citizen—an achievable goal—Jeronimo Yucra eventually obtained his visa as well.

She bought—again in cash, sight unseen (as she had done in Addis Ababa, when she bought the house in Italy)—an attractive home half a mile away from her son's house. She packed everything, except for a couple of suitcases, into an enormous wood crate the size of a small cottage so that nothing would be stolen during shipping.

She said good-bye to her friends and Peru, then flew to San Diego. It had been another difficult decision, but she felt that God had spared her from Juan Velazco Terry's Marxist Regime that dispossessed the rich without solving the problems affecting the poor.

Thirty

San Diego

When she reached the United States, Alexandra was seventy years old. English, Italian, and Ethiopian were the weakest languages in which she could speak. She could speak, read, and write perfectly in Russian, French, and German. Once in San Diego, she and Koka immediately settled in her home on the southerly slope of Narragansset Avenue with a partial view of the bay and, later, of the Coronado Bridge. The house was ideal for her, with a majestic palm at the entrance, a narrow access to the garage—typical of the houses built before World War II that required a mixture of art and science to drive the car in and out without scratching the house or the wall or the car.

The back yard had a birch tree to remind her of Russia and a big eucalyptus tree that reminded her of Ethiopia. She knew the eucalyptus would provide a good remedy against ants when they would show up in her house; a few branches of odorous leaves proved that it also worked in the New World. She would also inhale the steam of eucalyptus leaves soaked in boiling water to alleviate acute bronchitis.

She managed, with help, to disassemble "the big box" that contained all that she had brought from Lima. This took a whole week. Her oils, watercolors, icons, Persian rugs, Peruvian ceramics, and the bishop's furniture transformed the new house into Alexandra's uniquely charming domain. Very soon her dental equipment was used

Olik sitting open-mouthed in the bishop's chair patiently tolerating the pedal-driven drill

on Olik's teeth in the living room, Olik sitting open-mouthed in the bishop's chair patiently tolerating the pedal-driven drill, and the subsequent drying of the cavity with alcohol—in the form of Smirnoff vodka—prior to the amalgam filling.

Alexandra had no inhibition to let her tastes be known, which did not always make it easy for a daughter-in-law. She'd visited Olik and Frances in Oakland and the encounter produced moments of turbulence. With a little patience, Frances and Alexandra soon got together. However, not long after Alexandra's arrival, Frances began going blind because of diabetic retinopathy, and Alexandra's support was unconditional.

The next step was to get a car, a Chevrolet that time cost $2,000. She passed her driver's license tests, and never scraped the house or wall or car in getting into her garage during her twenty-three years of driving in San Diego. The next essential: She started attending the Midway Adult Education classes to improve on her limited knowledge of English.

To her surprise, she soon started receiving Social Security. It was the first time in her life that she was entitled to such assistance, but it was a surprise that was at variance with her notion of personal independence and self-sufficiency. "What a strange and great country," she wrote in a published article, "and cold and hot water at all times in the kitchen and in the bathroom." The news journal, *Novoe Russkoe Slovo* of New York, printed several of her articles.

With Koka, her faithful and inseparable companion, she could be seen walking early in the morning on Shelter Island and other parks. She started visiting Balboa Park and its museums, and got acquainted with the city.

Alexandra started painting again

She resumed her considerable correspondence. Taffara Deguefe had been doing amazingly well in international banking. In his meteoric rise from humble origins, he'd shaken hands as the Ethiopian government's representative with Robert McNamara, who was president of the World Bank at the time, and received a medal from the hands of General De Gaulle when he came to visit Ethiopia as President of France. Yet it was also through Taffara that Alexandra and Olik kept up with Birke, who'd been Olik's nanny.

"American women are heroes," she commented. "They don't know that in most of the places I lived, I could have somebody to do the chores. Here, you have all kinds of electrical appliances, but you still have to do the chores."

Alexandra had always delegated the preparation of meals to her domestic help, or as in Italy, to her parents, until she came to California. She then started to cook. Her favorites were borsch, won tons in chicken soup, Russian salad, pine nuts, and coffee mousse between ladyfingers cake. She despised "Soviet borsch" which was vegetarian, in absence of meats. "Borsch must have three varieties of meat: beef, lamb, and pork" besides the usual beets, tomatoes, onions, potatoes, cabbage, tomato paste, and ketchup.

Of course, her famous Russian salad (minced potatoes, boiled beets, pickled cucumbers, dill with mayonnaise dressing) was still great for picnics. Sweet wine and vodka were always present.

Chores and housekeeping took too much time for someone who had always had help. Jeronimo was the solution. He did not have to be convinced to follow her to California, but it was not easy to get him in. Alexandra even wrote a moving letter—in her own English—to the then President Richard Nixon to help Jeronimo get a permanent visa. His Americanized nickname became "Gerry."

She started painting again, now that she had more time and realized that, to supplement her income, rather than using oils and water colors, she would have a better chance painting Russian Orthodox and Byzantine-style icons. She perfected her technique of painted mosaic to enhance the beauty of her creations.

While icons traditionally must conform to the original, she created several that were unique, including the representation of the Russian Imperial family as martyrs of the Revolution, and the Ethiopian version of the Saint of Lalibela and Ras Desta Damtu—the Ethiopian guerilla leader executed by the Italians.[103] She never forgot this tragic patriot. She managed to sell over three hundred icons that are spread over the Americas, Europe, and Australia.

Creating an icon, for Alexandra, was a fulfillment of prayer and had a Spiritual dimension. The process was complex and might take a month or more.

First, one must find a dry, well-aged, non-resinous wood. To avoid warping, one or two hardwood planks could be wedged in the back of the board; or good quality, thick plywood would do. A carpenter can prepare a recessed area in the panel, for protection of the image. Then coat over with lime, then flatten with fine sand paper. Then, make contours with a hard pencil. Apply the gold leaf to the background and

---

[103] See photo of icon in color section.

Creating an icon, for Alexandra, was a fulfillment of prayer and had a Spiritual dimension. The process was complex and might take a month or more.

with black paint, outline the mosaic squares. Then use egg tempera and lacquer surfacing for the icon. Lastly, the decoration of an optional frame may include pyrography, a style of wood burning, and affixed semiprecious stones. Alexandra usually protected the finished piece with a glass-covered box frame. Triptychs would remain unframed or could be hinged to stand alone. It then must be blessed by the priest. Father Sergei who had both arms paralyzed from polio was a frequent visitor and usually blessed her icons.

For Alexandra, the creation of icons fulfilled her creative and spiritual needs, helped financially, and attracted new friends. She exhibited the icons locally and sold a number of them through the Jones Gallery in La Jolla. It was at the gallery that she met Ray and Beatrice Hutchinson.

Alexandra's life stories fascinated Ray, and he began collecting them while Beatrice was at the hairdresser. They met frequently to look at Alexandra's many photo albums and reminisce. The Timkin Museum in Balboa Park had a wonderful collection of Russian icons, and the three of them had many outings there. On one of the trips, Alexandra took Beatrice, a very religious lady, to a museum. Driving her car, Alexandra felt thirsty and asked for a bottle in the glove compartment. To Beatrice's consternation, the label said "Smirnoff Vodka," but the content was water.

While writing a manuscript about Alexandra's life, Ray succumbed to cancer. Beatrice generously passed his documents to Olik.

Alexandra had many slides of her icons and enjoyed being invited to give talks about them. On one such occasion, she met Marion Reupsch, a retired nurse, and friendship bloomed. Marion traveled around the world many times, helped evacuate children during the last days of the conflict in Vietnam, took a bus from Turkey to India, had gone to China twelve times, Indonesia thirteen times, and to the Antarctica twice in one year.

Alexandra standing next to her artwork

Despite her many activities and friends, Gerry's filial care, and the companionship of her dog Koka, Alexandra often felt lonely. She loved to travel and decided to take Gerry and Koka to visit friends in Phoenix—Father Gladkov, a Russian Orthodox priest, and his wife Matushka. With intuitive goodness bubbling from her heart, Matushka had survived unbelievable hardship and danger during the horrors of World War II, "when life was not worth a bullet, and only God knows how many times we would have perished had it not been for the goodness of people from the most unexpected sources," Matushka said.

On the return trip from Arizona, Koka died on a day parched with heat. Alexandra smuggled the canine body back to her home on Narragansset to be buried in a quiet corner of her backyard that became the pet cemetery. No less than seven of her and friend's cats and dogs found eternal rest, and the plants prospered.

Then came Ussia, Alexandra's long-haired dachshund, who was without a doubt the smartest dog in Point Loma. Ussia's companionship and the good material life in the United States could-n't entirely assuage Alexandra's loneliness. She wrote to her friend Elizabeth Meier—whom she'd known in Peru, but who had moved to Germany—and invited her to come for a visit. Elizabeth stayed for six months on two occasions.

Pilar Graña, a distinguished lady of Mexican and French descent, worked as an interpreter for Olik's medical group. She proved to be great company and traveled with Alexandra to Cancun and Hawaii.

Over the years, Alexandra and Olik had corresponded with Herman Dabbert, and knew he'd remarried soon after the divorce from Alexandra, that after World War II he'd made it to West Berlin where he'd become a professor at the Free University, and knew that his second wife had died and he'd remarried a third time. When Olik and his wife Frances visited Herman for the last time in 1973, Olik found his father polite and caring. He wanted to show his son and daughter-in-law the beauty of his homeland. After retiring from teaching, Herman had returned to two of his old loves: painting and model railroads. Model trains climbed mountains and crossed lakes through the rooms of his apartment. Though blind, Frances still enjoyed her travels. Sadly, this would be her last trip, as her health began to deteriorate.

In 1974, Alexandra became an American citizen and therefore qualified for rights that were denied to foreigners. Among such privileges was that of possession of firearms. Now, she could have a revolver, and Olik gave her one. She kept it for years under her pillow.

As Alexandra celebrated freedom in a democracy, sad news reached her about Ethiopia. Emperor Haile Selassie was deposed and eventually smothered, although other more sinister rumors surrounded his death. Afterward, Taffara—as director of the Ethiopian bank—was accused of being a "slippery stone" to the advancement of the Marxist Revolution of Mengistu Haile Mariam. Taffara was detained with many other political prisoners. Ironically, while in prison, his signature continued to show up on the Ethiopian paper currency that continued to be printed after the Marxist takeover. Political prisoners, to survive, had to be fed in prison by relatives—and when executed, the family was charged for the price of the bullet. Taffara's mother and other relatives brought him food every day. He sometimes shared his food with other prisoners who had no local relatives. Ironically, some of those he fed had been among his inquisitors. While in prison, he read all the books available. An interesting Russian book showed up, which his Marxist Ethiopians jailers assumed would have solid value as Communist propaganda. It was Solzhenitsyn's *The Gulag Archipelago*.

Alexandra's former patient, crown prince Asfau-Wossen, escaped to England where he later suffered a stroke. He went to Switzerland for treatment. While there, he met one of his and Alexandra's German friends, Frau Hertel's daughter, with whom he discussed old times. He also gave her some of the prized very hot Ethiopian pepper that had been sent to him from his native land. "Vilma sent a glassful of this pepper to me," Alexandra said, "but it is too strong for me, so I give it to a nurse from Ethiopia who works in San Diego."

The home in Addis Ababa became first a "spoil of war," and after the revolution was taken over by the dreaded kebele, equivalent to the Soviet KGB. Compare the house entrance to the Herman's sketch of the originally designed it (page 137).

ፕ

A call came from Rita Dabbert. Herman was eighty years old in 1979, and fell asleep reading in his chair and didn't awaken. He left Olik a hundred thousand dollars. Olik's cousin Eb wrote years later, telling Olik the stories of Hitler's coercion in keeping Herman in Germany in 1935, and also the following story of Herman's encounter with General Zhukov after the war—events that came as stunning surprises to Olik.

Though he'd visited his father before he died, Olik never learned this vital part of his father's story. Shortly after the end of World War II when Herman was the head of the Department of Works in East Berlin, General Zhukov—the great Russian general of World War II—called for a meeting, interested in weeding out former Nazis. An interpreter was present, but the general soon realized that Herman was fluent in Russian and let the interpreter go. The discussion changed and became quite personal, and when the interview was over, they rose, shook hands, and bowed in the old-fashioned way they'd been taught at military college. However, neither had tried this move in years. They banged their heads, and then had a good laugh. Zhukov finally told Herman that he was too open and would not last in the system of intrigue in which the Bolsheviks operated. He advised Herman to disappear to the West. Dumbfounded, Herman thanked him, not having expected such candor from a famous Communist general—even though Zhukov had been in the tsar's army before he joined the Bolsheviks. The general became Marshal Zhukov and was the commander of the Soviet occupation zone in East Germany.

Olik was flabbergasted that such a high-ranking Communist could behave so humanely and was glad his father had had such luck. To Olik, the quintessential Russian conformed to the old saying: A Russian will embrace you in the morning, shoot you in the afternoon, and at night, weep in grief over your death.

Thirty-one

Passages

In 1978, Frances' condition worsened. Alexandra was there, providing comfort and support till the end. She died of diabetic end-stage kidney failure, and Olik experienced what he described as bottomless grief. His spirituality and his work helped him endure the loss.

By an odd coincidence, Frances had received from her old friend Betty Turberville news of the death of Betty's husband only weeks before Frances died. Frances had written her a long letter of sympathy. Acting on the current correspondence, Olik sent Betty notification of his loss. It was the start of a new relationship.

Olik went to an orthopedic convention in Atlanta and met Betty for the first time. Beyond their mutual losses, they found many common interests. Betty impressed him in a subsequent letter by saying that her vacation to Jekyll Island started with blue jeans and the beach. In October of 1979, Betty and Olik married at the Montgomery Air Force Base in Alabama, courtesy of Betty's mother who had been the first congresswoman from Georgia in Washington.

Alexandra welcomed Betty and eagerly started showing her around San Diego and introducing her to Russian dishes. Betty skillfully maneuvered to make her relationship with her mother-in-law blossom into a system that worked.

In 1981 Taffara had been in prison for seven years. He'd survived and was released. He published his fascinating reminiscences in *A Tripping Stone—Ethiopian Prison Diary* and *The Gold is not All—Reminiscences of an Ethiopian Banker.* He and his Canadian wife Lara live in Vancouver, B.C., Canada. Through Taffara, Alexandra still kept in touch with Birke, Olik's nanny.[104]

By 1988, Assfau-Wossen still lived in England where he was maintained by the English government. "He is a very good person. He has a very big heart. I think the English recognize in him the royal blood. Perhaps one day, when circumstances are right, they will restore him or his son to the throne." Alexandra sighed and added, "But perhaps not."

One of Asfau-Wossen's brothers-in-law visited Alexandra in San Diego, brought to her by Father Sergei, a priest of the Russian Orthodox Church.

"What are you doing in San Diego?" Alexandra asked the prince.

"I am pumping gasoline in a filling station," he replied.

Two months after journalist Christopher Howse[105] drew public attention in 1988 to members of Haile Selassie's royal family who had been imprisoned without benefit of trial since the Marxist revolt in Ethiopia in 1974, seven of them were released. Most were friends or patients of Alexandra Dabbert, not merely exotic names upon a page. Princess Tenagne-Work, seventy-six, was the daughter of Haile Selassie, and closest to the former emperor of those released. She had been a personal acquaintance as well as Alexandra's patient.

Alexandra found out that the missionaries she'd left her property with in Ethiopia were using it as their own. One of these missionaries, not living in the San Diego area, invited her to his home to talk over old times. In the course of their conversation, she complained, "Did you know that I lost by your missionaries all my furniture and most of my dental tools and equipment, and even my dental chair, and never got it back?"

---

[104] Birke died of "old age" in 2004, not long after sending Olik her last letter wishing to see him one last time.

[105] *The Spectator*, March 19, 1988, p. 18.

He replied, "We lost more." The entire mission had been "sequestered" by the government about fifteen years before and given to some East German doctors.

She had remained friends with many of her patients, including a retired Dr. Manuel Sorenson, the Seventh Day Adventist missionary and the only one of her former patients still alive in 1989. His daughters, like her son Olik, were born in Ethiopia.

Alexandra had a Mexican maid by this time, and Gerry lived two blocks away. He never anticipated that his stay with Alexandra would result in such changes in his life. She had insisted that he graduate from high school and become an American citizen. He also trained as an auto mechanic, raised a family, and at Alexandra's urging bought a home with five garages that he rented to pay his mortgage. He called her "Mama" and helped her as if she were part of the family.

Alexandra continued her activities, especially painting. When Olik asked how much she paid for her dog Ussia's cataract operation, she answered, "No worry, I just finished and sold my latest icon."

When Ussia started losing her hearing, developed arthritis, and lost a few teeth, (an abominable event for a dentist to have a toothless pet), Alexandra reacted to this gradual decay by having leg pains bad enough to need Tylenol and Codeine. To Olik's consternation, he found when he examined her that she had absent peripheral pulses in her legs, obvious signs of peripheral vascular disease. Was she headed to eventual gangrene and amputations? When finally Ussia was compassionately put to sleep and buried in the "Dabbert Pet Cemetery"—and a new dog, Mussia was adopted from the Humane Society—Alexandra's symptoms disappeared. Even her peripheral pulses returned to normal till the end of her life.

Since the days of Ethiopia, Alexandra had rewarded Olik with sweets upon returning from receptions. Similarly, she loved to remember her horses and dogs with choice morsels. So Mussia, the Pekingese who understood Russian, was generously supplemented with morsels, as were her other pets. When these bits landed by Alexandra's dining

Alexandra and Mussia, sans Colt 38

room chair on Persian rugs, she said, "They only get richer in color from the scraps." Unfortunately, she applied the same philosophy wherever she was invited.

As with many small female dogs, Mussia alerted Alexandra to anyone approaching her home. It was not unusual for Alexandra to answer the doorbell with her Colt 38 in her hand, followed by Mussia dragging her big pillow. Alexandra frightened a few people, but it satisfied her aim to be able to protect herself. Mussia dragged a pillow because she slept on Alexandra's bed, and—to stay there when on guard duty—Mussia's collar was fastened to a big pillow until released early in the morning.

When Olik rang Alexandra's bell, Mussia came running to greet him with the leash in her mouth, hoping for a walk. As Alexandra was increasingly unable to take long walks, Olik made a point of exercising Mussia or taking both of them for a ride to Spanish Landing or Shelter Island. Alexandra would contentedly sit on a bench and watch or read her favorite historical and travel books.

At ninety-three, she'd stopped driving and lost the strength to power her trusted foot-operated drill and had to quit taking care of Olik's and Gerry's teeth. In all the years under Alexandra's care, Olik had never complained of a toothache and was sad when he had to switch dentists. Because she realized her capacities were declining, she resolved to paint one last painting after her cataract operation. It was an icon of Jesus Christ, which Olik promptly took to his office to encourage senior patients to keep trying and not to give up or give in to the challenges of old age.

Alexandra never stopped her avid reading and always had shelves full of books on art, archeology, history, and biographies—especially those related to royalty. Spiritual quests fascinated her, such as those of the Theosophists and Alexandra David-Neel's Tibetan experiences. This was an interest she shared with her dear cousin Oksana. They also shared a common background of suffering and sacrifice because of the Bolsheviks.

Oksana was the granddaughter of Katerina's sister Olga and Alexandra's only living relative besides Olik. Her father was a prominent philologist and a member of the Ukrainian Intelligentsia, quite outspoken in favor of an independent Ukraine, separate from Russia. After the Civil War that followed the Bolshevik Revolution, they were persecuted by the Communists. Her father was sent to Siberia. Miraculously they endured exile and toward the end of the Second World War, escaped to Germany. Oksana's first husband, a doctor, died in an air raid in Berlin when bombs hit the hospital where he worked.

Again barely surviving, the family eventually immigrated to the U.S.A. and settled in New York. Her father-in-law from the first marriage, an Orthodox priest, built a thriving Russian shrine and community—a beautiful church and cemetery in Spring Valley, New York. Through selfless effort and incredible labor at a fraction of minimum wage, working up to eighteen hours a day, the family made a success of their dream. They brought into existence the "Ukrainian Academy" in New York—real idealists.

Oksana's second husband, a prominent painter, also died, leaving her to take care of her three children, all of whom became independent professionals. She corresponded extensively with Alexandra and visited her. Oksana continued to work long hours, seven days a week, selflessly, devotedly, and generously at the Ukrainian Academy—an effort so prodigious it probably was the main secret of her continuing long life.

Alexandra's circle of Russian friends often shared their trying times in Russia. The librarian of the Russian Orthodox Library introduced Alexandra to Yuri Vetokhin, a graduate of the Soviet Naval Academy. He'd served in the submarines, became disenchanted with the Soviet system, and tried three times to swim to freedom. Finally, he took a cruise on a Soviet ship bound for the equator. When the charted course neared an island of the Indonesian archipelago, he jumped ship. After twenty-four hours of constant swimming, he made it to one of the islands and lived to describe it in his book, *Inclined to Escape.* He was committed enough to risk death rather than stay in the Soviet Union.

During the frequent gatherings among Russians, Alexandra showed a clipping from a journal called *The National Interest.* The article was entitled, "Relative Values."[106]

> Asked once whether Hitler or Stalin was worse, Isaiah Berlin replied, "My answer will surprise you. I am a Jew and I should answer that Hitler was worse. Yet not only did Stalin destroy tens of millions of human lives . . . he also installed slavish fear into people's souls, brought the intelligentsia to its knees, extolled lackeys, mediocrities. Apart from that he had a wonderful gift for playing on the lowly instincts of mobs."
>
> Yes, Hitler was worse for the Jews, but Stalin was worse for the rest.

"I am grateful to the Communists only for one thing," Alexandra said. "Without their menace, I would have never lived in Germany, Ethiopia, Italy, Peru, or America."

Looking back, she pondered the desperate times that she had overcome, times that in the long run shielded her from events that proved to be even worse. Without the Russian Revolution, she would not have left Russia and wouldn't have escaped the terrors of Stalin. Without Germany's post World War I hyperinflation, she would not have been able to repay the debt for the tools of dentistry in months rather than in years. Leaving Germany, she eluded the devastation of the Nazis. Leaving her beloved Ethiopia, and being barred from returning, she evaded the degradations caused by Mangistu Haile Maraiam's Marxist takeover. Leaving Italy, she avoided the leftist turmoil, inflation, and loss of property. Without World War II and the "Cold War," she would

---

[106] "Relative Values" from *The National Interest*, #59, Spring 2000.

have missed Peru and California. She left Peru just before the country fell prey to another harsh Marxist regime.

She lived her life running from an ever-encroaching shadow of Communism, yet instead of bemoaning her cycles of transcontinental uprooting and loss, she forged her own way, widened her circles of friends, and counted her blessings.

From cane to walker to wheelchair, Alexandra gradually lost ground. She became particularly anxious about losing her memory and her mind, but she would not let that happen to her. When time came for the caregivers to be in the house around the clock, then she had to accept, unwillingly, certain restrictions—one of the main ones being the use of blank cartridges in her pistol. Nevertheless, the pistol stayed under the pillow till the end.

Two months before her one-hundredth birthday, Alexandra had mentioned her fancy.

"I wish to ride a beautiful horse."

There were several horseback-riding clubs that would provide horses, but side saddles were not available because they were not insurable.

Yet when given the good news, Alexandra refused to ride. "No, absolutely not. I don't have a riding habit."

That solved the problem.

Alexandra's one hundredth birthday party

On September 27, 1998, the celebration started at 8:00 A.M. when Alexandra called Olik to wish him her happy birthday. Then, there were frantic calls from Elizabeth Meier, who at the time, was staying with her.

"Where are the table leaves?"

That is when Betty, who was the main brain in organizing the event, took charge. "We don't need any leaves. All is under control!"

By four o'clock the whole family and Gerry's family were all there to help. By five o'clock, the guests arrived and the living room became a florist's paradise. Alexandra was in a good mood, and between visiting and answering telephone calls, enjoyed the deviled eggs, caviar and cream cheese, cakes, pineapple pies, chocolates, coffee, and punch. Then all twenty guests, including Mussia the dog, sang "Happy Birthday." There were no tears.

When she required constant help at home, she had Celia, Jerry's wife, Fidelia, Elena, Isabel, Clara, Marcela, and Emma to give her comfort and care. Her dear friend Marion Reupsch was so dedicated that for a whole year, she would come to Alexandra's house at five in the morning to cover the hiatus between caregivers. Micki Head, the gifted English humanist-physical therapist by profession—an avid traveler with the widest range of interests—was her best friend till the end.

Alexandra had accumulated some twenty photo albums, which were always used to tell her story to new acquaintances and friends. She had the ability to make friends that stayed close to her all of her life. She believed in productivity and accomplishments, but by U.S. standards, she would have been considered poor. In her state of mind, comparative poverty never slowed her in pursuing happiness. She occasionally experienced the "loneliness of freedom," but never lost her autonomy.

Despite the hardships she'd faced, she wondered if they signaled the protective, invisible hand of God. She thought so. Alexandra seldom went to church, but some of her best friends and supporters were Orthodox, Catholic, Protestant missionaries, and Rabbis. She felt just as near to God while painting her icons or riding her horses in communion with nature.

"When I cannot sleep sometimes, I begin to pray for my family. I begin with my great-great grandparents and I recall their children and their children's children, all dead now. I never get to my parents before falling asleep."

Her favorite prayer was: God, let me break through, fend myself off without crashing. "It sounds better in Russian," she said.

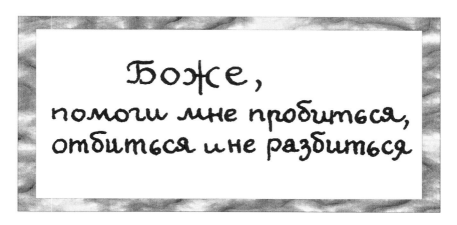

Боже, помоги мне пробиться, отбиться и не разбиться

Having bravely faced all that life had to offer for one hundred and one years, she lived at peace among the mementoes of all those tumultuous years, loved by many and respected by all.

With Oksana at the bedside, she died of "old age" the way a candle is slowly consumed, outsmarting the doctors who were bent on a specific diagnosis. Life just peacefully slipped away on March 9, 2000. Her decision to be cremated and her ashes scattered at sea were followed as she returned to the Source with a clear conscience of work well done. She made her world a little better than the one she had met at her birth.

About the Authors

$\mathcal{R}$aymond A. Hutchinson, a native of Little Rock, Arkansas, served in the U.S. Naval Air Corps and graduated from Marquette University. Following Seminary studies at St. Thomas in Denver, Colorado and the Catholic Seminary in San Diego, he was ordained in 1957 by Bishop Buddy. He left active priesthood in 1965 and become a writer. Ray's publications include *Diocesan Priest Saints* and *The Gospel according to Madison Avenue*. A great teacher and moderator of radio broadcast, he led a deep intellectual and spiritual life, firmly bonded to his beloved wife Beatrice, nee Weissberger. Ray died on December 12, 2000 and left unfinished his manuscript about Alexandra Dabbert.

The task of completing the work fell to Alexandra's son, Olgard Dabbert, M.D., better known as Olik. Born in Addis Ababa, Ethiopia in 1931, he learned Russian, French, German and Italian. He went to Medical school in Lima, Peru, completed his orthopedic training at Bellevue Hospital in New York and Duke University in North Carolina, and practiced his specialty in San Diego, California. He served on the editorial board and published many articles in *The San Diego Physician*, the official publication of the San Diego Medical Society. His special interests have included history, bioethics and spirituality, shared by his inseparable wife Betty Blitch Dabbert, from Homerville, Georgia.

Margaret Lang came to the project as an editor but also contributed to the text. Originally an English and art teacher for many years, Margaret is now an editor and writer in the San Diego area, co-founding Silver Threads, a publishing company specializing in memoirs and life writing. She teaches writing classes at the La Jolla Writers' Conference, the Learning Annex, and other seminars, and has written a spiritual gift book, *Academy of the Soul, Earth Campus* under the pen name Maggie Wingfield, book reviews and articles.